BLOOD, POWDER, AND RESIDUE

BLOOD, POWDER, AND RESIDUE

How Crime Labs Translate
Evidence into Proof

BETH A. BECHKY

PRINCETON UNIVERSITY PRESS

PRINCETON AND OXFORD

Copyright 2020 © Princeton University Press

Requests for permission to reproduce material from this work should be sent to permissions@press.princeton.edu

Published by Princeton University Press
41 William Street, Princeton, New Jersey 08540
6 Oxford Street, Woodstock, Oxfordshire OX20 1TR

press.princeton.edu

All Rights Reserved
ISBN 9780691183589
ISBN (e-book) 9780691205854

British Library Cataloging-in-Publication Data is available

Editorial: Meagan Levinson and Jacqueline Delaney
Production Editorial: Debbie Tegarden
Text Design: Leslie Flis
Jacket/Cover Design: Layla Mac Rory
Production: Erin Suydam
Publicity: Maria Whelan and Kate Stephens

This book has been composed in Arno Pro

Printed on acid-free paper. ∞

Printed in the United States of America

10 9 8 7 6 5 4 3 2 1

CONTENTS

Preface vii

Introduction: Welcome to the Crime Lab 1

PART 1: THE WORK OF CRIMINALISTS 13

Chapter 1. Forensic Scientists at the Lab Bench:
Taming, Questioning, and Framing the Evidence 15

Chapter 2. The Social Worlds of Forensic Science:
Science, Criminal Justice, and the Public Sphere 57

PART 2: THE CULTURE OF CRIMINALISTS 73

Chapter 3. A Culture of Anticipation: The
Consequences of Conflicting Expectations 75

Chapter 4. Creating a Culture of Anticipation
in the Crime Laboratory 98

PART 3: THE STRUGGLES OF CRIMINALISTS 111

Chapter 5. The Specter of Testifying: Forensic
Scientists as the Voice of the Evidence 113

Chapter 6. DNA Envy: Responding to
Shifting Scientific and Legal Standards 148

Conclusion 173

Appendix: Case Notes on an Ethnography of a Crime Laboratory 189

Acknowledgments 199

Notes 203

References 215

Index 225

PREFACE

While giving a plenary presentation to a packed ballroom at a statewide conference of criminalists, Tina, a DNA analyst turned homicide detective, recounted her first cold case.[1] She stressed that forensic evidence is critical to the investigation of such cases:

> I just got promoted to run with the big dogs up in homicide, and in my first month I got assigned a cold case, a sex crime case. Now that I am on the inside, I'm not wearing a white lab coat, I'm wearing a blue coat. Today I want to communicate how important it is for detectives to get information from you, the lab rats. Don't hold back—get it to us fast.

Displaying an image of side-by-side mug shots on the screen, Tina explained the background of the case:

> This caper stars "Big Thunder." Imagine this guy coming out of the trunk when you think you are going on a sex date, doing a stroll, as the call girls say. The two gals meet with suspect one, agree to sex, and then suspect two, Big Thunder, jumps out of the trunk. They beat the girls a little, find money on them, take them to a hotel room and rape them. On the way to the hotel they pick up a third assailant at a trailer park. The victims are repeatedly raped and beaten and the suspects take their IDs and cell phones. They think they are going to die.

In their investigation, the police tracked the calls made on the women's cell phones and interviewed a tow truck driver who identified two of the suspects. The investigators were familiar with these suspects, who had been arrested for a prior attack and for drunk and disorderly conduct. They found the two men and sampled their DNA for comparison with the rape kits from the women.

In her presentation, Tina projected a table of DNA profiles produced by the crime lab and took the audience through the results row by row:

The initial findings from the evidence kit from the victims shows semen on the vaginal swab and condom, amylase (found in saliva) on a neck swab. We have a huge amount of information, including DNA mixtures on a couple of these swabs. The profile on the vaginal swab matched the second suspect, Big Thunder, across the board, and the first suspect was a partial match to one of the mixtures. There are unknown profiles from some of the swabs and a condom.

Although the police were unable to identify the third suspect, the district attorney moved forward with the prosecution of the two in custody, typical in such situations. More unusual was what happened at the preliminary trial a year later. While telling the district attorney about the third man they picked up in the trailer park, one of the victims suggested that he looked like he could be the younger brother of the second suspect, Big Thunder. Hearing this, the district attorney decided to investigate whether the third assailant—the unknown source of DNA on the condom and other swabs—might be related to Big Thunder.

The police lieutenant asked Tina, as a former DNA analyst, to use her forensic science expertise to probe the details of the old case. Tina's work began with the DNA evidence. In her words:

I looked at the DNA results to do a familial DNA review. I compared Big Thunder's profile with the unknown profile, and it looked pretty familial: it matched at six loci and the remainder had shared alleles. Also, the transcripts in the file had the victims talking about a third assailant and we had a report in our database where all three of them were drunk and acting stupid, getting into fisticuffs.

Tina's familial DNA review was crucial for substantiating the hunch about the third suspect, and gave her the evidence needed to pursue him. As she described:

I do the legwork, find his driver's license and track him down in the Marines, which he had joined after his big brother was arrested. I lay out the "high degree of similarity" with a judge, who signed the arrest warrant.

I picked him up, submitted his DNA swab to the lab, and the victim picked him out of a photo array. Then I got the confirmation report back from the lab. In court, he was held to answer.

Tina's work enabled the justice system to convict all three suspects. In addition, her success in using her forensic expertise to crack a difficult case and find a dangerous suspect prompted the adoption of familial DNA profiling as a routine practice for cold cases in her jurisdiction.

Forensic evidence collected at crime scenes—DNA, fingerprints, bullets, and other materials—are a key tool for investigators in finding suspects, and stories like Tina's are commonplace. In one case that made headlines, the attempted 2018 pipe bombing attacks on US politicians and prominent critics of Donald Trump, a fingerprint on a package and DNA samples found on the devices in two others provided the clues needed for law enforcement officials to quickly locate and arrest the suspect.[2] More quietly, over the last several years thousands of backlogged rape kits have been analyzed through a funding initiative spearheaded by Manhattan's district attorney, which has so far resulted in sixty-four convictions.[3] Forensic evidence propels investigations forward, links suspects to crimes, and exonerates those who have been wrongly incarcerated.

The work of the crime laboratory is critical to the pursuit of criminal justice. As a result, the stakes of that work could not be higher. Lives turn on the claims made on the basis of forensic evidence. And yet the evidence and those who analyze it are not infallible. Instances of laboratory error and malfeasance do occur, and their effects ripple throughout the criminal justice system. Problems with forensic evidence can undermine justice, waste taxpayer dollars, and damage public trust.

Consider the scandal stemming from the work of Annie Dookhan, a chemist in a Massachusetts state drug laboratory. In 2013, Dookhan pleaded guilty to multiple counts of evidence tampering and obstruction of justice stemming from her work handling narcotics evidence. She admitted to "dry-labbing," to identifying drugs without actually performing any tests. Dookhan had also contaminated evidence samples with known drugs, combined case evidence before testing, and forged signatures of other criminalists and evidence technicians.[4]

Dookhan's misconduct did not only compromise the lab. Because prosecutors, defendants, and juries depend on forensic science work, her crimes thoroughly shook the Massachusetts justice system. She had worked on thousands of drug cases during her tenure at the laboratory, and challenges to the convictions based on evidence she handled began to be heard in special courts almost immediately.[5] The Massachusetts Supreme Court ruled that thousands of cases should be retried.[6] Many people had been incarcerated for years on the basis of tainted evidence, while others "who deserve to be incarcerated for a very long time are going to walk," according to one defense attorney.[7] Ultimately, over twenty thousand drug convictions in the state were dismissed.[8]

Errors in the analysis or interpretation of evidence have also led to wrongful imprisonment and individual harm. In one prominent example, Brandon Mayfield was jailed in Oregon in connection with the bombing of the Madrid commuter rail in 2004 on the basis of an incorrect fingerprint identification. In 2006, the US government formally apologized to Mayfield for his pain and suffering and awarded him a $2 million settlement.[9] DNA identifications are also fallible, as demonstrated by the release of Amanda Knox after four years of imprisonment in Italy for her alleged participation in the murder of her roommate. Geneticists working for her defense team argued that the amount of DNA found on the knife used as evidence to convict her was "vanishingly small" and could have been left there under innocent circumstances.[10] Each of these cases show that forensic evidence is less a matter of black and white than the product of complex science entangled in high-stakes legal battles.[11]

The cases we see in the news illustrate the significance of forensic science work: because it links suspects to crimes, this work has the power to change lives, making accuracy and expertise paramount. However, media stories largely obscure the true nature of the work of forensic scientists; their media portrayals as determined sleuths and unsung heroes are dramatically appealing, but they do not reflect what actually happens inside a crime laboratory.

The work of forensic scientists is both more mundane and more demanding than these images suggest. The analysis of forensic evidence is highly technical, requiring painstaking effort at the lab bench. At the same time, forensic scientists evaluate evidence at the behest of investigators and prosecutors, within a hierarchy of courts and law enforcement agencies. Forensic science is performed in the service of justice, which means it is complicated by the relationships between the science and the law. The scientific work is intertwined with the other parties in this system and cannot be considered without examining these relationships. In this book, I will describe how those relationships play out, the ways in which they lead to tensions in the work of forensic scientists, and their implications for criminal justice as a whole.

BLOOD, POWDER,
AND RESIDUE

Introduction

WELCOME TO THE CRIME LAB

When Allison tells people she is a forensic scientist, "they don't really understand. Everyone's watched *CSI*, and they think they know everything about it. I try to tell them it is not as glamorous, and it doesn't happen in fifteen minutes. Because a lot of people have the misconception that a crime occurs, and within two days they find the suspects and within a week and a half they are convicted and in jail. And it just doesn't happen that quickly or easily."

Contrary to the popular image, forensic science is not a glamorous job. Despite the crimes involved, the work resembles that of bench scientists or laboratory technicians. When dusting the whorls of a fingerprint on the handle of a knife, scrutinizing a slide under a microscope to locate sperm in a sample, or test-firing a gun to see if it was used in a crime, forensic scientists look like lab scientists. Of course, the science is more complicated and time-consuming, and less sexy, than what we see on television. Day in, day out, Allison makes sure her work table is sterile, her notes are meticulous, her samples uncontaminated, and her instruments calibrated and working properly.

The intricacies of the science are also embedded in the links between the work of forensic scientists and investigators, attorneys, judges, and juries. The science in a crime laboratory serves a specific function: to analyze the evidence on which the criminal justice system relies. The work forensic scientists do is constrained by this function. Unlike other scientists, they perform their work *only* for the criminal justice system. They struggle with the knowledge that the work they do is not ordinary science, but a science used by a complex system that assesses guilt or innocence. The people it affects are real, and the stakes are high.

In light of this knowledge, it makes sense that forensic scientists also refer to themselves as "criminalists." Every day, criminalists work in the shadow of the criminal justice system, which controls their budget, sets their agenda, and requires more evidence processed ever faster. Criminal justice permeates criminalists' ways of working and thinking; they write reports knowing a jury will hear their conclusions, worry about how to explain contamination on the stand, and analyze evidence for the purpose of addressing questions of criminal law. Criminalists do not relinquish their scientific standards, or allow outsiders—attorneys, politicians, journalists—to misuse science for their own ends. But criminal justice concerns penetrate their daily work.

Criminalists know that their work might end up in a court of law. What they worry about most is appearing in court themselves. Testifying is exceptionally rare, but the possibility looms. Despite all the thought and care criminalists put into preparing for court, they know that appearing on the witness stand can be risky and fraught. The courtroom is commanded by people who are not scientists, and they may willfully or ignorantly use the science in ways that criminalists do not intend. Defense attorneys can turn a small lapse in lab procedure into a challenge to the criminalist's job performance; prosecutors mistakenly believe they can twist a scrap of evidence into the missing link their case needed. And the jurors, of course, may misunderstand the intricate science completely.

Testifying is not just where the science meets the law, but is the main venue in which the science is represented in public. The courtroom is where outsiders judge, undermine, and occasionally attack the hard work of the crime laboratory—all part of the theater of criminal trials. In the lab, criminalists can spend hours or days polishing a report with the help of colleagues, making sure the science is presented accurately and impartially. In court, one misinterpretation could lead to important cases lost, innocent people convicted, and severe repercussions for their careers.

Given their understanding of all of these consequences, criminalists approach testifying with a mix of determination and concern. Anca, in a crime lab's DNA unit, noted that criminalists should always be nervous when they go to court:

> I don't care how many years of experience you've had because there's so much riding on your testimony and it doesn't matter how good you are at what you do here. It's relaying it to the jury that's the important thing, and you could be a great scientist but you could be a really bad witness, so [it's both] being able to do the analysis and the work and explaining it and relaying the message. I think that's it: Did I do a good enough job to relay the message? Did I explain it well enough? Could I have done it better?

In the words of Tom, a firearms examiner, "I walk in there with a sense of responsibility. I'm nervous. I think if you're not nervous in some capacity, maybe you aren't taking it seriously enough."

———

This book examines the culture of the crime lab, specifically the challenges of working as a criminalist within the criminal justice system today. It is an ethnographic account based on eighteen months of fieldwork I conducted within a crime lab of a major metropolitan area in the western United States. Metropolitan County Crime Laboratory (a pseudonym) is a mid-sized laboratory with about sixty criminalists, operating under the auspices of the county's district attorney. The laboratory is located in a bright new spacious building rather than the cramped basement spaces of other laboratories I have visited. The caseload is typical for the state in terms of the types of analysis performed, but the lab handles more than the average number of cases per year relative to laboratories across the state.

As an organizational ethnographer, my goal is to try to understand and portray the daily life of the people working in the organization. Doing so meant that I was a regular presence at the lab benches, computer screens, and meeting tables in Metropolitan County Crime Laboratory (MCCL): watching, listening, and asking questions. Apart from entering the evidence lockers, I was given full access to all areas of the laboratory and visited about three days a week for six to seven hours a day. I focused my attention on four forensic science units—forensic biology, chemistry, comparative evidence, and toxicology—and spent between three and six months in each unit.

I observed every criminalist in each of these four units for at least a day: not only watching them work, but also accompanying them to lunches, group and lab-wide meetings, presentations, professional conferences, and court. I augmented our informal work conversations with interviews of more than thirty criminalists at MCCL. During the workdays, I occasionally interacted with members of the criminal justice system, such as attorneys and police officers. However, this book is not a study of the entire justice system. This is a study of criminalists, their perspectives, and the work that they do.

To understand the tensions and challenges of a form of work, I find it illuminating to actually try to do it myself. Therefore, I wanted to learn some forensic science techniques. The crime laboratory presented an unusual constraint on my participation in because I was not permitted to touch any case evidence. To compensate, criminalists let me practice on non–case evidence: members of the DNA unit patiently taught me how to run my own DNA profile, and I test-fired weapons in the firearms unit. In a lab coat and gloves, I peered over shoulders and into microscopes as the criminalists worked.

In addition to participant observation at MCCL, I toured three other crime laboratories in the state and interviewed their directors. I spent a day in a county-level crime laboratory in an eastern state, where I interviewed the deputy director and observed the work of the units of forensic biology, controlled substances, and comparative evidence. I also attended both state and local professional meetings and workshops. Conversations with this wider set of criminalists, supervisors, and directors broadened my understanding of the field of forensic science. It also helped me to assess the representativeness of MCCL: while the lab seemed spiffier and better funded than average, the work done there was representative of criminalists' work everywhere I visited.

My study of MCCL coincided with a critical moment in recent forensic science history: the National Academy of Sciences issued its report "Strengthening Forensic Science in the United States" just after my arrival at the lab.[1] This government-sponsored scientific assessment was critical of the scientific foundations of many of the disciplines of forensic science, although it exempted DNA profiling from its criticisms. Its publication led to increased public scrutiny of forensic science, the impact of which reverberated throughout the lab. I had an inside view of the responses of laboratory members, as well as a fortuitous opportunity to observe the broader field examine itself in reaction to this critique of their methods, their thinking, and their very existence.

What I witnessed showed me that criminalists take their work incredibly seriously. They think of themselves as scientists first and foremost. I never saw anything that made me think that criminalists are the source of error within our criminal justice system. Instead, I saw criminalists expected to do more with less, conscious of being accountable to the law and the public and sometimes treated shabbily by law enforcement, attorneys, and judges. They are people, and, therefore, not perfect. But the standards to which they hold themselves are exacting.

Instead of directing blame at criminalists, this experience showed me that gaps can occur in translation. The process of moving the science from the lab into the courtroom is a worrisome fault line in the criminal justice system. The rigorous work of criminalists is used for purposes unique to this branch of science, and the outcomes of their work are judged on criteria outside that of scientific protocols. The disconnects between scientific findings and legal arguments create misperceptions, and scientific knowledge is difficult for nonexperts to parse. When scientific findings are used in the service of justice, misunderstandings can arise, and criminalists' translation is critical to averting and correcting them. Explaining this process of translation is the focus of the book.

This book is divided into three parts. In part 1, "The Work of Criminalists," I describe what criminalists do. I examine a typical day in each of the various disciplines of forensic science (DNA analysis, firearms examination, narcotics analysis, and toxicology), as they receive new evidence, process ongoing cases, write up reports, and worry about testifying. Although the particulars of their analyses are different, criminalists across disciplines face a similar challenge: navigating between the worlds of science, criminal justice, and the public sphere. Every day, criminalists need to first ensure that their work meets the threshold of good science, but they also need to communicate this science accurately to attorneys and judges as well as to jurors. Moreover, in an age when technology is rapidly advancing and criminal justice is under scrutiny, criminalists must work to convey their value, discipline, and impartiality to the broader public. Americans today order DNA tests over the internet and see criminal cases neatly wrapped up through science in sixty-minute TV dramas. It is no wonder the public is both wary and overly enthusiastic about the capabilities of forensic science.

In part 2, "The Culture of Criminalists," I explore how criminalists make sense of their work. Navigating the three worlds (science, criminal justice, and the public sphere) requires more than scientific acumen and individual initiative. Criminalists are aware of the gaps that may occur in translation and have evolved a particular workplace culture to address them, which I identify as a "culture of anticipation." The needs and expectations of outside audiences are never separate from the daily work of criminalists, and, as a result, criminalists anticipate the concerns of others. Anticipation makes their work more difficult; performing their analyses thinking of what the attorneys might ask for next, or what questions jurors might have about their processes, is a demanding experience. Criminalists craft their reports carefully, with language they believe will accurately deliver information to the court. The specter of testifying informs every step of examination. Anticipating a future attack on their work (and, by extension, themselves), criminalists need to be able to say: "This is what I did and how I did it."

The culture of anticipation is written into criminalists' daily practices and reproduced in their training, their meetings, and their casual conversations. Criminalists watch each other's courtroom testimonies to see how it is done. They develop a shared understanding of their role, assuring each other that the best way to anticipate is to be the "voice of the evidence"—an impartial, scientific, but lucid and clear translator of the lab into the court—and nothing more. Because of their position within the criminal justice system, they cannot separate today's work from how it may potentially be used tomorrow, and they have developed a culture that makes this position at the intersection of these social worlds tenable.

In part 3, "The Struggles of Criminalists," I investigate how criminalists confront the current challenges to their work, and I uncover the obstacles and conflicts that define their work lives, beginning with testifying. Attorneys may verbally attack criminalists, whose slip-ups on the stand can have terrible consequences, and, even in a relatively friendly courtroom, criminalists find it challenging to discuss details of science. Simply attesting to scientific results has become more complex, because technological breakthroughs have destabilized criminalists' footing. DNA testing has become America's darling: we are using it in our doctors' offices to predict disease and in our living rooms to find distant relatives, and we even use those same databases to track down serial killers. The rise of DNA profiling has raised questions about the science of many other disciplines, requiring criminalists across the field to examine and justify their standards and practices. The science of DNA seems obvious and irrefutable, and, not surprisingly, it receives the lion's share of attention and funding inside today's crime laboratories. Other disciplines are being pressured to emulate DNA's success and become more "objective." However, there is a degree of subjectivity in all their work, and differences in techniques make criminalists wary of comparisons. DNA profiling is only one technique of many needed to turn crime scenes into courtroom evidence.

What is the value of studying criminalists? One goal is to illuminate the inner workings of the American criminal justice system from an unexpected perspective. Seeing how messy crime scenes are transformed into clean scientific reports and courtroom evidence is key to understanding how ideals of justice are put into practice in the United States. There is also value in revealing how diverse methods of science are conducted in the real world with real consequences. The work itself is fascinating, difficult, and worthy of study: criminalists' translation of their expert knowledge is just as important as the science itself. Ultimately, studying criminalists matters because their struggles reveal the struggles of expert workers in numerous occupations around the world.

Expert work is currently under siege. Commentators warn that workplace applications of digital technologies—algorithms, big data, artificial intelligence—are going to gut the work of professionals,[2] everyone from lawyers to doctors to criminalists. These technologies track and amass data, processing and calculating information at lightning speeds, which reduces the need for the people who traditionally worked with data. Consequently, pundits and scholars suggest, the work of experts will necessarily move away from thinking and processing information, which will radically change their occupations.[3] At the core of their argument is an image of expert work as merely the cognitive processing of a body of knowledge. If expert work is simply pattern-finding and clear-cut decision-making, it can be easily overtaken by the power of algorithmic technologies.[4] With machines doing the work of analyzing data, we can expect a future with fewer jobs for experts, and those jobs that remain will require different, and less complicated, skills.

Yet, in this study of criminalists, I show how this conception critically misconstrues the work of experts. In fact, expert work does not just entail the mastery of a large, complex body of knowledge. Instead, expert work relies on *interpreting* and *translating* knowledge. Experts sit at interfaces where they must communicate knowledge to others who need it but may be unable to easily understand it. Cultivating the skills of interpretation and translation are all the more critical in our digital age. The ability to holistically understand data and what it can and cannot tell us is a vital human trait in the world of big data.

Professionals and experts develop their craft through hands-on learning within a community of like-minded others. Problems in the real world rarely present themselves in neat packages that fit either the formal knowledge found in a textbook or the information processed through machine learning. However, through extended apprentice-ships, experts are able to contextualize and enrich their knowledge with daily practice under the guidance of seasoned colleagues.[5] Expertise goes beyond formal knowledge to skills that are both tacit and embod-ied; expert work is a form of visceral knowing. Across a spectrum of fields, expert workers hone their skills through this process of learning by doing.[6] And they figure out how to apply what they know to the specific problems at hand.[7] Their interpretation of the problems they face is central to their expertise.

Moreover, expertise is often useless in isolation; it is through transla-tion that expert workers create value. In this process, experts translate their knowledge of the material world into more mobile forms, usually by inscribing it into documents, images, or other representations that can be used for communicating.[8] Experts are regularly called on to apply their knowledge beyond their own domains, sharing what they know with outside communities. Engineers need construction crews or production workers to execute their plans, and doctors must explain their diagnoses to patients. To make an impact, experts must convince others of the legitimacy of their knowledge, generate support for their ideas, and maintain their power in ways that that draw on shared lan-guage, materials, and conventions. Engineers bolster their expertise with drawings and prototypes, using these to convince others to sup-port their designs.[9] Similarly, doctors interpret the language of medical records in collaboration with patients to help them understand their conditions.[10] In these settings, and others like them, the fundamental burden on experts is to translate their particular esoteric knowledge in a manner that persuades nonexpert audiences.

These acts of translation also depend on the broader context of social relations. Experts are embedded in a set of relationships with interested parties who have perspectives about what knowledge is relevant and whose expertise is valuable.[11] These structures matter in how expertise is taken up, used, and assessed. When politicians and journalists talk about climate science, this affects the influence that climatologists have in convincing the public to accept the evidence of climate change. Public opinion then affects the future institutional funding for climate research as well as the ability to garner further evidence.[12] Such chains of influence also impact the everyday practices of scientific experts, who have to decide how and when they should talk to journalists or participate in government-sponsored activities.[13]

This conception of expert work is the foundation for my study of criminalists. Expertise is an interpretive skill developed through daily practical experience in a particular community, which needs to be translated to a set of people who do not share those experiences. Criminalists are expert science workers who are called on regularly to translate their findings for outside audiences. Unlike climate scientists, who can choose whether and how to participate in public science, criminalists do not have the autonomy to walk away from their audiences. They have to work in a state of anticipation and translation; their work is organized solely to produce findings for the criminal justice system.

Criminalists are a model case of what happens to expert workers like teachers, doctors, or engineers who have "good jobs," but are required to work within systems beyond their control. Perhaps securing expertise once promised some level of autonomy; this was particularly true for professionals, who often worked in partnerships managed through the collegial interactions of a set of peers. Today, being an expert worker often means that you report to nonexperts, or must justify your existence to those who do not know your field. Working with and depending on those outside of their occupational boundaries influences experts' work practices. Watching criminalists adapt to new technologies, invent new ways to communicate their science, and struggle to show how their subjective yet informed judgments are better than allegedly objective machines or automated algorithms is valuable; it offers lessons for other expert workers.

It is also important to understand the real way science is practiced, and the messy ways that knowledge is produced. Many want to believe that the work of criminalists is flawless, and that science itself is flawless. For example: *The bullet is a match. It is his DNA.* But looking at the real work criminalists do shows that even the most prized science— including DNA analysis—is interpretive, using tacit and subjective judgments to draw conclusions in context.

Unlike crime shows or courtroom pronouncements, the evidence rarely speaks for itself. Criminalists need to translate the realities of the science to outside audiences. Thus, instead of stating hard-and-fast truths, what criminalists say instead is more like the following: *These specific markings, at these particular locations, on this bullet found at the crime scene, match the markings on a bullet fired from the gun belonging to the suspect. The probability of selecting the observed DNA profile from a population of random unrelated individuals is expected to be 1 in 325,000 based on the alleles present in this sample.*

With this book, my hope is that by describing in detail the world of forensic science, you can see what is important (and representative) about the work of criminalists. In showing how vital interpretation is to the expertise and the judgments criminalists make about evidence, I make an argument for the value of communities of expertise, negotiated interpretations, and translation skills writ large. Examining how criminalists are situated within the worlds of criminal justice and the public, and the different expectations produced within these worlds, illustrates the challenges of working in a culture of anticipation. Criminalists are not simply free to do science; they cannot ignore the translation work that navigating worlds requires. In exploring the ways criminalists interact with these worlds—writing reports, talking to attorneys, testifying in court—I demonstrate what translating looks like for a set of experts, whose occupation is captive to another, and who have a commitment to serving the criminal justice community.

And, now, into the crime lab.

Part 1

THE WORK OF CRIMINALISTS

Chapter 1

FORENSIC SCIENTISTS AT THE LAB BENCH

Taming, Questioning, and Framing the Evidence

Forensic scientists are applied scientists who work in the service of the criminal justice system. In many ways, the work that forensic scientists perform in Metropolitan County Crime Laboratory (MCCL) resembles the work performed by laboratory technicians across the spectrum of science.[1] The analytic practices they use, in terms of biology or chemistry, are similar to those one would see in academic, industrial, or hospital labs. Yet the purposes toward which forensic scientists put these techniques are different. Unlike other scientists, their goal is to analyze possible material links between a suspect and a crime.

Forensic scientists work on analyzing evidence for use in the criminal justice system. As the term "forensic science" indicates, criminalists employ the methodical and systematic approaches of science and apply them to evidentiary materials used in the law. Their work therefore requires not only scientific acumen, but also an understanding of the standards and requirements of the legal system. Like all science, it depends on routines: scientists meticulously follow procedure to avoid contamination and produce consistent results. While rote practice does structure their work, they also rely on the aesthetics of their materials, using embodied aspects of their craft—that is, their five senses, along with their expert knowledge—to help them make judgments.

Forensic science work follows the same overarching path across all disciplines at MCCL. In each unit they analyze evidence from crime scenes by taming, questioning, and framing the evidence. The evidence arrives in the basement of MCCL wrapped in neat paper and plastic packages, belying the messiness of their contents. The items inside, often soiled from the crime scene, now need to be tamed, to be made more standard and orderly for scientific investigation. Forensic scientists carefully lay out the items on their benches, readying them while considering what analyses to do.

For example, in the process of screening evidence from a rape scene, a DNA analyst puts on gloves to remove a pair of underwear from a paper bag, scrutinizing them closely to see where she might find biological materials. She photographs them, cuts off small pieces to try to extract DNA, and draws a diagram in her notes indicating where the samples were taken. Firearms examiners and fingerprint analysts treat their evidence gingerly as well, first examining items thoroughly and carefully, so as not to accidentally fire a loaded gun or damage any potential prints. Care with materials is a hallmark of all scientific work and carries through every step of analyzing evidence at MCCL.[2]

In their approach to analyzing evidence, criminalists hold a neutral stance toward the interpretation of their results. Criminalists identify as scientists: they believe strongly in the tenets and practices of the scientific method, and, when expressing their views on their work, they speak in terms of the norms of science.[3] They remark on their own objectivity and neutrality as they pursue the results of their cases, making remarks such as "I don't have a horse in the race."

And, like science more generally, forensic science is organized communally. Criminalists rely on two scientific communities for guidance: the broader forensic science community and their local laboratory colleagues. Within the laboratory, criminalists review one another's work and rely upon their colleagues for training, support, troubleshooting, and decision-making. Additionally, laboratories communicate with one another about the appropriate protocols and practices to use, in online forums, by phone, and in person during audits by the forensic science laboratory association and at professional meetings and conferences.

After questioning the evidence to determine what it shows, criminalists narrow their findings in order to draw conclusions, which they share in written reports and courtroom testimony. These reports of conclusions require framing, in which criminalists represent their results and work processes in ways that will be legible to a broader audience: lawyers, judges, juries, and the media. To do so, analysts in the lab collectively craft reports and the statements within them, to present a compelling image of their expertise that is consistent across cases. They are scientists whose primary audience, in many ways, is the people outside of the science community.

This chapter will introduce you to the work of the criminalists at MCCL. Analysts tame the evidence that comes into the lab from messy crime scenes, question it with specific techniques to discern what the evidence demonstrates, and then frame the evidence in a report that is both a scientific and legal document. While all the work at MCCL reflects similar broad scientific conventions, the distinctions between the units' work are striking as well. I describe in detail the practices of each unit, which differ in their techniques, materials, types of output, and style of interpretation. This chapter investigates the different paths that evidence takes through these different disciplines, and the ways each kind of forensic scientist performs their work.

WHO ARE CRIMINALISTS?

Before describing the practices of the disciplines and units of the crime lab, we first need to know more about where criminalists come from.

Forensic scientists arrive at the crime laboratory with similar backgrounds: typically a bachelors' degree in biology or chemistry. After passing a battery of tests and undergoing a panel interview, they are hired into a specific unit, such as forensic biology or toxicology. The practices of forensic science vary by discipline, and criminalists use distinct techniques to examine different forms of evidence: in narcotics, wet chemistry is used to identify drugs, while firearms examiners use comparative microscopy to compare bullets. Consequently, once assigned to a unit, criminalists undergo extensive specialized training. Training is particularly intense in forensic biology (whose most common output is DNA profiling), where analysts train in-house for nine months before being certified to work on cases. And in firearms, examiners attend a statewide training program for a year, and then train in the lab for an additional year before even starting casework.

Because the complexity of the techniques, practices, and cases varies across disciplines, the time and effort criminalists need to create and report conclusions about the evidence also varies. Major cases, which include serious felonies like homicide or rape, are complex, involving extensive evidence collection requiring analysis of multiple items. Consequently, the DNA analysts and firearms examiners I observed who worked on these major cases were proud if they completed sixty to a hundred in a year. In contrast, toxicologists, in half a day, could analyze forty-five blood samples simultaneously for DUI (driving under the influence) cases, and narcotics analysts could assess many types of drug samples in only ten to fifteen minutes each. These specialized fields, then, while grouped collectively under "forensic science," actually exhibit striking differences, both in the science involved and in the daily work of their practitioners.

It wasn't always this way. Forensic science was once the province of generalists. Senior criminalists I met often spoke about their early years in the field, where "I did everything: blood typing, firearms examination, narcotics." This generational difference helps explain why, despite changes to the field, senior managers still expect all forensic scientists to have a similar skill base and regard them as potentially interchangeable across units. When the lab director at MCCL planned to swap two criminalists between the narcotics and firearms units, he reminded everyone at the monthly staff meeting, "You are all criminalists, and you should be able to work in any unit in the lab."

Despite such sentiments, over the last twenty years, as changes in science and technology have refined forms of analysis, criminalists have become specialists. Some do switch units, primarily as a result of their own interests and wishes. Among criminalists at MCCL, the most common career move is from toxicology into narcotics, since these units share analytical techniques. Only occasionally do toxicologists or narcotics analysts move into a unit that analyzes major cases, such as firearms examination or DNA profiling.

The differences across units—in techniques, work, and relationships within the broader system of criminal justice—result in distinct social practices within each unit.

Forensic biology is the largest unit in the lab with eighteen members, two-thirds of whom are women. The unit's nickname, "DNA princesses," refers not only to gender but to the status of DNA profiling. As the most recently scientifically and legally legitimated technique of forensic science, DNA profiling is held up as the gold standard of forensic evidence. Other groups envy the resources the unit commands in terms of equipment, funding, grants, and staff.

Comparative evidence, on the other hand, which contains the firearms examination lab, is the smallest: seven members, predominantly men. Also working on major cases, this unit practices the most traditional forensic science, using techniques developed inside law enforcement. The chemistry unit, which contains narcotics and trace analysis, and the toxicology unit handle much larger caseloads of simpler drug identification and intoxication cases. Even though the two units perform similar chemical identification techniques, they have discrete work practices. In toxicology, the nine analysts have less autonomy. The work is more rote and requires the least amount of training. The work of the eight narcotics analysts, on the other hand, is more independent and varied.

Thus, while the criminalists at MCCL share scientific assumptions and practices, these differences in casework, training and techniques lead to different work practices within each unit.

WORK PRACTICES OF FORENSIC BIOLOGY: LEGITIMATED SCIENTIFIC INQUIRY USING STATISTICAL INFERENCE

Ellie is leaning over a paper-covered square table in the DNA lab's screening room. She lays out a white dress, the evidence from a sexual assault case, underneath four large hanging ceiling lights. Two months earlier, Ellie had tested the swabs from the rape kit: the intimate swabs taken from a victim's body at the hospital. Ellie says, "Those were negative [for DNA], so as a last resort I have this grab bag of clothing."

Failing to find the perpetrator's DNA in the rape kit—the most likely place, given the details of the police report—Ellie extends her search to the victim's clothes. The victim, attacked in an alley, told the police that she did not think the man wore a condom. So, after the rape kit came back negative, Ellie next ran the underwear, because "the underwear would have draining because the victim wore it afterward." Again, no DNA.

Now she is testing the dress, she says, because "you start with what you think is the most probative." That is, Ellie started with what is most likely to result in evidence that would directly link to the suspected crime, and later moved to less likely evidence: the dress. This is because, Ellie explains, "on the dress, the suspect can say all sorts of things . . . if it is on the outside of the dress, that is easier to explain away. He can say, 'I did my thing on her' and then just get public exposure, a much lesser crime."

The dress has some reddish-brown stains on the front and back, as well as some hairs. Ellie removes the hairs with tweezers, puts them in an envelope, and adds to her running notes on the case their location on the dress. Climbing up a stepladder with a camera, she snaps several pictures of the front of the dress, and then flips it over to take several more pictures, again noting the locations of the stains. Then she turns the dress inside out and photographs it that way as well. Between each set of photos she replaces her gloves so that DNA is not transferred to the camera for the next analyst using it.

Because this is a large piece of evidence, Ellie first tries to pinpoint the location of any biological fluids by using an ALS, or alternative light source. Semen fluoresces (glows) at 460 to 470 wavelengths, so the light source is focused at that wavelength. Ellie and I both put on orange goggles; then she turns off the overhead lights and flips on the blue ALS. After checking the quality control item (a piece of cardboard with semen on it) to make sure it turns bright yellow, she focuses the light on the front of the dress. She sees several bright yellow spots and circles them with a black Sharpie. "Because I didn't find anything on the underwear, this is surprising," she says. "It may still be nothing."

Since other fluids aside from semen fluoresce at the same wavelength, Ellie, after scanning the entire dress with the light, moves on to a specific test for semen: an acid phosphatase (AP) test. We go out to the serology reagent refrigerator in the main lab, which holds shared chemicals for common biological fluid tests, to get the necessary chemical reagents (substances that cause or detect chemical reactions) for the AP test. Since there are so many locations on the dress to test, Ellie needs to make an unusually large amount.

Ellie mixes the reagents in the proportions required in the protocol and puts them in a large tube. Allison, sitting nearby at her bench, jokes about the amount of reagent: "What are you AP'ing, an elephant?" We laugh, and Ellie borrows a timer from her. She pulls a quality control strip out of the freezer, and we return to the screening room. The strip turns purple in the proper number of seconds after she drops the AP onto it. This means the test she has prepared can correctly identify semen.

And yet, when Ellie performs the same test on the circled locations on the dress, no purple appears. The dress, ultimately, had no semen on it that Ellie could find.

———

Ellie's screening activities are typical of the first step of casework in the forensic biology unit, whose primary focus is DNA profiling. All DNA analysts in the MCCL unit perform all the tasks in this process: screening the evidence, running the profile on the biological sample, interpreting the results from the instrument, and writing the report.[4]

The vibe of the DNA unit is that of any busy biology lab. Analysts in white coats sit or stand at their benches, peering through microscopes, wiping down workspaces with alcohol, pipetting samples and adding reagents under a fume hood, and moving samples to different instruments in order to amplify and then analyze the DNA. As they move from the lab to their computer spaces to work on their reports, conversations among analysts center on their interpretations of the output, concerns about contamination, problems with the instruments, and questions about statistics and language in the reports.

———

The first step to discovering a DNA profile from biological materials is to tame the evidence so that it can be analyzed. For major cases such murder or rape, the process of DNA profiling begins with items of evidence (primarily clothing, weapons, and swabs from bodies) that might contain biological fluids, such as blood and semen. As described above, when confronted with a piece of evidence from a crime scene, Ellie has to figure out where the biological fluid from the suspect and/or victim were likely to be before she can produce a DNA profile from it.

By methodically laying out and screening items, DNA analysts use the systems of science to create order from the messy materials of the crime scene.[5] This screening is a process teeming with uncertainty: Is there a biological fluid on the dress? Where? Of what kind? This uncertainty can be attenuated somewhat by reading the police report on the case, so as to try and understand where the biological materials might be. It is also managed through the systematic approach that analysts use. By following a specific order of analysis and using verified protocols, as well as carefully noting down everything they do, analysts ensure that they perform a thorough investigation and have a trail to backtrack if anything goes wrong.[6]

Analysts at MCCL tame items as varied as moldy pantyhose from a decades-old cold case to desiccated muscle tissue and teeth from a mummified body. More typical, however, are items like underwear from a victim or gloves and hats left at a crime scene.

Analysts share approaches with one another for collecting biological traces from such items. Jonah is an experienced DNA analyst who had worked in a big East Coast city for a few years prior to moving to MCCL.

He shared techniques with the unit, such as his practice of swabbing the inside of a t-shirt's neckline, because that is where skin cells are likely to gather. He also developed a method for carefully slicing open gloves to reach the inside where fingers regularly rub. Similarly, when Eden, one of the unit supervisors, was screening a large blanket, she showed new analysts how she mapped out a grid on the blanket and wiped each segment with a piece of cotton, creating a set of swabs numbered to match the grid drawn in her case notes.

———

After taking a sample through cutting or swabbing, the analyst is ready to analyze the DNA profile in the biological material. This process of questioning the evidence involves meticulous benchwork, careful interpretation, and often collective problem-solving. The analyst extracts the DNA from the sample by chemically breaking down and washing the cells in a small tube. Then, she amplifies the DNA in the sample, which requires multiple steps. First, she adds enzymes and proteins in a fresh tube to isolate particular regions of the DNA strands called "short tandem repeats" (or STRs), which are present in everyone's DNA. Next, she puts the sample on a thermal cycler, which heats and cools the sample multiple times. This replicates the STR fragments of DNA, so that there are many copies to ensure detection through capillary electrophoresis, the instrumental technique by which a DNA profile is developed.

Each step in this process entails standard laboratory benchwork: careful tracking of all samples, putting on gloves, pipetting exact amounts of reagents into small test tubes, changing gloves, centrifuging samples, wiping down the work surface under the hood, regloving for the next set of tubes, and so on. Every time they perform a new step, the analysts carefully note down which sample numbers they transfer to which tubes, and which controls they use. They log the expiration dates of reagents and other supplies.[7]

A portion of each sample is then loaded on an instrument that performs capillary electrophoresis. The preparatory steps in this process take several days; analysts batch the samples for multiple cases together in a run, which will ultimately be processed at one time. Because of ever-present fears about contamination, the lab's procedure calls for grouping samples expected to have high volumes of DNA (such as blood) together, and processing separately those samples with low volumes (such as contact swabs from places that are merely touched by an individual). This is to ensure that the low-volume samples are not accidentally contaminated with DNA from the high-volume samples.

In capillary electrophoresis, after the days of preparatory steps, the instrument separates the STR fragments, sorting the molecules by size and charge as they are forced by electricity through a thin glass tube. Here, the amounts of each DNA segment are detected with a laser, which identifies fluorescent markers that are attached to particular fragments. The instrument converts these amounts and records them as peaks on an electropherogram.

Each STR is drawn from a particular region of the DNA strand, called a "locus." This locus contains a known set of alleles that occurs throughout the general population (i.e., a locus is one of the points where analysts can easily compare the DNA of one individual to the DNA of another). The particular alleles in the sample are displayed in the electropherogram, a graph that shows peaks for the alleles at each location. After viewing these, the analyst identifies the peaks as the alleles for each locus and creates a table of sixteen loci to present in the final report as the DNA profile for that sample.

The report also includes all of their notes on the procedures followed, as well as a conclusion, which is often an attribution about the source of the DNA profile as it relates to population statistics. One report contained the conclusion, "The suspect is included as a possible contributor to this DNA mixture. The probability that a person selected from the population at random would be included in the combination of alleles present in this mixture is: 1 in 260,000,000,000 in the Caucasian population" (see figure 1.1, p. 25). In other words, DNA analysis is not only about identification but is also about probability. When presented, however, the conclusions seem irrefutable.

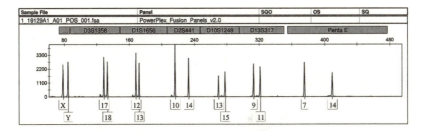

FIGURE 1.1. A sample electropherogram image with peaks representing alleles at multiple loci.

	Evidence bloodstain	Suspect A	Suspect B	Suspect C	Suspect D
D8S1179	13, 16	11, 12	13, 15	14, 14	13, 16
D21S11	30, 33.2	29, 30	32.2, 33.2	29, 29	30, 33.2
D7S820	8, 11	9, 9	8, 11	11, 12	8, 11
CSF1PO	12, 12	11, 12	10, 12	7, 8	12, 12
D3S1358	14, 18	15, 18	16, 17	15, 16	14, 18
TH01	6, 8	6, 8	9, 9.3	7, 9	6, 8
D13S317	8, 13	11, 13	8, 12	11, 12	8, 13
D16S539	10, 14	10, 11	11, 14	9, 11	10, 14
D2S1338	20, 23	18, 20	16, 24	16, 23	20, 23
D19S433	12, 16	13, 16.2	13, 15.2	13, 14.2	12, 16
vWA	14, 16	17, 17	12, 15	18, 20	14, 16
TPOX	8, 11	8, 8	8, 9	8, 9	8, 11
D18S51	14, 15	13, 17	16, 17	14, 15	14, 15
Amelogenin	XX	XX	XY	XY	XX
D5S818	11, 12	13, 13	12, 12	12, 13	11, 12
FGA	20, 21	22, 22	20, 21	19, 23	20, 21

FIGURE 1.2. A sample table of alleles at 16 loci for multiple individuals.

The tables and graphs that constitute DNA profiling reports look tidy and objective. However, DNA analysts themselves consider the process of profiling messy and in need of expert, but subjective, judgment: much like the work perceived to be "less scientific" performed in the rest of the lab. DNA graphs are marred by stutter, imbalanced peaks, drop-off, and spikes caused by technical issues with instruments, as well as dirty and degraded samples. These issues can sometimes make interpretation difficult. Analysts must evaluate these and figure out which markings represent the profile versus those generated by problems with the scientific process. Andy, an experienced analyst, listed some of the instrument problems that might prompt him to rerun a capillary electrophoresis test: "If there are artifacts [unusual markings in the graph], bubbles in the capillary tube might cause that. The number one reason is lots of noise, you can't make out the type when it is so distorted. Or a temperature change throws off the instrument, and everything looks bad, even the controls, the run just didn't work. Sometimes the dyes in the tube clump together, and it looks like a big hump or a spike when the laser hits that, the baseline looks elevated." In other words, the output created by the instrument is not inherently objective. Inconsistencies in the instrument itself, changes in the lab environment, errors in the materials employed—all this and more can generate surprising and unhelpful results, which require DNA analysts to understand and critique their techniques like any other scientist.

Contamination in the lab also creates problems, as I learned one day while working with Carly, a veteran DNA analyst. A junior member of the unit, Terri, came over to tell us about the saliva samples she had difficulty with a few weeks before. She reminded Carly, "Those were the ones where there was contamination in the control sample and an allele showed up." This shouldn't happen, because the control is created in a laboratory to be blank and have no alleles present. Terri went on: "But I reamped the control this week and now it is clear." Because the samples are amplified, the controls must be as well. When a control is contaminated, the analyst has to reanalyze the entire run of samples, including the control, performing the same full set of processes. After a long technical discussion about the work Terri did on this problem, Carly concluded, "Oh, yeah, sometimes contamination just happens and you do all this sleuthing and don't find an answer."

Such anomalies in the DNA profiling process are thoroughly investigated. As Carly noted, "You want to figure it out so that you don't have it happen again, but a lot of times you can't . . . this process is so sensitive, sometimes you can't reproduce it. So you write it up, and say whether it interferes with your analysis or not."

The careful notes that analysts make while they work through their analyses are included with the report on every case. These documents, along with the original data files from the instrument, are then technically reviewed by a second analyst to ensure accuracy. Analysts pore over Excel spreadsheets of statistics together almost as often as they scan electropherogram results. And, because interpretation of such results is complicated, analysts also spend much of their time at their computers, crafting their reports.

————

As the discussion of loci and alleles illustrates, statistics are a vital part of the conclusions in a DNA profiling report. Those conclusions depend on the likelihood of linking the DNA sample from the crime scene to the suspect, and this likelihood is determined by comparing their combination of alleles against a large set of DNA profiles drawn from the local population. These statistics are complicated by the fact that DNA profiles in crime scene materials are often mixtures: they have DNA from more than one person. This can be seen in a rape kit, where the DNA of the victim and suspect, as well as possibly other consensual partners, would be expected to be present.

Similarly, Jonah's report from a robbery case involving five different suspects has DNA profiles from multiple items such as gloves, bandanas, and hats. Explaining the results table to me, he said, "There's a lot of stuff here, a lot of mixed samples. I need to look really closely at the results and see if this person could be included, excluded, or if there's just too much DNA on some of these for me to say anything." Because every person has two alleles at a locus, when multiple people leave biological traces on an item, there can be many alleles appearing on the electropherogram at each locus. Jonah was explaining that for each suspect, he needs to analyze closely whether the DNA profile constitutes a tangible identification on a particular item. This can be difficult, he said, because sometimes there is "just too much DNA." This is reflected in the way the electropherogram shows the data: "The peaks on some of the samples are all at a balanced, equal level. Sometimes, you have a major set of alleles at a higher level, and can say that others are minor." This means that, while in some profiles alleles have a strong likelihood of coming from one person, other profiles are less definitive and the alleles could be linked to multiple people. "For one glove, I can make an ID," Jonah noted, "but the other one is a mixture, probably of four or five people."

Jonah continued to look at the tables, as some of the samples had six peaks or more at each locus. What he was looking for was whether certain peaks (representing a specific person's DNA) are prominent across multiple loci on one sample. Such "unbalanced peaks," in which two peaks in the output are more prominent than other, smaller peaks (assumed to be from the DNA of others) can indicate to analysts that this person was a major contributor.

For instance, assuming a bandana belonged to only one suspect (who wore it to cover his face), his skin cells probably rubbed off onto it. Such direct, sustained exposure would produce more of the wearer's DNA in the profile—more, that is, than the other two or three people who might have passed it along to him and just touched it briefly. So the high peaks *across* loci would be interpreted as belonging to the major contributor.

Again, far from an "exact science," DNA profiling is a highly technical, but highly interpretive, method of investigating evidence. Jonah echoed this ambiguity when noting he was not the last word on the conclusions of his tests. "That's what's good about our process," Jonah explained. "I'll make these calls, this conclusion, and I'm curious what other people who will review it will think."

Jonah expected his report to be checked by others in the DNA unit. In fact, multiple rounds of interpretation are needed to produce conclusions.[8] The technical review process not only entails back-and-forth discussions between the reviewer and the originating analyst, but also draws in other members of the lab to aid in making decisions about calling alleles, calculating statistics, and representing results consistently across reports.

When Terri reviewed Jonah's report from a different case, she visited her supervisor Eden's office to ask a question about the wording of the conclusion. In his report, Jonah used the word "source" about a DNA profile that was from an unknown person. This wording felt too definitive to Terri. Had there been an "official decision," Terri asked, about how to discuss such a situation in a report? Anca, a veteran analyst sitting in Eden's office, replied, "I would say, 'originated from.'" As we walked away, Terri explained to me, "It takes a lab to write a report!"

After the original analyst submits the report, the technical reviewer plasters each case report with sticky notes asking the analyst questions, which they talk through together. After the analyst makes changes, the report is returned to the reviewer for another look, and then goes to one of the three supervisors for an administrative review. If the supervisor suggests changes, the entire process is repeated. Once everyone is satisfied, the report is released for use in criminal justice proceedings: that is, the report is available for those outside the lab—attorneys, police officers, and others—for official usage within the criminal justice system. The forensic biology unit engages in these communal judgments to make order out of the messiness of the DNA profiling process, and to consistently represent the results of their work to the criminal justice community.

The forensic biology unit's elaborate communal review process creates a sense of comfort with the messiness of the process, as well as a willingness to admit mistakes. Analysts often tease one another while they review cases. When Kerry, a new analyst, reviewed a case of Ellie's, she started to laugh as she read the notes on the image of a pair of bloody jeans. "You dropped the swab on the floor?" she asked. "I know," Ellie said. "It's the one thing you dread! I had the skinny rack and the tubes were in there. It kind of fell over onto its side." Kerry asked, "Were the tubes open?" and Ellie turned a little red. "Yes, well, the swab didn't fall out of the tube. I was just happy that I could resample. It is my biggest fear."

Additionally, because they need details of the crime scene to make sense of their evidence, analysts in the DNA unit read the police reports on their cases. Their conversations extend beyond the technical analyses to encompass their speculations about the crimes themselves. They sometimes talk about what had reportedly happened at the scene, like Kerry and Ellie, discussing how a fight started in a car and then the suspect chased the victim around a park with a knife. In addition to the jeans, Ellie also tested swabs from the suspect's hands and sampled blood from a knife the investigators thought was used in the crime. Kerry said, "Those hand swabs were bloody? Gross! But there wasn't any blood on the knife?" Ellie said, "Yeah, I know. And the knife had all sorts of other stuff on it, so they obviously didn't wipe it clean. It was an odd knife too, it didn't close, so how were they carrying it around? On the report, it looked like the police came right after it happened." Kerry said, "They must have tossed the real knife. It's the first thing they do when the cops show up." Although the reports may not always be relevant to the analysis, sometimes they suggest a starting point for screening and testing.

DNA profiling is an important tool for analyzing evidence from crime scenes. However, while outsiders may view the DNA unit as the most important of the whole crime lab, they are not the last word in forensic science. Often DNA evidence is unavailable, and the work of other units in the laboratory becomes paramount.

The other unit that primarily encounters evidence from major crimes is firearms examination. Similar to the DNA unit, the criminalists in firearms work many hours on analyzing their evidence and communally reviewing each other's work. Yet, in contrast to the DNA unit, the analytic process is not biological and does not use complex instrumentation. Rather, these criminalists perform hands-on functional examinations of guns and sit side by side, examining evidence of toolmarks under a comparison microscope.

WORK PRACTICES OF FIREARMS EXAMINATION: PATTERN RECOGNITION AMONG GUN FANATICS

Early one February morning, Al sits at his bench with a cart of evidence beside him, examining firearms one at a time. Moving an envelope to the bench's surface, he writes the lab number, his name, and the date at the top of a new worksheet. From the chain of custody listed on the envelope, he copies the bar code, item number, type, and manufacturer from the envelope onto the sheet. He pulls out a Smith and Wesson gun and checks to make sure that the firearm is unloaded, looking down the barrel to see his thumbnail at the end. Al notes down that it's a model 457, caliber .45 auto, and shows me a brass mark on the magazine due to rubbing from the cartridge cases. He holds up the gun, checking that the magazine disconnect and the safety both work. Then he pulls the trigger.

The trigger works. Al records the serial number, replaces the gun in the envelope, and puts the envelope into a shopping bag on the floor at his feet, which already contains several other firearms. The lab has a reference collection in a back room, with thousands of firearms lining the library shelves; when a gun arrives at the lab that the unit does not have in the collection, they keep it. Al tells Adam, sitting at the bench next to him, that he just examined a Smith and Wesson 457. Adam asks, "A .22?" "No," Al replies, "a .45 auto. I don't think we have one of those."

Al's function exams—which check the usability of an individual firearm—are interrupted by the telephone. After exchanging greetings, Al says, "Ah, LIMS, what a piece of crap." Al is referring to the justice system's evidence database, which wasn't working. He was fielding a call from law enforcement to summarize what he had already input into his official report: "The gun was inoperable when it came in, it wouldn't fire. It was dirty, filthy! Old grease, oxidized oil . . . I cleaned it up. . . . Yes, it was legal."

Hanging up, he says to Adam, "It was a burglary officer. He called because he couldn't see my report, LIMS was down." Adam asks, "What was the point to the exam?" Al answers, "It was a convicted felon in possession of a firearm." Al explains to me that the firearms laws are complex, with strict restrictions for convicted felons. "Even just a frame and receiver [the housing for the firing mechanism] are considered a firearm under the law, so just those alone, a felon can't have." Adam says that he had a case a few weeks ago where a convicted felon just had ammunition. "They are not supposed to. Even just carrying a fired cartridge case is illegal if you are a felon."

Al pulls a gun out of the next envelope on his tray, a Sig Sauer. "This is a nice gun," he says. "Only about $300. It is a plastic frame, which I don't care for. But it has an aluminum barrel with a steel liner." He moves a clip on the side to try to release the barrel, but it does not work. "This is almost a new gun, it is .22 caliber." He slides it forward and peers down the barrel. "I wanted to pull the barrel out." He explains that it would be good to add this to their collection. First he'd have to figure out its particular quirks. "With a normal Sig," Al says, "you can flip this clip down and everything comes off up front." But here Al had found a modification on the gun: "Hmm. I can worry about it later."

He looks at the tag and again writes down the item number, type, manufacturer, serial number, model, and caliber. "This comes in multiple colors, this one is a black grip with silver, it also comes with the opposite. All of them have a plastic frame and a steel trigger, I think. I wouldn't own this. I outgrew plastic guns a long time ago." He moves on to two shotguns and is similarly cautious (and chatty) as he examines them. On one of these, he does not recognize the penal code number on the evidence tag, so he takes the penal code down from the bookshelf above his desk to investigate. Al discovers the code stands for resisting arrest.

Al then looks through all the morning's worksheets, notes down the ammunition he needs to take with us to the firing range in another room, and sorts it out from the ammunition drawer. Checking each piece to make sure it is clean, he places the ammunition into boxes that he labels with the case information. He loads these on the cart with the firearms, and we head through the door to the firing range to test-fire them.

The back area where the firearms examiners test-fire bullets is soundproofed, and the walls of both rooms are lined with metal: one contains a horizontal bullet tank filled with water, and the other is an eighty-foot-long firing range. Al brings the cart to the bullet tank in the first room, which has a yellow fabric pouch at the front opening through which the examiners fire, and a rubber ducky floating in the water.

We put on our headphones. Al pulls out the .45 from its envelope, loads one of the prepared cartridges, warns me, and test-fires it into the tank. He reloads, and after a second warning, he fires again. One of the cartridge casings has fallen into the pouch, but the other is missing. He uncovers the tank and finds it in the water. Taking a three-foot-long wand off the cover of the tank, Al dips it into the water, and the soft clay on the wand's tip molds around the casing. He lifts out the casing and the two bullets one by one, places them on the table, and returns the firearm back to its envelope. After firing several more guns and retrieving the bullets and casings, we hang up our headphones and return to the microscope so Al can start the examination.

———

At MCCL, Al is the most experienced firearms examiner, and his morning is characteristic of the way criminalists examine firearms prior to testing them. The main tasks of firearms examiners are to test weapons gathered from crime scenes and suspects to see if they are functional, compare bullets and cartridge casings of guns used in major cases, and compare the guns they receive in the lab against IBIS (Integrated Ballistics Identification System) to see if they can find guns used in other crimes locally and nationally. Much of their daily work entails physically examining firearms, firing them, and using a comparison microscope to examine the bullets and cartridge cases.

The firearms lab is a small, tight-knit group with a strong sense of the value of their expertise. Firearms examiners set great store in their deep knowledge of firearms and their manufacture. To acquire the knowledge for their judgments, firearms examiners spend two years in training, reading histories of the manufacturing of firearms, and visiting firearms factories. They pore over image after image of best-known nonmatches: close markings found on cartridge cases or bullets that have been fired by guns of the same model produced by the same manufacturer. Knowing the range of such markings enables examiners to develop a foundational understanding of the similarities shared by different guns from the same manufacturer.

Knowing nonmatches is crucial to the work of examiners, who use their knowledge of the types and quantity of markings made in nonmatches as a baseline.[9] Tom pointed to this training in firearms as the source of his expertise: "Each examiner has built in criteria for identification from their training and knowledge. And you build these every time you look at what matches and doesn't match, the orientation. You build an understanding of nonmatch, match, the internal criteria. In training, they show you close ones that aren't a match—what they call the best-known nonmatch. Like bullets from two consecutive barrels from the same manufacturer—they are going to be close but not identical." Even guns made in the same factory will differ (i.e., not match), so developing and maintaining a stock of knowledge of the best-known iterations of this difference not only allows examiners to better identify bullets but also gives them a deeper, holistic understanding of how guns and bullets are made and fired. This long experience gave them a personal sense of confidence in their judgment of matches and nonmatches in comparisons.

———

In the firearms unit, taming the evidence involves less mess than in the forensic biology unit, but more danger. Examiners are very aware of safety issues and treat the firearms, as Al did in the examination described above, with caution and care. However, injuries happen. According to Al: "No matter how safe we are around here, we still get bit."

During the examinations that morning, he also showed me what happened to him a few years ago on a pistol. "I was examining it and I had my left hand around the front, but the safety was broken. I accidentally chambered a bullet and shot it through my hand. It pushed a piece of bone right out! And Adam got bit just last week." Adam replied that it was over a year since the last time he was hurt while examining a firearm. He pulled the pistol out of a box in the middle of the lab to show me: "I was working with this pistol and the slide was a bit stuck. I was pushing it with a lot of force and it finally moved and bit me. And one of the public defenders got bit by the hammer on this one last week." Al added, "Last week Patrick had this cartridge case bounce back and hit him in the forehead"—while firing a test round, the bullet's case landed sharply on the examiner's face. "He didn't even know he was bleeding!" Patrick, a novice examiner who was not yet certified for casework, laughed. "Al gave me a devil smile for a full minute before telling me."

———

This function exam, which demonstrates that a firearm can shoot a projectile, is the first step in examining a gun suspected of being used in a crime. Next, firearms examiners question the evidence to see if it is materially linked to the crime. To do so, they compare the bullets and cartridge cases found at a crime scene to those of a gun found on a suspect, owned by a suspect, or discovered at the crime scene. They then look for matching patterns.

In this type of comparison, the examiner test-fires the gun in the range at the lab and collects the bullets and cases, because a gun, in the action of firing, imprints microscopic marks on them: marks created by the lands and grooves in the barrel, as well as the other mechanical parts like the firing pin. The examiners use a comparison microscope to compare the microscopic marks (called "striae") found on the test-fires with those of the striae on the bullets and cartridge cases found at the scene (see figure 1.3 p. 36).

MCCL firearms examiners value their pattern recognition abilities, subjective training, and experience, which enable them to make these comparisons. They invest great effort in training the newest members of the unit. Al explained, "You learn from experience. The new trainee coming into our department knows nothing, and she won't touch a gun in here for six months. First, I'll have her read the two-volume book by Thompson Wheeland with basic information. It is a technical volume on all aspects of firearms. And then read it again, and then a third time so she'll have a good basic background. Also maybe Gunther and Gunther. And Hatcher, the *Forensics Firearms Examination*. And maybe that English one, Burrard, although those English are so full of BS, they don't know what they are talking about." Al is reputed to have an encyclopedic

FIGURE 1.3. Images of striae comparisons on cartridge cases.

knowledge of firearms, which he has used to help lawmakers craft gun legislation. Throughout the time I spent at his side, he brought up prior cases in labs at other law enforcement agencies, specific details about the manufacture of many types of guns, and the detailed ways that people could modify weapons.

Mentioning the Burrard textbook reminded Al of a story about an examiner from London's Scotland Yard, whom Al had met and did not think was very knowledgeable. This examiner told Al about an exam he had performed on a Henry Rifle, a gun that was manufactured in England between 1863 and 1865. Ultimately, the examiner correctly identified the gun as a modern replica from Italy, but the process had taken him a long time. Al had a different way of identifying the gun:

> I asked, "What about proof marks?" He said that everything was re-
> moved. I asked what caliber it was, and the guy said .44 to .40. I said,
> "That should have given it away right there, those weren't manufac-
> tured until 1873"—the gun, therefore, had to be a replica, and not an
> original—"and you couldn't modify an original one for those, because
> they shot .44 rimfire." I asked him about the screws, because if it was
> made in Italy they'd be metric, and the Henry would have English. It
> had metric.

Al scoffed, "So this guy had spent all this time, and it would've taken me five seconds! Firearms experts can spot each other. Once, I met this guy in Russia, he didn't speak English and I don't speak Russian but we re-spected each other's knowledge even though we didn't speak the lan-guage. You can tell."

While personal expertise and knowledge are points of pride for firearms examiners, they also make a visible record of the matching striae in order to reinforce their judgments in the courtroom, creating detailed note packets as they make comparisons over the course of several days. In these packets, they save digital images of every set of matching striae, including those from the firing pin impressions, extractor marks, and chamber marks. As Adam, an experienced examiner, told me, "You want the note packet to support [your judgment] on the stand. Multiple outsiders have seen my work, reviewed it, and it has never been challenged." Firearms examiners pointed out how their practices had changed over time. "We used to say, 'I know a toolmark when I see it,' and 'I know it like my mother's face,'" Adam said. "This is no longer acceptable for reports or testimony. We can't do that anymore. Now we have to document. In today's lab, you better have the images to back it up." Questioning the evidence was done in parallel with framing it: creating images and supporting documentation for the report.

On an afternoon visit to the firearms unit, I found Adam sitting at his bench peering through a comparison microscope at two cartridge casings from different crime scenes. He called Tom over, telling me, "I try to keep him on board on my thought process. We have a verification, a second read, and have the other person sign off on the image sheet." Tom then took his place at the microscope, examining the striae on the firing pin impression. He adjusted the microscope, reversing the image of the firing pin to a different angle. Adam, looking at it on his computer screen, said, "I looked at it that way, and it is not as good, go back to the way you just had it. It is a challenge to image it, maybe adjust the light." Tom flipped it and pointed at a set of lines on the image on the screen. Adam said, "We're at 40x [magnification], you can see it better, there's a whole section of agreement, light and dark, you can see a whole set of them." Tom replied, "Too bad you can't rotate [the angle of the microscope] more, get light in from the side." Adam said that he wanted to digitally photograph it first and then saved the images of these two places to his notes.

Tom told Adam, "You are almost right there for identification." Adam disagreed: "I think it's an identification already." Earlier that day, Tom had told me that examiners could have slightly different standards for identification, but, as long as they agreed on the conclusions, he was comfortable with it. Now, he pointed out to me, "See, Beth? I might do one more picture. He is comfortable already." Adam elaborated, "I don't believe it is random agreement at this point. You want me to do one more?" Tom suggested that he look at the chamber marks, and Adam said that he planned to continue to that next. Tom, moving away, said, "I'm happy with this, and you probably will have extractor and chamber marks too." Adam finished, "I'm happy with the images I took. I'm moving on to the extractor; I will call you over then."

Technical reviews of firearms evidence are collaborative, like DNA profiling, but, unlike DNA profiling, these firearm reviews occur simultaneously with the initial analysis. In the firearms unit a second examiner follows the first during every step of a comparison, looking through the microscope at each set of striae, and signs off on every page of documentation, verifying his agreement with the first examiner's assessment. Technical reviews are therefore made through continuous dialogue, which is not only about the particulars of a set of striae, but also about how to create a digital image that will be more convincing. This joint work incorporates the examiners' trained judgment of the striae, as well as their interest in creating the clearest and most convincing images for the notes on the case. Analysts frame the report during the examination and imaging process, keeping the expectations of the audience in the courtroom in mind.

———

Most of the firearms examiners at MCCL are gun enthusiasts; they not only have expertise with firearms, but they love guns. Al often asked me when I was going to buy my first gun and had ideas about which gun would suit me. Moreover, they like to take novices to the range and teach them how to shoot. In the month and a half I spent in their unit,

I shot in their lab firing range twice and at the county's firing range once. The latter was at an event where the group invited county public defenders to join them for "training." They are proud of their knowledge and eager to share their enthusiasm.

Their personal knowledge of guns puts firearms examiners close to the crime, as they think about how the gun might have been used at a scene. Similar to the way police reports situate the DNA analysts with respect to the crime scene, firearms examiners draw on their embodied understanding of firing weapons. As Al described a case he had analyzed several years earlier: "A woman was picked up for murdering her husband, put in jail. They sent over his clothes, and her gun for a distance determination. I looked at the clothes, and the bullet holes in the shirt and undershirt on both front sides line up. But on the coat, the [holes] on the left front are there, but not the right. I asked the detective, 'By any chance, did the victim have a gun on his hip? Was he reaching for it?'" While talking, he actively demonstrated standing up and drawing the gun from his right hip, which pushed his coat off to his side, showing me that a bullet would not have penetrated it. This familiarity with the real-life experience of using firearms informs the examiners' scientific analysis and adds insight to their casework.

Unlike DNA profiling, which is based on importing a new technology from basic biology into forensic science, firearms examination developed directly to serve the criminal justice system (both in practice and in theoretical orientation). In his history of the early years of firearms identification, Calvin Goddard describes how, with others, he developed the comparison microscope in the early twentieth century for use in comparing bullets and cartridge cases and promoted it throughout the late 1920s to police and legal organizations. After his firearms identifications in the high-profile 1929 St. Valentine's Day Massacre case in Chicago made headlines, he received private funding to develop the first crime laboratory in the United States: the Scientific Crime Detection Laboratory, at Northwestern University.[10] Goddard calls himself a "gun nut," and the history of the field is populated by many similarly enthusiastic gun users.

The techniques and instruments used in firearms examination were developed internally, within the institutions of criminal justice. As we see next, this contrasts with the origins of narcotics' use of microcrystallography or toxicology's use of gas chromatography, both of which originated in disciplinary chemistry.

WORK PRACTICES OF THE CHEMISTRY UNIT: THE CRAFT OF ESTABLISHING CRISP DISTINCTIONS

Matt, a seasoned narcotics analyst in the chemistry unit, cleans his work surface and tools with soap and water and puts on a fresh pair of gloves. He reaches down to his box of cases and removes a large white envelope from the sheriff's office. The envelope contains a Kapak (a heat-sealed plastic bag) and a small paper bag. According to the tags the officer attached to each bag, one tested presumptively positive for methamphetamine, the other for marijuana. Matt puts the paper bag of marijuana aside, on top of his fume hood. He examines the Kapak, notices just a small amount of drugs in a baggie inside, and places a tear sheet of paper on his balance.

He opens LIMS (the evidence management software, which Al had trouble with earlier) on his computer to enter the item number and his description for this case, typing "one heat-sealed Kapak containing one ziploc containing crystalline powder." He pours the powder onto the paper, and the balance reads .4190 grams, which he enters into LIMS as a weight of .41. "We don't record the extra digits," he says, "and we never round up. This gives the suspects the benefit of the doubt."

Matt then prepares to do presumptive color tests. He takes a six-well white plastic plate from the top of the pile at the back of his bench and uses his spatula to put a small amount of the powder from the paper into each of the wells, saying, "I have powder so I don't have to crush the crystals." He puts cobalt thiocyanate into the first well—the presumptive test for cocaine—and tiny blue specs appear at the bottom of the well. These disappear when he adds a drop of 10-percent HCl solution. The Marquis test solution goes in the next well; the police also use this as the presumptive test for methamphetamine, MDMA, and heroin. Matt expects it to turn bright orange for meth, and it does. The next solution is the secondary amine test, which turns a bright blue for amines (ammonia derivatives). He drips Wagner's solution in the fourth well—a general test for all drugs. It looks "kind of like maple syrup" and turns "more cloudy and brown, it reacts with pretty much anything." The final two wells are for Dille Koppanyi, the test for barbiturates, and PDMAB, for hallucinogens, and both of those wells remain clear. Surveying the different reactions in his six-well test plate, Matt says, "Fading blue, bright orange, blue, brown, clear and clear, this is the standard for meth."

But this test is not sufficient to prove a substance is, in fact, methamphetamine. So he moves on to the crystal tests for meth. In microcrystallography, or crystal tests, a chemical reagent is added to a drug, causing crystalline precipitate to form. The size and shape of the resulting crystals, as seen under a microscope, are characteristic of particular drugs. For these tests, he uses an indented glass slide with a well in it for the methamphetamine. After placing a small amount of the powder in the well with his spatula, he adds a strong base reagent. Then he puts two different acids on the slide cover, a tiny drop of gold chloride on the left side and a drop of phosphoric acid on the right. The meth, when the cover is placed on the slide, becomes volatile and moves into the two neighboring drops. After putting the cover on, Matt lets the slide sit to give the drug time to move. As the meth moves into the acid, he says to me, "See, notice the gold starting to cloud up."

Taylor walks by the lab benches saying, "I need an opinion," and the other analysts turn to look at him. "I've got a bunch of prescription drugs. All of them are in the blister packages. They are totally sealed, some in all foil, and I can't see in them. A couple are ointment." Matt says, "If they are sealed, you are fine doing packaging." Jodi agrees that he does not need to open them, just list what it says on the packages: "They aren't punctured, right?" Matt jokes, "What sort of dangerous ointment is it?" Taylor says, "I don't know, these are all Indian manufactured. I've even got some Indian energy drink mix, that'll be a 'not analyzed.' And some medicated Band-Aids, some antacid." Taylor explains that the evidence in question is from "this guy's first aid kit that they took from him, so now he's got some serious heartburn in his cell. He was arrested for 11–350—drugs without a prescription." Billie suggests sending the investigator an e-mail to ask whether any analysis, beyond listing the ingredients from the packaging, was in order.

Taylor sits down at his bench, and the analysts return to their work. Matt picks up his slide, removes the cover, and places it on a flat slide on his microscope. For the gold chloride test on the left side, he looks for crystals through a polarizing filter, and sees the "clothespin" shapes, which indicate meth. Removing the filter, he adds a reagent to the test on the right side and sees "rabbit ears" crystals. In the LIMS software, he pulls down a menu to record the results for each test, then repackages the baggie into the Kapak and cleans his work surface to start the next sample.

———

Every morning, narcotics analysts at MCCL go to the property room in the basement and pick up large boxes of Kapaks of potential controlled substances (illegal drugs) dropped off by law enforcement officers. Returning to their lab to analyze them, they use wet chemistry techniques, performed at the bench, as well as instrumental analyses, performed with instruments and computers, to confirm that the submitted evidence is a controlled substance. The law requires a short turnaround time for narcotics cases, and analysts are expected to have all of their assigned cases completed within ten days, and 70 percent in five days.

Over half of the controlled substances submitted to MCCL are confirmed as methamphetamine, with another 20 percent cocaine and the remainder a mix of other substances. In 5 percent of cases, no controlled substances are detected. Although methamphetamine is the most common substance encountered, the daily box of Kapaks typically includes marijuana, cocaine, ecstasy, prescription sedatives, hashish, psilocybin, and more. Analysts excitedly relate their identifications of unusual substances to one another (and to me): "Check out these mushrooms!" As a group, narcotics analysts are curious and thorough about hunting down the identity of the different substances they analyzed, and they hold fast to ideals about scientific investigation.[11]

Unlike in forensic biology or firearms examination, narcotics analysis does not require as much cleaning and preparing of evidence. Although occasionally the lab receives drugs that have been hidden in people's bodies, most of the time controlled substances arrive neatly in bags or packages. Analysts are attuned to the physical attributes of different drugs, and use indicators such as color, texture, and odor to get a sense of what the substance might be. As a result, they frequently told me what the controlled substance "probably" was as they took it out of its container or bag. As Billie examined a baggie with white powder stuck on the sides, she said, "This is what cocaine salt looks like. If we had a lot of it, it would have a very vinegary kind of odor, not like vinegar but the same sense."[12]

Narcotics analysts are sensitive to the aesthetic dimensions of their work. While DNA analysts are faced with body fluids on a daily basis and rarely seem disgusted, narcotics analysts are more squeamish. They are grateful that their supervisor "spreads out" the rare cases of drugs that have been exposed to body fluids, assigning them to different analysts in a rotating sequence as the drugs come into the lab. They are also attuned to odors and stash cases with large samples of marijuana or methamphetamine under the fume hood while working, "or it just stinks up the whole lab." I heard the most complaints in narcotics, that aspects of forensic science work are "gross," and several analysts told me that they would never work in the DNA unit, since the work there is too "icky."

As in the description of Matt's casework above, each controlled substance analysis begins with weighing, since the specific charges for suspects depend on how much of a substance they had in their possession when arrested. Then, analysts perform presumptive tests, called "color tests," with a small bit of the sample. These tests, in addition to the analysts' sense awareness, help them to determine what class of substance it is, and then they move on to confirmatory testing specific to each drug.

Narcotics analysts at MCCL primarily use wet chemistry techniques to confirm the identity of controlled substances, assessing, identifying, and recording their crystalline structures. Crystal testing is a long-standing method of identification. In the lab, analysts perform these tests in minutes: the preparation of the slide is straightforward, and the crystals precipitate rapidly (see figure 1.4, p. 45). They examine the slide under the microscope as the crystals form; then, when the slide gets overcrowded, they dispose of it. They note the crystals' distinct shape in their reports by both naming the shapes ("feathery Ks"; "rabbit ears"; "clothespins"; "hockey sticks"; "daggers"; "3-D jacks") and drawing a picture of what they see.

Some drugs, such as marijuana, crack cocaine, and MDMA, cannot be confirmed with microcrystallography. For these cases, as well as for "unknown" substances for which the presumptive tests and physical examinations leave analysts uncertain about their chemical makeup, they turn to instrumental methods. To confirm MDMA or cocaine salt, analysts use an instrument called a "gas chromatograph/mass spectrometer" (GC/MS).

The GC/MS instrument decomposes and detects the individual chemical components of a particular drug, which makes it possible to give the drug a formal identification. First, a suspected drug is put into a solvent. One part of the instrument, the gas chromatograph, separates the mixture's individual components, distinguishing substances by the time they take to travel through a narrow tube. The second part, the mass spectrometer, hits the material with a beam of high-energy electrons, which creates positively charged ions that decompose the substance into fragments. Under these conditions, no two substances create the same fragmentation pattern, which means that the analysts can employ the two aspects of this instrument to clearly distinguish the suspected drug from other known drugs. Both the results from the GC and the MS are recorded as output graphs

FIGURE 1.4. Image of cocaine microcrystals as would be seen under a microscope.

from the instrument, and the substance is matched against the instrument's drug library and a known sample of the suspected drug (see figure 1.5, p. 46).[13]

In the narcotics unit, reports are supported with drawings of microcrystals and documentation from the instrument. During crystal testing, analysts record what they see under the microscope by drawing it, and, as Matt noted, "In the report, we describe what we see, we don't just say, 'This is meth.'" These reports are simple and short, especially when compared with the lengthy notes and supporting documentation of DNA analysts, or the digital images of firearms examiners. However, because there can be unknown compounds that produce similar-shaped crystals, crystal tests provide "less certainty" than instrumental tests. As a result, the guidelines of the narcotics national scientific working group require that two different crystal tests be performed on each sample, using two different solvents. MCCL practice is therefore to provide verification of the results of the first crystal test with a second, different

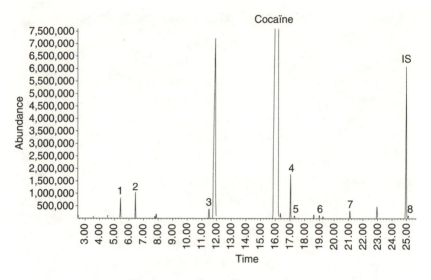

FIGURE 1.5. Chromatogram obtained for a typical cocaine sample.

crystal test. Once these tests are complete, they are technically reviewed by the supervisor of the unit.

———

Narcotics analysts value careful science, although they do not need to be as concerned about contamination and, consequently, are less neurotic about gloving up than in the forensic biology unit. However, they are very prickly about assumptions and standards and worry about their science being represented appropriately. For example, the police often do a presumptive test at the crime scene and submit case evidence with a phrase on the label such as "confirm meth." Analysts do not like this. As Robin pointed out, "I am always uncomfortable when they write that on the label. That's not exactly what we do, even if we end up confirming it. It isn't quite right." Robin's point is that the police, in these cases, have already "proven" to themselves the chemical makeup of evidence and are implicitly asking the lab to merely confirm their conclusions. That, to Robin's mind, is hardly scientific, and it devalues the expertise and scientific authority that criminalists bring to evaluating evidence.

The difference between their stances came through clearly on a day that an undercover police officer, a district attorney, and two defense attorneys visited the lab, intending to go through a huge amount of evidence from a drug bust. The defense attorneys, as might be expected in service to their clients, were not excited to have the forensic scientists positively identify a controlled substance. After Jodi removed about twenty baggies from a Kapak and laid them out on the table, one defense attorney pointed to them and asked, "That's the alleged coke?" Tim, the supervisor, replied, "*Not* alleged. Jodi tested it, it is cocaine." The lab did not want to diminish their scientific authority before their peers in the criminal justice community. They had followed their procedures to scientifically demonstrate the substance was cocaine, and it was important to their whole unit—not to mention Jodi's reputation— that they clearly reiterate that conclusion.

The defense attorney continued, "How pure is it?" and Tim answered, "We don't quantify it. If [the suspects] processed it again, it might be chemically slightly purer. I wouldn't attest to that, though." The defense attorney, looking chagrined, sighed and said, "I know, this is like when I talk to my own experts. I should know better than to talk to a scientist, it is maddening." Tim pointed out, "It is kind of like your 'alleged' versus our scientific certainty." Here, the defense attorney was lamenting that criminalists would not make any claims unless they had the scientific results to back them up.

During the meeting, one of the defense attorneys asked a lot of questions about the chain of custody and where the evidence had been kept; afterward, I asked the analysts about this. Their answers reflected another value of forensic science: careful documentation. Tim replied, "Yeah, if the best argument he's got is [that we have broken the] chain of custody, he's screwed. That's what we do day in and day out, we dot our i's and cross our t's." Taylor added, "Redundancy up the yin-yang."

In narcotics, the care they take to document their work is sometimes at odds with their need to be efficient. Because of their requirements for rapid turnaround, narcotics analysts strongly value efficiency in processing cases. In fact, at least one or two analysts time themselves on "typical" cases, getting teased by colleagues about their race with the clock. When the information system for filing case reports was changed, the new data entry process was slow and complicated, which caused a major slowdown in narcotics case processing times. The unhappy analysts met with the IT representative to discuss the specific problems with the new system. At the end of the meeting, one analyst, Billie, said, "We have efficiency concerns, will we talk about those?" Taylor added, "These are not small things." They discussed several problems with the wait times for particular data entry screens to open. Taylor ended with, "If we could fix all these, I could cut it down to seven minutes, which is just one minute longer than [the old system]." Billie joked, "We don't want to set our bar quite as low as that!"

Thus, narcotics analysts are thorough and efficient, but also curious, prizing variety and autonomy in their analysis. Analysts contrast their craft-based chemical identification work with the analysis done in toxicology, which they see as routine and boring: "It's mind-numbing, you press buttons and open tubes all day." Several of them had worked in toxicology and had been eager to move to another unit. In Taylor's words, "I took a job in tox because it was what was open in the lab at the time, and it took a long time to get out. . . . Too much paperwork and not enough benchwork! So I convinced management to train me in other areas."

WORK PRACTICES OF TOXICOLOGY: THE EFFICIENT "OCD UNIT"

As he has every other day that week, Jason, when he first arrives in the toxicology lab at 8 a.m., downloads a set of forty blood alcohol cases on the computer. A newcomer to the lab but an experienced toxicologist, Jason prepares to put these samples in a batch on the gas chromatograph.

First, he prints out the list of samples and creates a sequence list for the instrument. Then he takes multiple boxes out of the refrigerator and removes the samples by number, placing them in a rack in the order they appear on the list and making a checkmark next to each sample on the page as he does so. Jason labels each of the vials with his initials and date and checks the numbers again against the sample list as he loads the vials one by one onto an instrument to rock them, ensuring that there are no clots when he draws the sample for the instrument. While they are rocking, he sets up the instrument, checking the sequence list and choosing the appropriate method for blood alcohol.

It is now around 10 a.m. Jason draws samples and adds an internal standard (n-propanol) to aid in quantifying the result, using a mechanized pipette to draw both together and put a small bit in each small vial in a tray. He pulls the sample from its tube, draws the standard from another tube, moves to the tray, fills two vials from each sample, and wipes the pipette clean. After eighty back-and-forth iterations, repeating his moves with the pipette between the sample rack, the standard in the tube, and the tray, Jason is done setting up the samples.

He repeats this process for the quality controls and the acetone markers, the results of which tell the analyst if the instrument functioned the same throughout the run and distinguishes between alcohol and acetone (acetone, which can be found in blood or urine, can be mistaken for alcohol, and therefore needs its own test).[14] When the tray is finished, about an hour and a half after he started filling the vials he seals all the vials and loads the tray into the instrument, checking the vial numbers against the sequence list yet another time. He begins the run, which will take about four hours, and leaves for lunch.

The next morning, Jason conveys the list of quantitative gas chromatography results from the instrument to the lab's computerized report system. He prints and checks the one-hundred-page report, both to confirm sample accuracy and to make sure the instrument performed correctly (noting internal standards and retention times). He transfers his written information about the standards and instruments to a digital log the lab keeps for traceability.

———

Forensic toxicologists detect and identify drugs and poisons in body fluids, tissues, and organs. Every day, the toxicology unit at MCCL receives multiple boxes of samples of blood and urine to test. It analyzes over fifteen thousand samples a year. Like Jason, each analyst is assigned to an instrument upon arrival in the morning, where they download a computerized list of cases to analyze for a particular class of drug. Because samples come to the laboratory already in a tube, the evidence needs little processing before toxicologists start their analysis. The most important aspect of preparation is keeping vigilant track of the samples and making sure that none of them are transferred incorrectly.

Toxicology requires careful attention to detail in analyzing many similar samples simultaneously, which instills values of error-free, obsessively organized processing. In toxicology it is vital that the hundreds of samples they receive each week for analyses are not mishandled in any way. My first day in the toxicology lab, the analysts joked with me that they are the "OCD unit": the most important aspect of their job is making sure that they match the correct samples to the individuals on their analysis list. Every step taken in the analysis process is checked off this list as the toxicologist looks at the labels on the vials, makes new matching labels, moves samples from place to place, and, finally, replaces the original vials in their boxes in the refrigerators.

Thorough, error-free documentation and sample tracking is critical in every unit of the laboratory. But it is a particular fixation in the toxicology unit, where samples for blood alcohol analysis or enzyme immunoassay screening have to be analyzed within four to five days. As Jason and his colleague Neha pulled samples out of the refrigerators one morning, Neha complained that a third toxicologist, Jorge, had not yet shifted the samples from the temporary property boxes to the neatly ordered and labeled toxicology boxes. "No, that's my fault," Jason said. "Jorge got tasked to do something else and I have been doing it the last couple of days. I'm a bit behind, I ran out of time last night." They noted to me the importance of having compulsive organizational skills to work in toxicology. Neha said, "Occasionally you get a normal person in toxicology and they annoy the rest of us by not putting things back in the right place or forgetting to label something."

The most common analyses toxicologists perform are blood alcohol analysis (called "BAC"), and drugs of abuse testing. Blood alcohol analysis is done through gas chromatography (as noted, it is also used in narcotics identification), which separates alcohol from other volatiles in the blood, and compares the suspect's alcohol peak to ones obtained with known blood alcohol standards. The toxicologists' work consists of preparing the samples to be analyzed; loading and starting the instrument; making sure the instrument operates properly; and checking the results of the analyses to see whether samples exceeded the chemical threshold for DUI (see figure 1.6, p. 52). Drugs of abuse testing starts with an enzyme immunoassay screening (called "EIA") for methamphetamine, cocaine, opiates, and/or PCP; this is sometimes followed by confirmation on a GC/MS instrument. Toxicologists program the instrument for EIA screening with positive and negative cutoff points for detecting a "dose" of a drug; any samples in the "inconclusive" range go to GC/MS for exact confirmation.

The results created by these instruments are far more straightforward than the electropherograms produced in DNA profiling. In fact, little interpretation is required. Moreover, although the type of instrumentation in toxicology overlaps somewhat with that used in narcotics analysis, in toxicology there is far less variety. Toxicologists work for several months at a time with a particular method (a procedure for analysis), such as BAC; like Jason, they run multiple samples on the same method each day.[15]

In toxicology, talk radio plays in the background while the analysts work at their individual benches preparing and running samples. While they do not frequently consult one another about interpretation, they gather together to troubleshoot and complain about their instruments; because their analysis is extremely reliant on them, analysts pay close attention to how the machines are functioning. Kanthi sat down next to her instrument as it began a run, saying to me, "I will sit and do some reviewing near the instrument so I can keep a watch on it." About ten minutes later, she jumped up to check something. "It doesn't sound right?" I asked. "No," she said, recognizing a sound from the instrument that was out of the ordinary. At the instrument, she leaned over to look at the samples. "It didn't put the right amount of sample in this one."

FIGURE 1.6. Image of GC/MS instrument for BAC testing.

She circled the well on the plate with a red Sharpie. "We have no control over this instrument, I can't stop the run. All I can do is note it and re-run the sample."

Several toxicologists are expert troubleshooters and share their knowledge with their colleagues. When Hank was analyzing samples from the coroner, he was troubled by the way the peaks in the output graphs were being called (the chemists use the term "call" when refer-ring to how a test labels a controlled substance). He picked up the phone and said, "I'll phone my lifeline. Taylor's a talented analyst, he trained me." When he hung up, Hank said, "He'll come over. This is what gets us through, our collective efforts. Just last week Oscar had an instrument problem. It was either skipping samples, or picking them up and putting them in the wrong place. He and I had to shut it down . . ." He was interrupted by a knock on the door. Taylor entered the room, fiddled with the settings on the instrument's screen for a minute or two and figured out how to change the peak threshold so that it would recognize the controlled substances accurately. Hank thanked him. Taylor said, "Call me if you have any more problems," and returned to narcotics.

Toxicologists employ short, standardized reports, which are batched for release to the criminal justice community. After a toxicologist transfers results into the lab's evidence tracking system, another toxicologist qualified in that method downloads the report, which includes all of the samples in a particular run, and technically reviews the printed results. This analyst carefully scrutinizes the lists of samples to make sure the report sample numbers match the initial lists. She also checks to make sure that the controls worked properly, and she calculates some of the calls the instrument makes to check its accuracy. Then she sends the packet to the supervisor, who releases the results to the district attorney's office.

The reports on individual cases are not lengthy, but they include comparisons to standards, and the notes on the report contain identification and dates of standards as well as instrument information. Toxicology reports are relatively short and simple, and the parties in the legal system are very familiar with their standardized structure. Consequently, toxicological analysis requires little framing.

However, testifying in toxicology is more intricate and sophisticated for analysts who are certified as Forensic Alcohol Supervisors (FAS). While all toxicologists are certified to testify to the analysis they performed, five have the additional FAS certification, which enables them to testify not just to the chemical composition of drugs and alcohol, but to the *effects* of alcohol and drugs on the body.

This type of testimony is universally acknowledged to be the most complicated and challenging done at MCCL. Criminalists attribute this to the "big business" of defense against DUI charges. In general, defense attorneys have more experience in DUI cases than many of the district attorneys. One veteran chemist, Peter, explained, "In the district attorney's office, a lot of newbies start off in drunk driving and drugs. DUIs can be harder to prosecute, and they have defense attorneys who are more practiced at defending. It can be quite tough. Also, a newbie district attorney won't know what to ask . . . defense attorneys have classes they take on how to attack or defend against DUI." The criminalists who testified to drug effects therefore spend a lot of time thinking and discussing with one another how to testify in court.

It is relatively easy to learn to do toxicology casework, given the chemistry and biology background of incoming analysts. New toxicologists are ready to work on cases using a specific method, such as BAC, after as little as one month of training. However, remaining vigilant and attentive to every step of toxicological analysis is difficult, given the repetitiveness of the process. When Jason was pipetting the internal standard and a urine sample into a vial, he pointed to the air gap in the pipette tip that indicated that the pipette was ready to pull up rather than dispense and said, "If it isn't there, the pipette will dispense the internal standard into the sample and it is ruined. Not only do you have to write a long report, but the lab gets to make fun of you for a few weeks." Toxicologists are adroit and careful, obsessive about record keeping, and unwaveringly attentive while performing multiple repetitive tasks.

TAMING, QUESTIONING, AND FRAMING ACROSS THE METROPOLITAN COUNTY CRIME LABORATORY

Criminalists' work entails applying science in the service of justice. Inside the laboratory, they receive evidence from crime scenes that needs to be put in order and made amenable to analysis. They question the evidence through a set of forensic science techniques, and they have a skeptical stance, relying on their procedures to convert evidence into findings that reflect the natural world. However, the evidence also needs to be useful in criminal proceedings. Thus, framing the evidence so that the legal parties could understand it and use it is also an important aspect of their work. While specific tasks, technologies, and practices vary across the units, the processes of taming, questioning, and framing the evidence are consistent throughout MCCL.

These processes all have methodical, legal, aesthetic, and routine dimensions that are the hallmark of forensic science work. At MCCL, criminalists in all areas followed careful, rigorous scientific methods. In DNA profiling, techniques were surrounded by a regime of order that analysts applied not only in their protocols for extraction or capillary electrophoresis, but also in screening to ready the evidence and documentation to avoid mistakes. Toxicologists paid careful attention to documentation and to logging reagents and other materials. Narcotics analysts checked their instruments' standards every Monday before casework to ensure their tests were accurate. While different in each unit, technical reviewing to catch errors was the norm in all parts of the laboratory.

Attentiveness to legal standards permeated the work of all the forensic scientists at MCCL. Firearms examiners were familiar not only with the best-known nonmatches of particular bullets, but also knew the penal code. In DNA profiling, analysts considered how their work would be perceived in court, as in Ellie's understanding of the order of screening in which she first tested the swabs, then the underwear, and finally the dress. Narcotics analysts were aware of the charges that attached to each controlled substance, and knew which weights brought higher penalties.

While narcotics analysts seem the most aesthetically sensitive, intuiting drugs on the basis of their smell, all forensic science work is similarly embodied. In firearms identification, the comparison microscope enables them to make judgments based on visual cues, and they light up their digital images expertly. Firearms examiners feel the inside of the barrel of the gun to sense a blockage, and toxicologists hear problems with their instruments.

Routine is the acknowledged province of toxicology, the "OCD unit." However, routine is the foundation of all forensic science, where the implications of mistakes can cost people their freedom. In all areas, protocols are followed religiously at all points in the process. In the firearms unit, I received a routine set of safety instructions for test-firing, one that I saw repeated by Adam, Al, and Tom every time they entered the firing range. DNA analysts complain about the routine aspects of their work: extraction takes days of pipetting, centrifuging, and washing, all of which requires documentation for every sample. When Taylor finished his narcotics case with the Indian pharmaceuticals, he said, "I wasted half my day just to document it. That's the drawback of forensic science. You can't just do the fun stuff, you have to document it thoroughly. Other scientists can be a bit more rough with their case notes. Attorneys are not always so forgiving."

As Taylor's comment suggests, criminalistics is not just bench science; it is also forensic science. The work is permeated by the way the science is embedded, and entangled, within the social world of law and criminal justice. Moreover, forensic science is performed in the service of the public; therefore, the laboratory intersects with the public arena as well. The next chapter describes the relationships that forensic scientists forged at the intersection of science, law, and the public.

Chapter 2

THE SOCIAL WORLDS
OF FORENSIC SCIENCE

Science, Criminal Justice,
and the Public Sphere

Forensic science is an applied science, but it is one whose outputs serve the justice system. However, the social worlds of science and criminal justice each possess different structures, norms, practices, and understandings of what science is for, how it is performed, and what its limitations are.[1] Moreover, since they are a part of the criminal justice system, criminalists are also accountable to the public, which adds a third set of expectations to their work. Criminalists therefore navigate three worlds: science, criminal justice, and the public arena.

Let's take an ordinary American crime committed with a gun and see how complex the analysis of evidence can become, as criminalists seek to explain their examination to their scientific peers; to police officers, lawyers, and judges; and to the lay people of the general public and jury.

When a gun is fired, gunshot residue (GSR) can linger on the person who pulled the trigger: on their hands, clothes, and more. When the police suspect someone of firing a gun, they collect samples from the individual's hands onto a specially treated stub (see figures 2.1 and 2.2, p. 60). In the trace evidence area of the chemistry unit, criminalists use a scanning electron microscope to analyze whether these stubs contain GSR. The microscope detects particles of the characteristic size and shape and then does an elemental analysis, looking for the unique combination of lead, barium, and antimony that together demonstrate a gun may have been fired.

How to make a scientific assessment of GSR requires one kind of skill; how to *display and discuss* the evidence in the service of the criminal justice system requires another. One morning when I arrived at MCCL, Robin was complaining to Jodi, another member of the chemistry unit, about the way the lab wrote up the GSR report. Robin and her teammates Meredith and Taylor wanted to change the way they reported GSR analysis, but Sam, the deputy lab director, thought they should keep reporting the way they had been.

Meredith's suggested method was, in Robin's opinion, more accurate. She combined the separate results for the stubs from the right and left hands into one overall conclusion about whether or not the suspect tested positive for GSR. The information from each stub analyzed was detailed in the notes that accompanied the report, but this was not needed for the report itself. Since, after firing a gun, GSR might be found anywhere on the body, Robin felt that separate reporting of the particles' location was technically precise, but not likely to deliver a true understanding of the science to those outside the lab.

As Robin said, "What you are reporting is just whether the person has GSR, not what hand it is on. Nobody is actually shooting with just one hand." Jodi joked, "Maybe some gangbangers are," striking a pose in which she extended her arm out with her hand "gun" pointed horizontally. Smiling, Robin continued, "Well, it isn't really right to report it out that way. I'm going to talk to [our supervisor] Tim about it." Robin noted that not only does GSR travel, but most people shoot with two hands, further limiting the necessity to report which hand was which.

Robin and Tim met later that morning. Tim had reviewed the procedure manual that governs trace evidence like GSR and told her, "The procedure manual says we report stubs by hand, but we can change that. Do Ellen or Dave [trace analysts at other labs in the state] report out the left hand and the right hand?" Robin said that, regardless of the protocols of other labs, continuing to separate right from left hand GSR was confusing, with potentially big implications: "It implies that one hand is shooting versus another. For lay people I think it will be misleading."

Robin went on to explain that they check both hands, because GSR doesn't land only on the "hand that fired." Even those particles that do land on the firing hand might not stay stuck to that hand, but move and stick to other parts of the body:

The only reason we even run two [stubs in the instrument] is that they lose tackiness, as time goes on, so you want to make sure that you don't miss potential GSR. If both are positive, we report that. But when one is positive and one isn't, it is still the same human being with GSR on them. It'll be weird and confusing to a layperson to report them separately. I shoot with both hands, plus, all the parts of your body are connected, so people have GSR where they touch.

Underlying Robin's argument was the belief that scientific methods and understandings of the natural world (i.e., which particles were found where) had to be considered alongside the questions and ambiguities of criminal justice—who would hear this information, and to what end. Robin combined the scientific and social concerns into one: how best to perform the analysis mattered, but so too did how the analysis would be received.

Robin returned to the lab and checked in with her GSR colleagues Meredith and Taylor. She decided that she didn't want to call the analysts at the other labs. Instead, she created a question for the online Yahoo group forum for those who worked with trace evidence, a place where such nuanced questions were frequently discussed. Taylor, looking over her shoulder, read part of the message aloud: "Is it necessary to be specific in the report about the right and left hand stub?" He thought it looked fine, so she posted it to the group.

But the story didn't end there. The following week, I ran into the lab director; in our conversation, the GSR reports came up. He told me,

We've been around a long time, Sam [the deputy director] and I, and we've reported out GSR on right hand and on left hand. The staff is concerned that the DA might use this to mislead the jury in terms of the interpretation. But I tell them that they can't worry about this, this is out of their control. The DAs can do what they want. Our role

FIGURE 2.1. Image of gun firing.

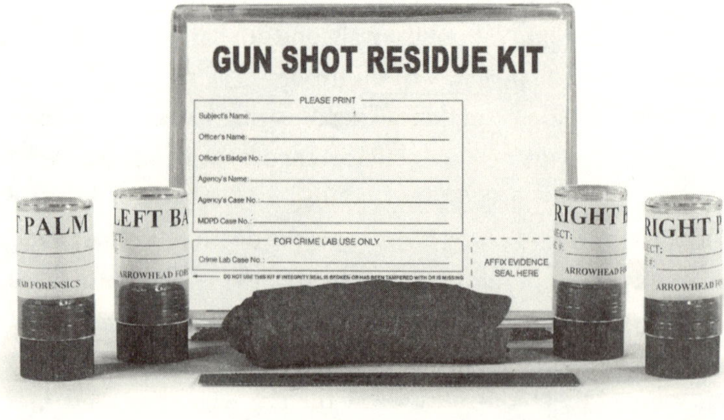

FIGURE 2.2. Image of Gunshot Residue (GSR) collection kit.

As in most scientific worlds, criminalists work as part of a community.[2] They rely on their local colleagues to help at every stage of their analysis. Moreover, the extended community supports their work both formally and informally. When questions arise about their protocols, as in the discussion of the GSR report, criminalists often connect with their counterparts at other laboratories throughout the country, either by phone or e-mail. They know these colleagues from their joint participation in formal professional activities: conferences run by professional associations, audits of their laboratory (typically staffed by supervisors or veteran analysts from other labs), or prior work experiences.[3] Criminalists also keep MCCL's procedures current by referencing best practices at other laboratories. When questions about how the lab could be accredited for crime scene investigation (CSI) arose in a meeting of the supervisors, Tim, the leader of the CSI team at MCCL, asked, "What does it take to be accredited?" The supervisors agreed that they would need to develop a procedure manual, which would be complicated to create. To address these complications, Neal, the lab director, told Tim, "Check into it. Reach out to the community to see what they do."

Given their regular participation in and socialization into this world of applied science, the members of MCCL strongly identify as scientists. As noted, they often express the values associated with science, such as communality and disinterestedness,[4] and comment on their neutrality with phrases such as "It doesn't matter to me what the results say." As we saw in chapter 1, typical practices of bench science constitute the daily work or criminalists: validation of methods, cautious following of scientific protocols, and obsessive prevention of contamination.[5]

When I first started talking with crime lab directors, I was swiftly corrected when I referred to criminalists as "technicians," and instructed to use the term "criminalist."[6] Although they have a similar education as many technician-level scientists in universities and hospitals, criminalists' control over their own work, as well as their participation in specialized professional associations, creates a more professionalized identity than that of some other technician occupations.[7] In particular, criminalists at MCCL are not overseen by PhD or MD scientists, as is typically the case for technicians in other locales. Because criminalists run the lab, they are responsible for decisions about new analytic domains. These decisions entail instrument purchases and the development and validation of protocols for the instruments. In academic, industry, and hospital labs, these tasks are usually handled by scientists with an MD or PhD.

Criminalists describe this as one of the advantages of working in a crime lab. In toxicology, Oscar and Stan worked together on validating and creating protocols for a new gas chromatograph/mass spectrometer that would be able to precisely identify over six hundred drug compounds. As Oscar told me, "When I worked in a biotech laboratory, I did extraction, and I learned the technique, and after that there wasn't anything new to do. The PhDs in the lab were doing validations and the cool stuff. We don't get a lot of PhDs in crime labs so I have the opportunity to do that here." Acknowledging the skills of forensic scientists by providing opportunities to do autonomous work creates a community of engaged, proactive experts in the laboratory.[8]

This involvement in all of the activities in the lab produces criminalists who develop deep expertise in forensic science and a sense of identification with science. Billie, a narcotics analyst, told me a story that exemplifies this; it involved a case in which Billie reported that the evidence submitted to the lab was hashish. Later, she was asked to testify to her conclusions.

> What I got was this greenish, fluffy powder that had little, tiny fragments of leaf in it, but was mostly powder. And I called it hash. The law is very vague as to the difference between marijuana and hash, or concentrated cannabis. It says hash is the separated resin, refined or crude from the marijuana plant. So to me, if the marijuana looks like it's been processed at all, like if anything has been done to refine it, it constitutes hash. And there weren't any whole leaves, it didn't look like marijuana anymore, so I called it hash.

For Billie, the law here was almost an obstacle to good science. "I hate [hash] cases," she admitted, "because it is the only drug where the difference is not a scientific difference. It's a legal difference." The difference between hashish and marijuana is not a scientific distinction at all, but, instead, a legal one in which different sentences apply to different drug types. She went on to explain:

> It's not like coke and coke base, where there is an actual chemical difference that you can quantify. Between hash and marijuana the law says it's just a question of what does it look like, which bothers me because it's not like it says hash is 50-percent THC, it says it is processed.

The problem was that the DA then called Billie, explaining that the suspect was insisting it was *not* hash. The attorney wanted to double-check, but the question put Billie in a bind. The science was ambiguous, and the law full of consequences for the suspect. To be careful, she confirmed her initial assessment:

> So I talked to my coworkers and half of them said they'd call it marijuana and half of them said they'd call it hash. I'm like, "That's a big help." But my supervisor agreed with me, so in the end I told the DA, "Here's what I see, and here's what the law says, and I think that it looks like it's been processed."

The matter continued, because the DA now had further information:

> He said, "Yeah, the guy actually says he put it through a screen." So I said, "Okay, I'll come testify." But I didn't really want to because I was really worried about this. What's the judge going to think the difference between the hash and marijuana is? I can't say as a chemist, "This is this drug.""

Billie was uncomfortable with hash cases because there was not a chemical way to identify hash. She relied on her colleagues to help her feel comfortable with her conclusions, but she was worried about what would happen with her results in the world of criminal justice, which had different expectations about evidence and science, and where her conclusions might lead to different outcomes.

She was certain of her analysis as it related to the lab's standards and to the principles of science, but things were liable to get much less clear when she entered the courtroom. Criminalists first navigate the social and technical demands of the science world, but, as noted earlier, theirs is a science whose outputs are the exclusive domain of the criminal justice world.

FORENSIC SCIENCE IN THE CRIMINAL JUSTICE WORLD

The results of the work done in a crime lab are a direct input to the criminal justice system. Thus, while the criminalists at MCCL primarily identify as scientists, they are subject to the standards of the legal system in which they are embedded. Forensic scientists believe in the pursuit of justice, but they perceive legal norms as contrasting with the neutrality of science: instead of the scientific pursuit of truth, lawyers pursue *convictions*, and they do so by using evidence as proof in an adversarial system. Criminalists claim that "all the lawyers care about is winning," and they often worry about how their results might be represented in court.

The place of forensic science in the world of criminal justice is encapsulated by the motto of one professional organization of criminalists: *Fiat justitia per scientiam* (justice done through science). However, although both law and science are knowledge-building systems, they have different goals. Fact-making in law is about creating knowledge related to justice in a particular case. But in science, fact-making is about seeking the truth of natural laws, which generalizes beyond the situations in which such truths are produced.[9]

Forensic science in the United States is organized in a patchwork quilt of multiple types of criminal justice agencies, which supervise different kinds of crime laboratories in various locales. The Federal Bureau of Investigation and the Bureau of Alcohol, Tobacco, and Firearms both oversee public crime laboratories throughout the United States, the Department of Justice runs laboratories at a state level, and local jurisdictions such as city police departments; sheriffs' offices, and county district attorneys' offices often have their own laboratories. These agencies control the budgets of the crime laboratories that report to them; the directors of the laboratories are accountable to the agency for the decisions they make regarding hiring and other priorities.

At MCCL, the laboratory director reports to the DA, an elected officer of the county. In addition, a deputy DA serves as a laboratory liaison and has direct contact with the laboratory director and deputy director on a regular basis as well as attending occasional case meetings at the lab. In other jurisdictions, laboratory directors report to police or sheriff's offices. Directors of such labs informed me that laboratories reporting to district attorneys the way MCCL did were ones in which it was "easier" to obtain resources, primarily because district attorneys did not have to make "tough tradeoffs" between buying a new instrument for the laboratory and putting additional officers on the street. In the words of one lab director, "In some respects, crime laboratories don't fit well into the police functions of patrol, investigations, detention. They are sort of the odd stepchild, and thus they are hard to fit in."

At MCCL, criminalists interact with members of the criminal justice community, such as district attorneys or investigators, regarding the evidence they are analyzing in their casework. Particularly in units such as DNA and firearms, which analyze evidence for major cases, criminalists are familiar with the district attorneys and some of the investigators that work on the cases. They talk with them about evidence during the analysis process and see them in court. They are also familiar with the public defenders and independent expert witnesses who work in their area, with whom they sometimes interact during cases that go to court. Toxicologists who are certified to testify as Forensic Alcohol Supervisors also know the attorneys who are regularly involved in DUI cases. Though there are a few exceptions, most criminalists at MCCL do not know these attorneys and investigators well, since they have infrequent interaction with them on a case-by-case basis.

Despite more or less familiarity with the criminal justice colleagues who utilize the output of their work, all criminalists have to navigate the different, sometimes conflicting, standards of both worlds. Fundamentally, the pursuit of facts related to justice in court is quite different from sitting at a laboratory bench and coaxing conclusions from samples taken from the natural world.

The adversarial practices of law contrast with the ideals of the objective neutrality of science as well as with the communal approach criminalists adopt in their analytic work. Moreover, attorneys sometimes draw "bright lines" around results when arguing for the guilt or innocence of a defendant. That is, for criminalists, evidence is always open to interpretation: the DNA profile comparison is a question of probability, the difference between hash and marijuana one of subjective, if expert, judgment. Attorneys in the world of criminal justice do not think that way, apparently: for the sake of their argument, the DNA must absolutely match, or it must absolutely not. The substance must unequivocally be hash (perhaps for the DA), while, on the other hand, the substance must unequivocally not be hash (perhaps for the defense attorney). This can be seen in the infamous O. J. Simpson case, which, in one important respect, hung on the question of a glove found on the scene, and whether it did—or did not—fit the suspect. Simpson's attorney Johnnie Cochran created his own bright line around this evidence, with his argument to the jury: "If it doesn't fit, you must acquit."[10]

In court, evidence is employed in a manner different than in the crime lab. When making scientific assessments of evidence, criminalists perceive these lines as messier and more ambiguous. This can make criminalists uncomfortable with some types of requests. When the DA's office wanted MCCL's firearms examiners to help perform a function test on a baton that had been used in a crime, Holly, the supervisor of the comparative evidence unit, was not excited about the idea. A function test determines how a tool might be used and whether and how it works, given any modifications the user might have made to it. None of the examiners in the unit were familiar with batons, and so Holly felt uncomfortable asking them to draw conclusions about a type of weapon for which they lacked expertise. The DA handling the case had decided to bring in an outside expert, but still wanted the lab's help, both in terms of expertise and space. Holly called him to talk about it. The DA said, "The expert will likely set up things to manipulate the baton, and he will write a report. I know Adam [a senior examiner]. He can provide the imprimatur of the lab." Holly said, "I haven't spoken to Adam yet. I would rather the criminalists not issue an opinion."

The DA and Holly disagreed about what the criminalists at MCCL should do. The DA argued that the lab might issue "an opinion about functionality," while Holly maintained that, as they had agreed, the DA was bringing in the outside expert to express an opinion, rather than the MCCL's criminalists drawing a conclusion. Holly said, "My guys do not have the experience to issue an opinion." The DA responded, "There have not been many forensic examinations of batons before. There is lots of interest in this case, and I want to demonstrate that we are being thorough." Holly agreed to provide space and materials, and to talk about having Adam sit in on the examination. The DA ended by thanking her and saying, "I won't bully you guys. I am sensitive to your issues. Adam is a guy I know, I can talk to him. The expert knows a lot about use of force, and Adam is a mechanical guy. I think he would be helpful to have there." The DA was eager to have the crime lab validate his legal analysis of a piece of evidence; the criminalists were not eager to risk the lab's credibility over a case that involved a weapon about which they were not experts.

Providing expertise to the criminal justice system sometimes puts criminalists in a position where their identity as scientists clashes with the expectations and norms of criminal justice. In addition to concerns about the forensic scientists' level of expertise, this particular case illustrates how the criminal justice community depends on the scientific legitimacy of the lab's experts. The DA was not merely interested in the scientific opinion about the baton's functioning; he also wanted to leverage the laboratory's scientific opinion in court and in the public eye. Being a part of the criminal justice system thus embeds criminalists' work in yet another world: the public sphere.

FORENSIC SCIENCE IN THE PUBLIC SPHERE

The criminal justice system is accountable to the public, and the crime lab is therefore subject to public attention. Public expectations of science and evidence are made clear to criminalists both from a remove, through television and the news media, and in close quarters, through courtroom interactions with juries, victims, suspects, and their families. The straightforward explanation of the science of an investigation gets entangled in this other world. What does it mean to do science not only for a criminal justice audience, but for a criminal justice system that is working in the interests of the public?

Cultural tropes in the media about criminalists draw on logics from both the scientific and criminal justice worlds. When there are problems with the work of a crime laboratory or its personnel, commentary in news outlets often repeat a popular cultural notion: that criminalists, in their efforts to be fair and impartial in the service of criminal justice, should be held accountable to the public. When a crime lab in New York State was audited in 2010, problems with some of their training protocols were brought into public view. The *New York Times* reported statements such as these from government and academic representatives:

> "Cutting corners in a crime lab is serious and intolerable," said the state's inspector general, Joseph Fisch. "Forensic laboratories must adhere to the highest standards of competence, independence and integrity. Anything less undermines public confidence in our criminal justice system."[11]

> "It is a wake-up call to the forensic community," said Barry Scheck, director of the Innocence Project and a member of the New York State Commission on Forensic Science, which monitors all the state's crime labs. "What's alarming about this report and others that we've seen like it is it's not so much the bad actors, it's the fact that the system didn't detect them earlier."[12]

Here, the intersecting worlds of science and criminal justice that criminalists inhabit are exposed to and brought into conversation with a third world: the public, and its expectations of how criminalists should do their job. Far more complicated than a single question of putting select evidence before the public, this incident illustrates how the entire discipline of forensic science is dependent, to some degree, on its engagement with this third social world.

Expectations about the science of forensic science are multifaceted. In a general sense, cultural expectations of science demand an objective and rational way of reporting truths about the world.[13] Forensic science therefore encounters scrutiny on the basis of perceptions of how "scientific" it is: that is, whether it is objective and rational enough. This question became particularly pressing following the release of the 2009 National Academy of Sciences report on the status of forensic sciences. The report, "Strengthening Forensic Science in the United States: A Path Forward," called into question the scientific validity and standards of forensic science.[14] It noted that, troublingly, many jurisdictions do not require criminalist certification or laboratory accreditation for work in a crime lab; it also indicated a worrying lack of standardized operational procedures, not to mention the lack of a scientific body of research on the measures, variability, and sources of bias for much of forensic science.[15] Specifically, the report compared other forensic science disciplines unfavorably to forensic biology: it excluded DNA profiling from its criticism that many disciplines lacked a scientific basis and scientific validity. The NAS report suggested that "with the exception of nuclear DNA analysis, no forensic method has been rigorously shown to have the capacity to consistently, and with a high degree of certainty, demonstrate a connection between evidence and a specific individual or source."[16]

The resulting media attention gave the strong impression of a problem with the scientific practices of forensic science, and it generated calls to make forensic science more scientific. The *New York Times* reported, "Forensic evidence that has helped convict thousands of defendants for nearly a century is often the product of shoddy scientific practices that should be upgraded and standardized."[17] National Public Radio's Science Friday devoted a show to the NAS report, and Ira Flatow's promotion was similarly critical: "Up next, it is the not so scientific world of forensic science. . . . Our country's forensic sciences 'have serious problems and we need to overhaul the current structure.'"[18]

But beyond the concerns of the National Academy of Science and those of media outlets, there is another complication. Specifically, popular entertainment may have raised expectations for forensic science to achieve impossible results. In recent years, forensic science has vividly entered the public imagination with the *CSI* TV franchise, in which superscientists, who also function as intrepid investigators, solve crimes and apprehend suspects. Other dramas such as *NCIS* and *Bones* followed, along with many forensic science reality shows, all of which provide vibrant yet unrealistic portrayals of forensic science: extremely quick turnaround times, impossible instrumentation, and unlikely results. As a result, the public's belief in the ability of crime laboratories to develop conclusions about physical evidence may now be greater than even state-of-the-art practice in forensic science warrants.

This "*CSI* effect" has raised concern in criminal justice circles and the public. Attorneys worry that jurors now expect forensic evidence to be on display at every trial. While it does not appear that the *CSI* effect actually influences the outcomes of trials,[19] it is certainly the case that the criminal justice community believes that it has affected juries' expectations, putting pressure on them to use forensic evidence in court. Being in the public sphere, then, further adds to the public profile and perception of criminalists work and what it does and should do.

———

Crime laboratories are situated at the place where science, law, and the public interest overlap. Being embedded in these multiple social worlds has an impact on the work of criminalists. Because these worlds differ in their interpretations of evidence and perceptions of criminalists' work, straddling them creates ambiguities for criminalists. Moreover, there can be grave consequences for making mistakes; since evidence is used in adjudicating guilt or innocence, errors carry implications for suspects, victims, and for criminalists themselves. These tensions are ameliorated by the creation of what I call a "culture of anticipation" at MCCL, which structures criminalists' interactions across these worlds. I describe this culture in the next chapter.

Part 2

THE CULTURE OF CRIMINALISTS

Chapter 3

A CULTURE OF ANTICIPATION

The Consequences of Conflicting Expectations

The work of forensic science is structured to anticipate the concerns of attorneys, who in turn anticipate jurors and the public at large. The culture of anticipation can be seen first with the criminalists themselves, who take great care to balance the tenets of science with the expectations and interpretations of the other two social worlds. This culture is expressed through laboratory practices that anticipate the interpretations of the criminal justice community and the public while simultaneously projecting their scientific expertise into these worlds.

This balancing act at the boundaries of science, criminal justice, and the public sphere requires paying attention to the understandings and expectations of these communities while exhibiting a strong backbone under pressure. Scientists both believe and enact the image of themselves as the neutral voice of the evidence all the while knowing that being "captive" to the criminal justice world means routinely responding to law enforcement expectations and requests as they go about their work of analyzing, reporting, and testifying.

HOW EXPERTS ANTICIPATE

For criminalists, working at this intersection of worlds has consequences for the process of producing evidence, as well as for life in the lab. It means managing not only relationships with the criminal justice system, but constantly anticipating potential hiccups in the ways their evidence and their work are seen by the law and the broader public.

This anticipation, in itself, is not uncommon. It is often the case that expert workers, especially scientists, must convince others of the legitimacy of their work. This is true within the boundaries of scientific fields,[1] and becomes even more salient for experts whose work is used outside of a purely scientific domain.[2] Consider the climate scientists mentioned in the introduction: within their field, they have to convince one another of the veracity and importance of their work and come to some shared conclusions. This is a complicated process, but it unfolds within a space of (relatively) shared values and interests. In contrast, when climate science enters the sphere of politics and the media, scientists must convince people who do not share their values and may have diverging interests. Additionally, when expertise is used by outside audiences, those audiences can influence not only the ways experts communicate, but also their daily practices. As communications scholar William Barley notes, scientific weather experts perform this type of "anticipatory work," which often results in changes to the design of the scientists' research questions and the experiments they undertake.[3]

But, unlike Barley's weather scientists, whose output is used by a myriad of scientific audiences on a project-by-project basis, the crime laboratory's expertise is dedicated to just one user: the criminal justice system. Forensic science is therefore a captive occupation, structurally embedded in the world of a higher-status occupation that is fundamentally unlike it.[4] Others in expert occupations, like nurses, sometimes work in organizations such as hospitals, where higher-status doctors have authority over some of their work, but they also work in other domains, such as clinics, where they have more autonomy. The occupation and the work of criminalists does not exist outside the criminal justice system.

As a consequence, the work of criminalists is always anticipatory: it is structured to meet the expectations of this system (which in turn, is oriented toward anticipating the public in specific ways). For the crime laboratory, being embedded in the world of criminal justice means that the requirements of that world permeate not only specific tasks and outputs, but the culture of the laboratory. This culture of anticipation can readily be seen at MCCL. Because criminalists expect that their conclusions may not be seen as legitimate by attorneys, judges, and juries, they actively work to reduce multiple perspectives around evidence.

———

How does this anticipation manifest in the culture? In anticipating outside perspectives, criminalists take action in two ways: through incorporating these perspectives into their work and educating outside audiences about their work.

By incorporating, criminalists bring the perspective of the criminal justice community into their analysis, by integrating the expectations of their criminal justice peers into their work. They do not think of attorneys and juries during every aspect of a particular scientific task, but they test many of their reports and notes to ensure that a nonscientist could read them. Through educating, they take their identity and training as scientists and use them to change the hearts and minds of their peers in the criminal justice community, as well as those of the public. They hold public tours, provide training sessions for DAs and other members of the criminal justice community, create "protocols" to guide prosecutors' questions about scientific evidence, and encourage attorneys to meet informally before going to court. In so doing, forensic scientists work to share their own scientific knowledge as deeply and as widely as possible, in order to increase understanding, change perceptions, and conquer uncertainties around the interpretations they make.

This tension between anticipating criminal justice expectations and, at the same time, maintaining the integrity of science, is most evident in instances where criminalists negotiate the requests of members of law enforcement. One example of this can be seen in the last chapter, when Holly resisted the district attorney's request for the laboratory's opinion about the baton's function. Criminalists defend their time and effort by negotiating with DAs over what, when, and how evidence should be analyzed, questioning the usefulness and efficiency of particular requests.

They also push back on representatives of the criminal justice community when worried that their science might be compromised. In these moments, we see the internal tug of war that characterizes captive occupations.

Anticipating by Incorporating Outside Expectations

A major part of the work of criminalists is documentary; the formal laboratory reports they produce are routinely used in criminal proceedings. As we've seen, reports not only summarize the analytic process but also include detailed lists of results and conclusions about what the evidence showed. Criminalists know that reports are critical to communicating scientific determinations about evidence to lawyers, judges, and juries, all of whom represent a nonscientific but highly interested public. Therefore, when writing reports, criminalists anticipate the expectations of these audiences, and integrate those expectations into their reports.[5] In the trace analysts Robin, Meredith, and Taylor's discussions of the GSR report, they incorporated their concerns about jurors' interpretations of the results—possible misattributions about which hand fired the gun—to their ideas about how to change the report.

Forensic scientists at MCCL, in anticipating their lay readers, are as concerned about their language as they are about their science. I spent a day with Meredith as she wrote up a report for a GSR case. In this case, the gloves she tested arrived at the lab in a paper bag with a couple of other items in it: a hat and a sock. The suspect did not have GSR on his hands two years earlier when the crime happened. Now the case would be going to court, and the DA wanted the lab to test the gloves. Meredith found one GSR particle on each glove. But she would not be able to say that the GSR came from the gloves, because they were packaged together with the other items. In her conclusions, she typed: "Particles containing lead, antimony and barium were detected—considered characteristic of gunshot residue." She followed this with two sentences that she copied from a list of GSR conclusions pinned to the wall above her desk: "The area may have been exposed to a discharged firearm or been in close proximity to the discharge of a firearm. The area may have been in contact with a surface bearing gunshot residue."

This example elaborates on some of the tensions described earlier in the GSR reporting process. Meredith detailed her concerns to me about the way to word her conclusions: "I said particles, plural, because I recorded the two particles. . . . Sometimes we spend more time talking about our English than the science, it is frustrating." Two particles, as she noted, are not "very strong" results, and they came from two gloves. The gloves were packaged with other items, so the particles could have moved from one of the other items, which makes the attribution of where those particles were found a bit uncertain, from her scientific perspective. Because wording is so important in terms of incorporating a sense of what the legal system and the public might perceive, the GSR analysts developed and used this "cheat sheet" in their report protocol in order to standardize the wording of their conclusions.

This example is typical of MCCL practice: developing standard terminology inside each unit for reporting on repeated analytic processes is one way of anticipating their outside audiences. For instance, the forensic biology unit only runs a *presumptive* test for human blood before analyzing the DNA profile from a stain or sample, which leaves some interpretive space for error, as blood from other species may also produce a positive result. In their reports, DNA analysts therefore avoid claiming that the evidence is human blood. Instead of referring to samples as "blood," they write descriptions such as "I swabbed the red-brown stain on the dress" to refer to the sample they took.

The terminology for a DNA profile extracted from blood or stains from a crime scene has changed over time. As one rookie analyst prepared for a mock trial practice on a case, she told me, "We used to say 'the presence of human blood is indicated' from the combination of tests that we did: OTOL, stain, quant values. But we've been talking about it and we are not sure we should say that, because we never confirmed it was human blood. On the stand, you could say 'possibly,' but attorneys hate when you say that." Later, discussing this case in the mock trial, her supervisor pointed out, "I think that as a unit we'll have to come up with a way to address blood confirmation."

It was important to the group to find a way to word their conclusions to avoid questions in court that required claims about the blood being human. Since some of the other tests they used could report positive results for other substances, DNA analysts did not want to make an inaccurate statement. This highlights a concern for the group: reports are read by legal parties who might not understand their carefully worded findings and conclusions. At the same time, analysts' allegiance to the norms of the scientific community obligate them to represent their results as accurately as possible, so they worked collaboratively to find acceptable language.

The DNA unit's collaboration around finding appropriate language surfaces similar tensions to those that surround criminalists' discussions of GSR reporting practices. The science of GSR suggests that the hand from which the stub was collected is irrelevant: GSR particles are very mobile. The analysts' anticipation of the possible legal arguments around the results raised concern that a report listing the results of each hand could be confusing or misleading to the public, who did not have scientific knowledge about the movement of these particles.

Toxicologists encountered the same tension with respect to the detection of controlled substances in the blood. One toxicologist explained to me that it is not always straightforward to say when a drug is or is not present. That is, when quantifying the amount of drugs in a sample, there is a lower limit; above the limit, the scientific community agrees that the sample is clearly positive for drugs, but, below that limit, this measurement is not as reliable. However, in toxicologists' reports, they don't explain this fine distinction, and instead simply use the terms "detected" and "not detected." This was initially confusing, the toxicologist told me, because he "could detect it at a low level"—that is, he might find the presence of drugs, but the amount would fall below the lower limit—"and then it would be reported as not detected." This strict distinction contrasted with his understanding of the scientific quantitation process, which allowed for more nuance. When he asked his supervisor why they used these terms in the report, she said this was the language that the district attorneys wanted.

Navigating between the different demands of these social worlds can result in awkward compromises, as seen in the curious wording around relatively simple elements of a crime scene: the presence of blood, the use of a drug, the firing of a gun. These examples show how criminalists carefully craft their reports to ensure standard wording, hoping that the language they use will satisfy the expectations of the criminal justice system while being as true to science as possible.

———

Forensic scientists are also scrupulous about documenting their actions in the case notes, in anticipation of future interactions with attorneys and the public. Allison, a DNA analyst, described to me how the thorough documentation of everything she did served the purposes of both science and justice:

> With science, it has to be reproducible and it has to be credited, so of course, we want to be as open as possible. We don't hide anything. So if we write down everything, that way someone can come behind us and get the same results that we do.

But this wasn't just to serve the ends of science. For criminalists, such documentation is also a way to control the chaos of unruly crime scene evidence, and to manage their anxiety in the face of outside scrutiny. Documentation, continued Allison,

> is also for ourselves, because if we go to court it can be a year or so later, so we want to be able to jog our memory. It helps me to know that if I go to court, I'm going to feel confident with what I testify to. I'm glad the documentation is so thorough. It is a downside because I feel that all I do is write all day. But I wouldn't change it because it does give me confidence and I know that if someone has to testify behind me, it would give them confidence to testify to what I did.

Documentation is a standard of science, but, for criminalists, it is also crucial for anticipating the future demands of the criminal justice system.

In this way, documentation incorporates nonscientific perspectives into a scientific context.

Documentation is also needed to verify the criminalists' communication with members of the criminal justice system. During my time at MCCL, criminalists began to be more careful about fully documenting all case-related communications with anyone in the legal community. As Eden, a supervisor in forensic biology, noted, "We've gotten burned in the past. The DA's office has said we'd do something when we didn't agree to it. So I write a summary of any phone conversations plus any commitments that I made on the call. This is why I prefer e-mail [with the DA's office]. Then you don't have to rewrite it, it is clear what was said."

Criminalists told me that they spend more time documenting their work than they do at the lab bench; several suggested that about 70 percent of their time was taken up by documentation. Because documentation includes tracing the science while also crafting output for the legal world, it is more complex than documentation for benchwork alone. Also, criminalists collectively use documentation to try to reduce the tensions they feel about the overlaps of these social worlds. Documentation is an activity that criminalists can control, inside the laboratory; therefore they invest a lot of effort into it. Once they move outside their own domain, they have much less control, as will be described in chapter 5.

———

Criminalists also anticipate the needs of the criminal justice community in the process of analyzing evidence. As Jodi examined two samples of cocaine base in rock form from one case, I noticed that to do her analysis she chose the rock in the baggie that was knotted multiple times, and I asked why. She said that the police officer had marked the unknotted baggie "tested presumptive positive for cocaine," and, since both were about the same size rocks, she analyzed the untested one. "That gives them extra information to use in court," she went on. "He can say he did the presumptive on one, it came back coke base, and the one I analyzed also is coke base." Criminalists not only maintain awareness of what analysis is most useful on current cases, but they also try to keep abreast of changing legal requirements and standards. They read relevant legal cases in order to figure out if their analyses are acceptable, and they communicate with one another about them.

During my time in the lab, a significant legal case regarding forensic evidence was decided by the Supreme Court: *Melendez-Diaz vs. the State of Massachusetts.*[6] This decision held that the chemical narcotics certificates (the reports prepared by narcotics analysts in the lab) used as evidence in Massachusetts courts violated the Sixth Amendment, which requires that defendants have a right to confront their accusers. This means that, rather than attorneys presenting narcotics reports in the courtroom, more criminalists might need to appear on the stand to explain and defend their conclusions. This decision had potentially wide-ranging implications for how criminalists would be required to testify in court. In many jurisdictions across the United States, including Metropolitan County, forensic scientists testify on behalf of one another in court (under the business records exemption of the hearsay rule). This is necessary sometimes because the work for a case is distributed across multiple members of the unit, or because the criminalist who performed the analysis is unavailable to testify.

At MCCL, this happened most often in forensic biology, so the DNA analysts posted a question on the forensic biology listserv to see if other laboratories in their state had been affected yet by the outcome of the case. They received an appeals court case from elsewhere in the state; one analyst read it immediately, forwarding it to the rest of the unit with a note saying, "If you don't want to read the entire case we just got, start on page 31. Our cases in Western State differ from Melendez-Diaz, so hopefully we'll still be able to testify to business records." This was not the only time MCCL members worried about the Supreme Court decision. Legal rulings and requirements are regularly discussed in the laboratory.

In other instances, the legal requirements and processes in their jurisdiction did not always keep pace with the lab's ability to identify controlled substances. Criminalists are therefore attentive to how they might efficiently provide analytic results that meet the urgent needs of the criminal justice system. The toxicology supervisor, Flora, explained to me that when DUI samples come into the lab, toxicologists automatically set them up to be run for blood alcohol. However, if the BAC assay came out negative, Flora then had them set up the sample for an enzyme immunoassay screening, even if this screening for drugs had not been requested. As she noted, "I tell these guys to set it up for drugs, because there must be some reason [the suspect was] stopped for DUI, and so if we don't do it now, they are just going to call us a week from now and ask us to do it." By doing this, analysts would not have to rework cases later and could provide results more quickly for the legal system.

In the narcotics unit, the legal schedule of controlled substances specifies all illegal drugs and how they are prosecuted. However, because new drugs are constantly being created, the legal schedule is not always current. Billie explained some of the intricacies of the law:

> Once they realized that all these designer drugs were being made, the laws couldn't keep up. So they worked into the federal law that anything that is an analogue to one on the schedule is also illegal. It is vaguely written, but drugs like MDMA are therefore illegal even though not similarly named. The analogue to MDMA is meth—the MA is the same root.

Billie means that the law allows new drugs that are chemically related to older, illegal drugs to be treated as similarly illegal. Thus MDMA, with a chemical similarity to methamphetamine, is illegal in the eyes of the law. Consequently, criminalists need to bring their subjective, but expert, knowledge to bear on identification.

> A couple of drugs that are scheduled federally but not in the state are not analogues of anything. It's up to the district attorney what to do with those, but we call those and report that information to the DA. For instance, a drug called "foxy," which is 5-methoxy-diisopropyltryptamine. For a couple of months we saw that a lot. Lately we've been seeing more BZP, that is another one. Again, those we call, even though they aren't on the schedule.

Narcotics analysts are careful to report the full set of drugs found in the evidence, even when they are not sure if the DA will choose to prosecute the use of that substance. By completing and reporting additional analyses, even when not asked to, members of the toxicology and chemistry units provide what they believe the legal community might need.

As these examples show, in many of their everyday practices criminalists anticipate how both the criminal justice community and the public might perceive and respond to their work. With these practices, criminalists incorporate the expectations from the legal and public world into their analysis and reporting, but, as they do so, it is also essential that they project their scientific expertise outward, to educate members of other social worlds.

Anticipating by Educating Outside Audiences

MCCL has multiple ways of promoting understanding of their techniques. The lab regularly holds tours for the public in which a criminalist gives a presentation describing the different forms of evidence analyzed, and, at the end, the attendees are allowed to walk through the hallways and peek into the windows of the different units.

Willow, who led the tour I attended, offered explanations of the evidence the lab analyzed, often pointing out the differences between what the public might see on television and what criminalists actually do. Regarding firearms examination, she said, "On *CSI*, they put the bullet under the microscope and say, 'It's a match.' But it can actually take eight hours sometimes to match a bullet, looking in a microscope." She offered a similar debunking of how much time it takes to develop a DNA profile and about how GSR works, commenting, "We never wear leather pants to crime scenes, either."

Criminalists also regularly reach out to educate the world of criminal justice. They interact one-on-one with district attorneys and investigators, both when attorneys have questions about analyses or specific items of evidence and when analysts go to testify. From these interactions, criminalists have developed a shared, durable impression that police and attorneys do not understand the process or requirements of their analyses, nor even know the types of analysis that the lab could perform. With an interest in reducing this ignorance, MCCL developed formal training sessions for members of the criminal justice community. The initial sessions were held in the lab and open to everyone in the community: prosecutors, defenders, investigators, and police. In these sessions, forensic scientists tried to teach justice system representatives what they felt they should know about science.

The training sessions were specific to the practices of each unit in the laboratory and usually began with an introduction to the job of a criminalist in that area and an explanation of the examinations and analyses the unit was able to perform. The firearms training began early one morning in the conference room on the first floor of the lab, with humorous pictures and videos of firearms displayed on a screen. About twenty people made their way to seats in the room: defense attorneys dressed in suits, investigators in jeans, and a group of uniformed officers from the Metropolitan County Police.

Adam, a veteran firearms examiner, began his presentation by introducing himself and the other members of the unit, including their educational credentials and past experience. He then provided an overview of the tests they do, followed by a summary of different types of firearms. He added, "We have a lot of different people here today—police officers, private investigators, attorneys. I want you all to sound as professional as you can when reporting on firearms; you have to talk about them in court." He went into detail about the types of tests the unit performed, with his colleague Al joining in to discuss the penal code and firearms classification.

They spent about an hour on this overview of examination types, answering questions throughout to clarify both the extent of the testing and the technical details of some of the work. While discussing distance determination—an examination that relies on measuring the distance that gunshot residue has traveled—one attorney asked, "There's more [gunshot] powder in a 9 mm than a .22, would you get GSR as far as 6 feet out for a .22?" Adam replied, "I can't say. I need to know the exact gun, what are its characteristics. That would affect it. I'd need the gun." The attorney asked if the examiners could guess if he gave them the rounds, and Adam, reinforcing the limits to which he could scientifically attest, said, "No, I won't do it. I could pull the firearm out from our reference collection, but it really wouldn't be the best information. We won't know the barrel length. I wouldn't want to do it."

After Adam and Al finished the overview, they reminded the audience of some important issues to think about when handling firearm evidence and sending it to the lab: "Remember, safety first. We've received loaded firearms in the lab. It happens. Assume it is loaded and don't put your finger on the trigger. . . . Limit your interaction with the firearm. . . . Do GSR as soon as possible, a big problem is waiting for too much time." Then they opened the floor to general questions and wrapped up the session at about the two-hour mark.

Similar training sessions were held monthly at the laboratory. In each, the criminalists provided an overview of tests, answered questions about specific aspects of their analysis, and cautioned the audience about important aspects of evidence handling. These ranged from "When collecting DNA evidence, do not use plastic baggies" in the DNA training session to the advice in crime scene training to "Collect everything you can before you call the hazmat team or the fire department. We call them the evidence eradication team."

Unhappy with the low turnout among district attorneys, the lab director and the criminalist who organized the training sessions talked with the lab's DA liaison; together, they instituted a similar set of private sessions just for the DA's office. To encourage participation, these sessions qualified for continuing legal education credits for the attorneys and were held at the DA's office on court holidays. Turnout did improve. Although the content was similar to that of the monthly laboratory trainings, criminalists emphasized reports and testifying, since those were the main interests of the district attorneys. The laboratory director kicked off the first overview meeting with a slide titled "Forensics for Dummies" that showed images from *CSI*. He said:

The *CSI* series is great drama, but is it really what goes on in a crime lab? Cases are solved in an hour, they use the same instrument to analyze DNA and narcotics, and everyone is found guilty. Great drama, but not reality. On the positive side, it has raised awareness, from O.J.

to today. Now if you tell people you are a criminalist, they know what you do. But the big problem is the *CSI* effect. You may see this as attorneys: jurors are now expecting to see some sort of scientific evidence during a trial, which has put a lot of burden on crime labs. Now, on cases where normally you wouldn't put up any forensic evidence, they are expecting it. We are trying to get past that through education and everything else.

As the attorneys nodded along, he continued by providing a history of the laboratory and the role of the crime lab, followed by an overview of the "services we provide."

The lab director also discussed communication between the crime lab and the DAs, which he suggested was the "biggest issue." In addition to coordinating in order to meet deadlines and decide what evidence to analyze, he said, "We want you to know what our limitations are, what we can actually do. You need to understand what an exam can or cannot say." He remarked that pretrial meetings in which DAs talk with criminalists before court are very important. "You can meet to go over reports, talk about what questions you want to ask. We are happy that we have been seeing more of this. I can't stress this enough. In the past analysts would show up at 2 p.m. for a trial and would have no idea what [questions] they are going to get [asked] up there on the stand." In these training sessions, the criminalists brought the lab to the attorneys, demonstrating how they could be useful to one another. In so doing, they carried their scientific expertise outward into the world of criminal justice.

In this introductory session, the DA liaison also introduced the idea that specific scripts would be created to prepare attorneys for courtroom testimony, "so you will know the questions to ask. This is not in place of talking to crime lab personnel but to give you some ideas." The forensic scientists, however, were skeptical about these scripts. When I asked Brenna, a DNA supervisor, about them, she said,

> The DA wants us to make up lists of questions that the prosecutors can ask [criminalists in court], in the order they should ask them in. And those might be helpful, but it is pretty difficult to do them for the DNA unit, because there are so many different analyses we do,

and different types of statistical tests. And also, people may perceive us as biased if they find out we are using these scripts.

They had well-grounded concerns that the DAs would use the script as a substitute for speaking with them about the particulars of the case on trial. One DNA analyst complained to her colleagues about a telephone conversation she had with a DA who had asked her to testify: "I told him I had three questions. He tried to hang up after the first one! He clearly didn't want to hear what I had to say or to answer my questions. It is too bad they don't let us help them understand what kinds of things to ask; they just want a short script. Talking to us could be really helpful to them." While scripts would help provide expectations of the appropriate questions to ask about the scientific analysis, criminalists preferred pretrial meetings so that they could address the actual evidence in the case.

In pretrial meetings, criminalists talked about their specific results and what conclusions could be drawn from them. As I will elaborate in chapter 5, they worried that the attorneys would misrepresent the science, either deliberately to support their argument or inadvertently because they did not understand it. As Greg pointed out, "What's really helpful is to meet with them beforehand. I've met with defense lawyers. I've met with the DAs, too. It helps with the whole education side, because you can say something in the meeting and see that the lawyer didn't get it. Then I think, 'Maybe I need to step back and ask how I can say it so everybody gets it.'"

Most analysts agreed that pretrial meetings not only helped courtroom communication but also promoted outside understanding of their scientific constraints. Taylor suggested, "I get the sense from district attorneys that they think they know what we're going to say so they just call us in [to court]. And we don't really get a good meeting with them ahead of time so that we can explain what's going on." He continued by saying that his "best testimony experiences" happened when the DA "has sat down with me and we've gone through all the potential pitfalls of my testimony. And they actually did the right thing to find out what exactly I could say and what I couldn't" about the results. Criminalists were very appreciative when the attorneys contacted them in advance of their appearance.

In one of Andy's cases, he had several pretrial hearings on a DNA analysis he performed on swabs from a gun found by police during a car stop, in which several people were apprehended. These hearings ended up playing a big role in the case, but they did not proceed in the way that Andy expected. One morning, he was preparing to testify in the pretrial hearing for the woman who was driving the car; he had tested the swabs of the gun's cylinder release, hammer release, and trigger, and the results showed mixtures of multiple sources of DNA that were too complicated to be linked directly to the DNA profile of just one defendant. However, on the swab from the grip of the gun, he had found a major profile that matched with the DNA of the driver.

The DA called with some specific questions about Andy's testimony: Would he be able to say at what time the defendant touched the revolver? Andy looked at the table of sample comparisons in his evidence report. Andy replied, "[You mean the profile] on the wooden grip of the revolver? I wouldn't be able to say exactly when that occurred . . . the only thing I can really say is that she came into contact with it, I can't really say how or when. And on the mixtures, she was included but I couldn't say she was the source." The reference sample from the woman matched at every locus with the swab from the grip.

A half hour later, the DA called Andy to come to the courthouse. We went over with two other criminalists from the unit and waited outside the courtroom for over an hour before the DA invited Andy in. However, Andy did not testify. Instead, we watched as the defendant waived her right to a preliminary examination. Afterward, the DA and the arresting officer explained to all of us what had happened. "You aren't just here for nothing," the DA said. "I don't want you to go away thinking the testimony wasn't important." The arresting officer chimed in: "We put on the bright light when we stopped the SUV, this girl was driving and the other guy was in the way back seat. With the light, we saw the guy in the back bend over and put something under the seat, which we figured was drugs but turned out to be the gun."

"The driver was in the front seat," said the DA, "and she had borrowed the car from someone else who lives in Suburban County [the next county north]. So, that's why I asked Andy those questions about if he could tell when she left her DNA on the gun. If she touched the gun in Suburban County, then we can't prosecute it in Metropolitan County. Andy can't say exactly when and where she touched it, and it isn't against the law here if she says she touched it in Suburban. And I'm after the other guy. He's the really bad guy, and I'm trying to get her to testify against him. The officer saw him reach down so we don't have the jurisdictional issue with him. And she's small potatoes compared to this guy." Andy's inability to say when the driver touched the gun informed the DA's strategy. He would not immediately charge her if she was will-ing to testify against the other guy, the "really bad guy." But Andy needed to be there to show that the lab had definitely linked her to the gun.

The DA explained to us why he did not proceed to a trial for the driver, saying that he was not certain what would happen if the case went to trial. He commented that Andy "has educated me enough to know that I've got some small issues on this case. I'm no scientist, but he put it in terms for me to understand. So I know what I can and can't do." In short, because the attorney had learned from the criminalist more of the technical details about his analysis, he was able to make better decisions about how to proceed within the overall goals of the criminal justice system.

After we left, one of the analysts said, "I thought it was great that the DA explained it all to us." Andy agreed: "Well, he didn't want us to feel bad that we all came over here for nothing." Criminalists were more comfortable when they had the chance to explain their conclusions and the limitations of their results to attorneys in advance. Andy was grati-fied that the DA in this case had discussed the limitations of the DNA results with him, and was therefore able to understand how those results could and could not be used in his courtroom proceeding. However, pretrial meetings were not typical, as Peter, an experienced chemist, pointed out:

> I have had DAs meet with me the hour before court and take a copy of the report and say, "This is what I want to ask you, what do you think about that? And are there any other questions you think I should ask?" But that doesn't happen all of the time. It is kind of more

on the rare side. I realize that sometimes they are in a rush but still in terms of preparation they should do that.

In my time at MCCL I only observed one pretrial meeting, the one Andy had over the phone.[7]

In Metropolitan County, the DA realized that communication with the crime lab was important and was proactive about making it happen. As DNA supervisor Eden told me, "When the new DA started, he wanted to manage the process [of communication] and assigned a DA liaison to the crime lab. The liaison came over, and of course, he felt that we should prioritize the active DA cases. But when the police department has a homicide investigation going on with no suspect, that is a big deal. It's more important. I sat him down and explained it to him several times, and finally he understood how we worked." Like all criminalists at MCCL, Eden felt a strong compunction to educate the district attorneys; projecting the science outward could help them understand the work happening in the lab and thus would prevent inaccurate expectations.

By reaching out to the criminal justice community and the public to explain their work, criminalists hope to project their expertise and teach these communities not to expect too much of the science. They are aware that the users of their work have a minimal understanding of its limits. Moreover, they realize that some of the norms and standard practices of criminal justice are in tension with those of science. As Oscar, a toxicologist noted,

> We don't work [for the DA], it should be separate. Of course, the law definitely is on our mind. I mean, it just has to be. The word forensics, it is the use of science in law. So, it's probably halfway down [in our mind], almost. You can mix the two together. There are obviously things you have to work around—it's different, it really is a different feel from just regular science.

By projecting science, as well as by incorporating legal expectations, criminalists try to maintain their allegiance to telling the scientific truth while also anticipating the needs of criminal justice. These tensions were most palpable in their negotiations with criminal justice representatives about whether, how, and when to analyze evidence.

Anticipating While Negotiating and Resisting the Requests of Criminal Justice Representatives

The supervisors are the criminalists who most often negotiate with criminal justice representatives, balancing their requests with what is scientifically appropriate, efficient, and likely to be probative. Since their job entails assigning cases to the members of their unit, they engage with the district attorneys early and often about how items of evidence should be analyzed.

One Monday morning in March, Eden led me through some of her notes on her backlog of cases to be assigned to the DNA analysts. In the first case on the list, her most recent notes said that the item was a knife, and that she would wait for further instruction from the deputy DA assigned to the case. As she dug deeper into the major case forms, it became clear to me that this had been an ongoing conversation, sometimes one-sided, with the DA's office. She said,

> When I got the case in September, I determined the trial was six days from when he submitted the evidence. I called, he said wait for further notice. I then sent him an e-mail in late October, and he never got back to me. In February, I looked again and there was a new DA assigned to the case. I called him and he said he'd talk to the defense and see what he thinks. I told him we didn't have a victim or suspect reference to test against the knife.[8] He suggested we might have a reference sample already in our database so I checked and told him we didn't. I never heard back. So now, in my database, it says the case is closed. So I need to look and see what is in his notes to see if I can tell what to do next.

Eden then looked in a different database belonging to the DA's office and printed out his notes. She said, "Regardless of what it says, I'll have to get in touch with the new DA to confirm that they don't need anything else. You can't really go by what it says in the notes." She sent him an e-mail asking him the status of the case, and if she could now return the knife.

The next items on Eden's list were part of a case that also included firearms comparisons and GSR analysis. She said that, when she had first reviewed the evidence, "my initial concern was around testing this ejected .25 round. My concern is that this is contact DNA and the round was ejected onto the ground. What if it went into a puddle? Who picked it up, and were they wearing gloves?" The messiness of the crime scene and the low level of DNA would complicate the analysis. Eden continued:

> In September, I sent him an e-mail asking him all this, and asking who he believed the DNA was from. I didn't hear back, so I asked the same question a month later [in October], with even more specifics about why I wanted to know. Then we played phone tag, and on December 22 he called and said hold off. In early March, I asked again. He said he needed it in a month, so I told him again that we need a reference sample to check against the potential DNA. Nothing. Currently, the database says that the trial is on March 30th, which is less than a week from now . . . but I've done my due diligence. Reading this, I feel like such a pest. I'm not calling any more. When he calls wanting to know why it isn't done, I'll show him my communication log and tell him this is why.

As Eden's logs show, she spends a good deal of her time thinking about what evidence the DA might need, when it was needed, and whether it made sense for her unit to perform the analysis.

When they receive requests for analysis, criminalists within every unit also anticipate the value of the evidence for the justice system. In the forensic biology unit, analysts frequently talk about the types of analysis that will offer legal proof in a case. Maureen complained about a case in which the police had submitted hundreds of beer cans for DNA profiling that came from a party where a knife fight had broken out. Performing the analysis on every can would take months to complete, and she thought it would provide no insight into the details of the fight. Similarly, a group of DNA analysts chatted about recent requests they had received, and one noted, "The police submitted some bottles from a burglary which they picked up off the road, not in the house. They don't even know if the suspect was there!" Another replied, "I had a case recently with four different [brands of] cigarette butts, they put them all in the same evidence envelope." The cigarette butts posed a question not only about whether the analysis would provide useful evidence, but also about scientific accuracy, because DNA can transfer from one piece of evidence to another.

In the chemistry unit, Taylor described a trace evidence case where he had explored the possibilities for analysis:

> With a major case, we can read the police report and see what they are trying to gain, what they are looking for. We can look at the details and see if there are better things to test. For instance, I've got this domestic violence case—the suspect basically pulled her out of the car and kicked her in the back, he broke her tailbone. They want me to test for any fibers from her clothing on his steel-toed boots. But that is only a test for association, and it won't tell them anything more, because they already have both of them reporting the association. They both say that this happened in a parking lot. It can't prove the action of the kick. So I need to talk to the DA and tell him that.

Taylor later discussed this case with the supervisor, Tim, in a short group meeting in the chemistry lab. He said, "On the domestic violence case, I want to make sure I know what to do with the fiber evidence. First off, fibers only provide association, and they both admit they were there." Tim said, "This is the ridiculous one we talked about last week?" "Yes," Taylor said, and reminded him of the details and said he would call the investigator to tell him the evidence is not probative, since comparing the clothing to the trace evidence on the boot only provides a test for association. They continued discussing the merits of the analysis, and Taylor said, "They are looking for us to solve their case. This won't show that he kicked her, finding evidence of a garment on his boots." Tim added, "It could have happened anytime, or just be secondary transfer." Taylor said he would call the DA and tell him they would not analyze the evidence.

As these examples show, while criminalists anticipate the requirements of the criminal justice system, they also resist performing tasks that do not meet their occupational standards. This was true with respect to issues of legal proof and efficiency, but they were particularly sensitive about their scientific and technical standards. Scientific validity is not only a core tenet of their professional beliefs, but a point of pride for criminalists. Therefore, as in the example of the GSR report in the previous chapter, criminalists are proactive about asserting what is scientifically accurate. As Robin, Meredith, and Taylor argued earlier, the presence of GSR on a person indicated that they were near a weapon that had been fired: the hand on which a particle was found was not relevant. These cases also illustrate how the *CSI* effect influences what happens in the crime laboratory. As district attorneys experience increasing pressure to provide forensic evidence in courtrooms, they channel those pressures toward the laboratory with frequent requests for analysis that criminalists believe may be inefficient, scientifically inaccurate, or not useful for proving facts in a case.

Criminalists are particularly assertive in protecting their scientific credibility, and they could not be swayed by what the district attorneys wanted, if such desires did not match the scientific results. In the year and a half that I observed at MCCL, I heard about one DA who tried to convince a DNA analyst to change her conclusions about the results of a specific profile.[9] The analyst involved stood firm. Talking about it in the hallway with several other criminalists, one analyst said, "Of course she refused. I would have loved to have been a fly on the wall during that discussion. She's not someone I'd ask to do something like that!" Al, a firearms examiner, told me a story of a past case he handled in a different laboratory, when he had also been pressured to change his conclusions.

I had a gun and the question was, did it go off? No, it didn't, and it hadn't gone off for a long, long time. The barrels of the chamber were full of dust. There was no way the guy fired this gun. A deputy DA wanted me to change my report because he didn't like what I was saying because it didn't support the prosecution. So, I basically told him to go fuck himself. If he didn't like my report too damn bad. So I got a letter of reprimand for my language, which I couldn't care less about. It went in my file with all of my other letters of reprimand for my language. My report stayed the same. Nobody was going to tell me what to write in my report.

Thus, while they anticipated the expectations of the criminal justice system, criminalists balked if legal representatives wanted them to change what they saw as the scientific truth of their results. Anticipation did not equal blind obedience.

As these negotiations demonstrate, criminalists experience a tug-of-war between their commitment to science and the pressure to meet the expectations of the criminal justice community and the public. Balancing the two does not always work for criminalists, who frequently complain about needing to act in defense of the science. Moreover, the pressures of being a captive occupation were not constant. They were most prominent during moments when the translation from science into criminal justice was required: when criminalists wrote reports for use in the courts and when they appeared to testify.

While working in the overlapping space of three social worlds is difficult, the culture of anticipation in the laboratory made it possible to navigate these tensions on an everyday basis. Criminalists were accustomed to it; they knew that their job was to educate the members of these other communities about forensic science as much as was possible. And they were prepared to negotiate and resist demands that impinged on what they thought was scientifically and legally appropriate. The means by which this culture of anticipation is created is the focus of the next chapter.

Chapter 4

CREATING A CULTURE OF ANTICIPATION IN THE CRIME LABORATORY

In the crime laboratory, criminalists receive mixed messages about their role. Their symbolic position as champions of science and accuracy entwines with their practical function as captive experts whose outputs are oriented toward and consumed by criminal justice. Sorting out how to live within the ambiguity of these three intersecting worlds, while still maintaining their first duty of scientific rigor, is no easy task.

Leaders in the laboratory, forensic science community, and criminal justice community frequently characterize the job of the criminalist as directly speaking for the evidence. This top-down rhetoric suggests the symbolic position of criminalists as neutral experts in the criminal justice system. In their regular practice, in contrast, criminalists receive strong indications that they need to modulate their speech, such that they anticipate the expectations of those around them and actively manage those expectations.

Within the lab, criminalists are encouraged to go to court to watch the testimony of their colleagues and report back on their performances. As part of their training, new forensic scientists participate in mock trials, using their findings from case reports, with supervisors playing attorneys and the lab director as the presiding judge. Informal talk about testifying permeates the hallways, reinforcing the feeling that criminalists must always be ready to navigate these multiple worlds. Through these daily practices, criminalists become attuned to the expectations of the criminal justice system and the public.

RHETORIC: CRIMINALISTS ARE NEUTRAL EXPERTS WITHIN THE CRIMINAL JUSTICE SYSTEM

In my time at MCCL, I often heard at meetings, and even in casual conversations, that criminalists are the "voice of the evidence." This figure of speech contains the notion, familiar to scientists, that they serve as the conduit for information from the material world. Forensic science and criminal justice leaders frequently contrast this with the active role of advocacy and justice-seeking played by attorneys in the system.

At the first training conducted by the laboratory in the district attorney's offices, the lab director spoke about MCCL's principles of professional responsibility: professionalism, communication, competency, and proficiency. He said:

> We want to make sure lab staff are impartial, detached, and not influenced by department or political pressures. Our conclusions are based on generally accepted tests. The staff is trained and we review them annually to make sure they are competent. Clear communication is one of the concerns we've had—we want to provide accurate and complete data in testimony.

After presenting their professional principles, he again emphasized the lab's neutrality: "One thing I want to get across. We don't work for you as an attorney. . . . We are not here to prove guilt or innocence. We're looking at evidence, we let it speak for itself. We are just here to provide information, not to prove guilt or innocence."

An academic scientist and director of a state forensic training program made a similar statement in his keynote address at a statewide professional meeting of criminalists. In his words, "We must consider our audience, but we must also meet the requirements of good science.

However attorneys use the information we provide, it is incumbent upon us to be scientists. The public thinks forensic science is the handmaiden of law enforcement. We are not—our mission should be to carry out good science regardless of the outcome."

Good forensic science means achieving impartial, objective outcomes without influence from law enforcement. In public forums, I heard attorneys repeat these ideals of neutral science. A DA presenting at a local criminalists' workshop discussed the notion offered in the Melendez-Diaz Supreme Court case that criminalists should be available in court to be confronted as "accusers" under the Sixth Amendment. He said, "Do you have a reasonable expectation that your report will be used in trial when you work in the lab? Yes. But are you doing it to be accusatory? No, the answer is no, your answer should be no!" The room broke out in laughter. "You are objective," he continued. "You present scientific data that is neutral. You are not advocates; you are impartial. Criminalists have a narrow focus on objective scientific facts about the state of affairs in the world and not in order to incriminate people."

Another DA took this notion a step further in front of hundreds of criminalists at a statewide meeting. He recalled the history of his local laboratory:

> What has always been most important to me about criminalist testimony? It is not about the numbers or the methodology or can I make a match, but what is most important, whenever our criminalists came in to testify, is scientific integrity.
>
> Results are helpful, but the ability to withstand scrutiny is the most important thing when testifying in front of a jury.... With the scrutiny that is being placed on our community, you need to always go back to that integrity, that's what's important. There will be pressures that will challenge your scientific integrity, and a lot of that comes from law enforcement. A district attorney wants a specific example: "I need you to say x so I can argue y." We need you to stand in that gap and argue, "No, it is x, not x + 1." We need you to train us, to say, "It is x, it'll always be x." We train attorneys not to think that way,

but in the midst of the battle, they will forget, and it all comes down to you.

What criminalists hear, therefore, is that they should be neutral scientists directly reporting their results from the evidence they receive. And, as the lab director told me, he also told the members of MCCL that they only need to be comfortable with their analysis and should not worry too much about what the attorneys might do with it.

But the balancing act of hewing to scientific integrity in the face of external demands is not always straightforward. Criminalists' daily experiences suggest that more is expected of them than mere scientific expertise. What their interactions within other social worlds communicate instead is that they really are required to anticipate the needs of criminal justice: that their role "serving" justice is a subservient one.

Reality: Waiting and Making Anticipation Routine

Quotidian encounters with the criminal justice system indicate to criminalists that scientific integrity and unvarnished information are not enough. The captive aspect of criminalists' role with respect to this system overshadows their expertise: within the criminal justice system, criminalists are near the bottom of the hierarchy. One significant indicator of their captive status is that criminalists are often kept waiting.[1] Moreover, the notion of serving justice is routinely reinforced in daily interactions as not merely working toward justice, but doing so in a way that anticipates how the criminal justice system and the public might interpret their work.

The time criminalists spend waiting is particularly noticeable with respect to court appearances. Although criminalists' reports are used regularly in criminal cases, that does not mean they are required to appear in court. In fact, they are rarely called upon to testify on the stand: criminalists claim that they testify in less than 2 percent of their cases. For one thing, many cases do not go to trial, and for those that do, attorneys on both sides can stipulate their agreement to criminalists' conclusions, while some conclusions can be reported on the stand by police officers in the criminalists' stead. Also, defendants often plead out before a full trial is held.

At MCCL, of the almost 20,000 cases completed in 2009, analysts testified in just 87 of them (a third of these were major cases and two-thirds were in toxicology or narcotics). For major cases, a firearms examiner at MCCL explained that he had analyzed about 200 cases each year for the last 10 years, and, of those 2000 cases, he had testified in 40; similarly, a DNA analyst had testified 4 times out of the 260 cases on which she worked in the last several years.

However, unlike the daily routines of analysis and report writing, which criminalists feel are performed relatively independently of the DA's office, when criminalists testify, they are at the DA's beck and call. For every case for which a trial date is set, the criminalists who reported results of evidence testing are sent a subpoena. Each unit, then, has a bottomless supply of subpoenas that criminalists sift through, generally on a weekly basis. Criminalists are aware of the fact that they probably will not to have to attend court. As Jason in toxicology went through his pile one morning, I asked, "Is it like in the other units I've been in? You are not often called to testify?" He answered, "Of these, about 2 percent of them the attorneys might actually call you on; and of those, you testify at 30 percent." On the other hand, advance notice is not always forthcoming; sometimes attorneys call for the criminalists to appear in court later the same day. As Andy, a DNA analyst, told me about one case, "Originally, [the attorney] subpoenaed me for Monday, and I had written (on the form) that I wasn't available for [that Monday]. But he apparently didn't read the form because on Monday he called me and left one message saying at first that he wouldn't be needing me, and then later that I needed to come in."

Knowing the uncertainty of the process, criminalists have adapted to being at the mercy of the district attorneys with a variety of tactics. Since subpoenas are not reliable indicators, they are treated nonchalantly. In fact, Jason stood directly over the trash can while sifting through his pile, dropping each of them in after he had read it. However, they are also prepared to go to court at a moment's notice. The lab's dress code requires closed-toe shoes, and, although they wear lab coats over their clothing, criminalists typically dress casually in case of spills. Therefore, they stash business suits and "courtroom" shoes in their cubicles to be prepared in the event of a last-minute summons.

The waiting continues once criminalists arrive in the courtroom.[2] The district attorneys do not know how the action in the proceedings will unfold; they cannot predict the results of their own maneuvers nor those of opposing counsel and the judges. Therefore, their estimates of when a criminalist will be needed are not very accurate. When Andy appeared for the case whose subpoena he described, he and two other criminalists waited in the hallway outside the courtroom for an hour. They began wondering where the DA was. "It would suck if he called us over here and he's not even in the courtroom," said one of Andy's colleagues. It was another fifteen minutes before the DA came out to let Andy know that he would not need him to testify because they were holding off on charging the suspect.

Criminalists' captive status is also reinforced when they reach out to the criminal justice community to provide training or information, and find that their time is treated as less valuable. As described earlier, Eden's log of cases requiring contact with the DA to determine priorities illustrates that the supervisors spend a lot of time making requests of DAs that go unacknowledged. This experience was echoed in a conversation that Holly, the comparative evidence supervisor, had with Eden in her office one afternoon. Holly brought up a case in which a sheriff asked the lab to check some cartridge cases for both latent prints and DNA. Eden said, "What? They know that we don't do latents or DNA on anything that's been fired!" Holly said, "I called him about it and he said, 'It was worth a try.' Can you believe that?" Eden and Holly agreed that it would be a lot easier if law enforcement representatives contacted them to ask what is appropriate, instead of imposing assumptions. An assistant director of another crime laboratory reported a similar problem with investigating officers:

Investigators are very eager to solve their cases, and you can tell them six ways to Sunday that testing a certain kind of evidence won't help, but sometimes you have to just do the test to show them. And hope next time they won't ask again, although a lot of times they do. And you can't just say, "Well, we've got twenty other cases where the evidence is going to be more probative." Swabbing handguns for DNA is an example of this. Because people shed DNA at different rates: some leave a lot, some hardly any. It is really questionable that if you find DNA on a gun, it belongs to the person who shot it. Also, you can't tell if they were the last ones to touch it. You get information back but you may be answering the wrong question. But it can be hard to convince the investigators of this.

In this case, the issue of wasting the time of criminalists dovetails with other concerns, including how to communicate their scientific knowledge so that important resources are not wasted.

MCCL criminalists also perceive a lack of interest in their work from the DA's office in training sessions. Those held in the laboratory were open to everyone in the criminal justice community; as noted earlier, district attorneys only sparsely attended these. At the four trainings I observed—firearms examination, toxicology, blood spatter analysis, and crime scene investigation—less than a quarter of the audience were district attorneys. It wasn't until the inducement of continuing legal education credit was added that attendance improved, but, notably, during the toxicology session the DA's office still reinforced the criminalists' low status. One afternoon at 1:30 p.m., the entire toxicology unit and I arrived at the DA's office to find the meeting room empty. We sat down, and the toxicologists engaged in some annoyed banter, making jokes about what Jason, the main speaker, would say to the DAs after he spent all these hours preparing the slides. "If they don't come, we'll just leave." "Any questions? I have one. Why weren't you here at 1:30?" After about ten minutes, Flora, the supervisor, called the DA liaison, and he told her he changed the time to 2:00 p.m. but forgot to let her know. A veteran toxicologist, Parvaneh, said, "Why is it always tox they do this to?"

How Anticipation Is Made Routine

At MCCL, criminalists hear rhetoric from the leaders of their communities suggesting that their position requires scientific integrity and their role is to provide unvarnished information to the criminal justice world and "not worry" about what the attorneys do with that information. This accords with their own beliefs about the truth of the natural world and their values of neutrality and objectivity; they believe in performing careful scientific analysis without taking an interest in the outcome. However, many of the daily routines and practices of the lab emphasize the importance not of pure science, but of anticipating the perceptions of the criminal justice system and the public world.

This is particularly true with respect to testifying. Because criminalists most often have face-to-face encounters with the public and the justice system in the courtroom, this is the locale where these expectations are most salient. Forensic scientists begin their jobs at the laboratory without much background or interest in public speaking; consequently, both within the lab and in the larger forensic science community, they receive a lot of training about how to testify in court. All of the criminalists at MCCL are members of the state criminalists association, and newcomers are encouraged to attend a two-day courtroom testimony workshop offered regularly at the organization's biannual conference. This workshop included classroom discussions about testimony, exercises using "mind maps" to chart their expertise, instruction on creating visual aids for the courtroom, and a day of practice in a county courthouse in which each attendee participates in a mock trial.

The workshop I attended was taught by two retired criminalists, Donald and Jacob. Both had worked in state laboratories and one also served as an independent expert witness. On the day of the mock trials, the attendees arrived in court wearing suits and carrying their visual aids. Donald played the role of the defense attorney; Jacob the judge; and Sarah, a senior criminalist from a Department of Justice laboratory and Jacob's former colleague, the prosecutor. I played the defendant and sat at the defense table up front with Donald. The students in the class, all relative newcomers to forensic science, used what they had learned the day before to take turns testifying. After each student performed, they received detailed feedback from the veterans who led the trial, as well as the other students, who were taking careful notes.

During this training, the veterans explicated not only the logistics of testifying, but also the expectation that the "voice" of the evidence should convey more than scientific accuracy: it also needed to be confident and credible. After one DNA analyst said in response to an attorney's question that she was "looking for the victim's blood," Sarah told her, "As a forensic scientist, you are not 'looking' for anything. You are examining for the presence or absence of blood, testing for presence or absence. Not looking, not looking under the bed, not looking for anything, ever." A credible criminalist is not "looking," but "testing." And their statements should be short, clear, and loud. In Donald's words, "You have a small voice. You need to fill this grand stage. Be confident."

The veterans suggested that criminalists should use precise but not too scientific language, and, at the same time, they should not speak casually. Thus, every time a criminalist used a scientific term without defining it clearly, they pointed it out. Jacob told one, "You said 'amylase' without defining it," and he complimented another for explaining concepts well. Criminalists were also advised not to use slang or street language: "Remember it is 'cocaine,' not 'coke.' This is not the street." Finally, criminalists should exhibit understanding of court procedures, as Donald told one participant: "You have to know the rulings of the court. Twice I paused and you jumped in. You have to wait." These forms of feedback helped criminalists understand that they could not just present unvarnished scientific results to the court; instead, they should anticipate juries that want clear and polite explanations for concepts, attorneys that want loud and decisive answers, and judges that want courtroom procedures to be followed.

Criminalists participate in similar mock court proceedings in the laboratory during their training. When they complete their competency exams (comprising analyses of realistic cases created by a third-party organization) enabling them to do actual casework, criminalists then testify in the lab using the details from their competency case. They prepare extensively for this testimony with guidance from their more experienced colleagues. When Kerry, a novice DNA analyst, finished her competency case, she spent an entire morning preparing for the afternoon mock court. Other analysts had provided her with lists of questions that might come up in a standard DNA profile testimony. On a notepad, she drafted answers to the questions that she felt were most relevant to her case. Jonah, an experienced DNA analyst, had given Kerry a set of slides he used for training other analysts in DNA profiling and bloodstain analysis, and she drew on some of his definitions to compose her answers. Afterward, Kerry went through the sixty-page report, remarking, "This is a long report, so it is good to mark up the pages with sticky notes so on the stand you can easily flip to them if there are specific things you think they'll ask about. Like the electropherograms for specific items, or where there are artifacts or stutter." Like the criminalists in the workshop, Kerry paid close attention to her language, looking for terms such as "spikes" and "artifacts" that she might need to define on the stand.

While she prepared, Kerry told me about questions the attorneys were likely to ask. She said:

> They'll also sometimes ask crazy questions like, "Can you show that this was a nonconsensual act?" We joke about this in the lab. You can't tell happy consensual sperm from angry sperm. So we have a lot of sexual assault cases, and imagine that both the victim and the suspect were drunk—they agree that they had sex but disagree about who said no. The lawyers will try to get you to make up their story for them. So you have to be careful how you answer—you keep your answers short, say that you are not able to assess that. So, [in my case] they might ask, "The blood on the shirt, is that from the knife fight?" and I'd say, "It is possible, but it is also possible to be there from other reasons."

What is notable about Kerry's explanation to me is that Kerry was a new criminalist. She had never testified before in a DNA profiling case. Her colleagues in the forensic biology unit had told her about their own testimonies and prepared her for questioning in court, giving her the expectation that "crazy" questions might be in her future when she took the stand.

Criminalists also discover the types and styles of questions they might encounter by accompanying their colleagues to court. Criminalists walking back to the lab together often debrief the testimony, discussing the questions and answers and complaining about the attorneys.

When Carolyn, a DNA supervisor, was in court testifying in a pretrial admissibility hearing, I accompanied Yvette to hear her testify. When the three of us left the courtroom together afterward, Yvette and Carolyn discussed the questions the defense attorney had asked. Yvette said, "She doesn't know what she is talking about. I couldn't believe she was confusing volume with low level! How did you not yell at her?" Carolyn said, "I was going to correct her but I didn't want it to get too off track. I wish I could help her. We could have a pretrial conference and I could explain all this to her, and then we wouldn't have to spend all this time in court."

When criminalists return to the lab, they give a detailed accounting to their colleagues.[3] When we got back to Carolyn's office that afternoon, Anca came in, saying, "Another one walks the street!" and they discussed their recent experiences testifying. Anca was upset because a DA e-mailed her about a robbery case for which she had testified and said there was a hung jury. The defense attorney had argued that there had been secondary transfer of DNA across pieces of the evidence, and Anca worried that she had not done a good job testifying. "They said his DNA could've been on the handkerchief and transferred to the gun. And we never tested the handkerchief, we should have done that! But the DA didn't request for us to." They discussed the details of the defense attorney's questions, and Carolyn reassured Anca, "There's nothing you could do. . . . You do a good job of explaining things, and you did the best you could." In this manner, stories about testifying made their way through MCCL, contributing to criminalists' understanding of what to expect in the courtroom.

The stories that spread through the laboratory also serve as cautionary tales about the potential consequences of criminalists making mistakes in this forum. The tale I heard most often in the lab concerned what had happened to Peter, a criminalist who was removed from doing casework due to a mistake in court. Peter had testified about a piece of evidence that the DA argued placed the suspect at the scene of a crime. Peter's report may have been scientifically accurate, but it was presented in the courtroom in a way that was later challenged by other legal actors, and a higher court overturned the decision in the case.[4] The laboratory removed him from casework after an investigation of his work in the case.

Peter's situation illustrates the tensions around the difference between the rhetoric of scientific information and the reality of having to balance the interpretations and expectations of other worlds. The evaluation of his work was not simply based on his report, but also his testimony. However, this testimony was guided by lawyers' questions and framed by their interpretations and arguments. Inside the laboratory, the telling of this story was one way that criminalists expressed their concerns about how the expectations of the criminal justice system pervaded their work. The forensic scientists at MCCL attributed Peter's mistaken testimony to the prosecutor's overzealousness in interpreting his report rather than to a problem with Peter's expertise. They valued his scientific opinions and believed him to be one of the most skilled criminalists in the laboratory. However, the consequences of a courtroom error can be grave. As one supervisor told me, when he was involved in a case where the attorneys questioned his competence, "If I was ever determined to be wrong enough that it constituted an error, it would become an issue for [my career]. Everybody makes mistakes. We're not allowed to. Doctors have malpractice insurance. Forensic science is the only career where you can't make a mistake."

The stories criminalists tell about their own work, then, reveal both their understanding of their role in anticipating criminal justice and the consequences of failing to do so. This understanding is created in the course of their daily routines: interacting with members of the criminal justice world, being trained by their supervisors, and gossiping with their colleagues. While they subscribe to the rhetoric about the ideal of forensic science as a neutral conduit for truth about evidence, the reality of their daily experience suggests otherwise.

From the moment criminalists begin their work in the laboratory, the culture of anticipation reinforces their service to the criminal justice system. In this way, the lab culture is complicit in emphasizing the ways that forensic scientists need to balance multiple social worlds, metrics of truth, and styles of engagement. Rather than present a purely scientific truth, the anticipatory work done by forensic scientists serves to incorporate public and legal views about evidence and best practices that color their collective reports and public testimony. The consequences of not anticipating could be embarrassing or worse, resulting in grave harm to others or themselves. However, criminalists' desire to be true to their commitments to science often conflicts with the expectations of criminal justice. As a captive occupation, criminalists cannot avoid this tension, which is most acute at times when they face members of other social worlds outside the lab. The most critical moment, as I describe in the next chapter, is testifying.

Part 3

THE STRUGGLES OF CRIMINALISTS

Chapter 5

THE SPECTER OF TESTIFYING

Forensic Scientists as the Voice of the Evidence

Providing courtroom testimony as an expert witness is a vital part of a criminalists' job: how cases are decided can rest on the scientific analysis of physical evidence, and criminalists may be called to the stand to explain their conclusions about the evidence. Though a rare event, testifying takes on an outsize importance for the work and identity of forensic scientists. On the stand, criminalists' expertise is exposed to scrutiny.[1] Testifying is therefore the moment where the differences between the worlds of science, criminal justice, and the public are laid bare.

Tim, the supervisor of the chemistry unit at MCCL, described these differences and their impact on him:

> The other piece of our job is, I've got prosecution over here trying to get their story told. I have the defense over there trying to get their story told. I've got the judge doing God knows what. Sometimes he's on his own team. Sometimes he's on the jury's team. Sometimes he's not even paying attention. He's staring at his desk. So, among all those players, I always go there with the intention that I'm there for the victim. I'm there to be their voice, or the voice of the evidence. I want to be the voice for the evidence, and it's my responsibility to try and get that out in my written report, and in my testimony or any communications to the attorneys, but some of the players in that courtroom don't want to hear the whole truth and nothing but the

truth. So that's where we come in conflict with the judicial system. I haven't been censured, but I have pissed off a few attorneys. And I would do it again. I'm the voice of reason in the courtroom sometimes.

Testifying is when criminalists are most anxious about being members of a captive occupation: experts whose expertise is taken out of their hands, to be used and possibly misused with uncertain consequences. Exploring how criminalists experience testifying—how they prepare for the event, and how they respond to the tensions surrounding it—reveals what happens when criminalists need to anticipate the judgments of three distinct worlds. Tracing how analysts become, in Tim's words, the "voice of the evidence," helps us understand the boundary work done by criminalists: the ways they need to navigate the boundaries of different disciplines. We see what it takes to stay true to the science, while trying to serve justice.

THE CONSEQUENCES OF TESTIFYING

Because trials are a rare exception in criminal cases, given the prevalence of plea bargaining, it is not surprising that criminalists go to court for less than 2 percent of the cases on which they work.[2] And within this small number of cases, there are nuances in what a court appearance means for criminalists. Attorneys sometimes use the threat of forensic evidence and criminalists' testimony as part of their courtroom strategy. They may call for a criminalist to appear in court, without intending to have the criminalist take the stand, in order to intimidate a defendant to take a plea or testify against another person.

As noted in the last chapter, Andy, a DNA analyst, was called to a pretrial hearing in a case involving gun possession: he entered the courtroom, but never took the stand. According to the district attorney, having Andy there for hearing was helpful in convincing the gang members in the gallery that there was forensic evidence to support the case. The defendant, according to the district attorney, would consequently believe that the gun possession charge was not an empty threat. In a similar strategic move, Jodi, a narcotics analyst, described a set of court appearances in which the defense attorneys in Metropolitan County were calling her to testify in multiple cases, yet they did not seem to have any meaningful questions. It turned out that a new DA had just started his job and the defense attorneys called Jodi to the stand just to "give [the new DA] a hard time."

———

While infrequent, court appearances place criminalists exactly where the three social worlds of forensic science intersect. For actors within the legal world—attorneys, judges, bailiffs, court reporters—the courtroom is their everyday workspace. Therefore, each day in court is a routine day. The regular participants in a courtroom know one another as coworkers.[3] Attorneys on both sides of the argument relax, along with judges, in the backstage of the chambers. In contrast, the high theater of court proceedings is designed to intimidate the defendants and laypeople present, and it intimidates criminalists as well. Legal actors set boundaries around their domain, and criminalists are only allowed inside when called to the stand.[4] They are not coworkers but guests, and their experiences in the courtroom are anything but typical for them.

For the public, the courtroom is a different space, one of strain but also of judgment. Comprising not just members of the community, but often even the victims and their families, the public has vested interests in what happens and expectations about outcomes. This makes testifying a high-stakes event for criminalists: the outcomes affect people's lives. When Brandon Mayfield was arrested in connection with the Madrid train bombings on the basis of an incorrect FBI fingerprint identification, he said that the time after the arrest was "the hardest and darkest that myself and my family have ever had to endure."[5] For criminalists, testifying makes plain their role in determining defendants' guilt and innocence.

Criminalists directly confront the implications of their work when they enter the courtroom and see the people who are affected. Chris, a young DNA analyst, described the first time he testified. While Chris waited outside the courtroom before testifying, the victim herself came out of the courtroom and sat near him, visibly upset and "close to the edge." She asked him, "Why are you here?" When he said he was there to testify, she said, "Are you testifying for me?" Chris felt awkward, because he believes he testifies about what the evidence demonstrates, not for or against a particular person or side of the case. As he remarked, "I was uncomfortable talking to her. I felt bad. We aren't supposed to talk to anybody, but of course there is a human side to what we do." Anca, another DNA analyst, described a "gruesome" kidnapping and sexual assault case in which she testified, after which the suspect "was sentenced for a long time." She said, "I looked at the work I did and thought, 'I did a thorough job on this.' It took me back to why I got into this field to begin with . . . to give something back and do something good while doing science at the same time."

Although criminalists can be called to testify by either the prosecution or the defense, they almost always appear at the behest of the prosecution. Regardless of who calls them, as Tim notes, criminalists feel a responsibility to accurately report the results of their testing, which can indicate whether the evidence shows the defendant was physically present at the scene or committed a crime. Criminalists point to the importance of carefully interpreting the evidence, not only from the perspective of their scientific techniques, but also in considering implications for defendants. Maureen, for example, described the first time she testified in Metropolitan County. The suspect had been pulled out of a small lake, and the police had swabbed his hands and sent the swabs to the DNA unit to see if they found any evidence of the victim's DNA profile on his hands. Maureen explained her thinking while on the stand:

> I think the defense attorney meant to prove a point, which was the victim's DNA was not on this guy's hands. And I feel as an analyst that it can go either way. He could have never had her DNA on his hands. He could have washed his hands. In that case, you have to give him the benefit of the doubt, because he's innocent until proven guilty. So it's like if there's no evidence, that's more weight toward him being innocent, and my results were neutral. And neutral goes toward the defendant.

Al, a firearms examiner, also mentioned the importance of doing careful analysis to help people:

> Sometimes I think that I get more satisfaction out of helping a sus-pect to not be put in prison, when I know somebody has been wrong-fully charged and he is scared and he is sitting in jail. An unbiased impartial report, I think, that would clear him, that's what we need to do. Most of the time the guy is guilty as charged. But if I can help someone, I feel that I've earned my money.

Analysts expressed a sense of dedication to providing accurate results to help adjudicate defendants' guilt or innocence.

Testifying also has significant consequences for the forensic scien-tists themselves, in terms of their pride, integrity, and professional standing. Carly, a veteran DNA analyst, described a moment on the stand that was personally embarrassing:

> I've had to admit mistakes on the stand, which is not a nice thing to do, and you feel real stupid, [even when] it comes across well to the attorneys and to the judge. And you know, I have felt mortified on the stand when I have to admit a mistake. It's not a pleasant thing to do. One case I remember, it was a jury trial, and there were several items in the sexual assault. There were several pairs of panties and I mixed up the results from one pair of panties to the other. And I caught it, and I said "Oh. I have to go back to these questions, because I was looking at the results from this item, and I gave totally the wrong answer. And I'm so sorry I didn't catch it."

Carly testified about evidence she analyzed, but, while still on the stand, she realized that she'd made an error in her earlier statement. In seeking to correct, she feared that her honesty and confusion would be used against her in the courtroom.

> And the defense attorney said, "She's not an expert," and ranted and raved. "She's obviously making mistakes. She doesn't know what she's talking about. She can't even read her own report." And the judge just said, "She's the one who caught her own mistake. She's the one who's saying, 'Oh, I messed up.' She's correcting it. It's fine." You know,

"Let's get on with it." But I felt two inches high, and I'm sure I was beet red, and I'm sure my voice started shaking after that.

While Carly's mistake was minor and merely distressing, mistakes are always scrutinized, and more significant errors can derail a forensic scientist's career. The results of criminalists' proficiency and competency exams are a part of their file; they are discoverable by attorneys and can be discussed in court. Moreover, if a mistake is found to have been made on the stand, it results in firing, forced retirement, or suspension from casework (as was the case with Peter, discussed in chapter 4). More pervasive problems with analysis in a laboratory often make news; the chief scientist of the District of Columbia Department of Forensic Sciences resigned in 2015 in the wake of a laboratory audit, and the senior manager of the DNA area was dismissed.[6] Criminalists are keenly aware that their mistakes can have consequences for their careers.

As mentioned in the introduction, their awareness of these consequences means that forensic scientists treat testifying with gravity. They feel a sense of responsibility both to get the science right and to approach the situation of suspects and victims with the seriousness they deserve. As Marina, a DNA analyst, remarked, "It can be upsetting. [But] I feel like I give back to society in a positive way and in some ways give closure. For me, it isn't just the next case that comes across the table. That's somebody's life that's been impacted."

THE SPECTER OF TESTIFYING

Criminalists worry about many aspects of their jobs: following protocols, detailing and documenting their work, making sure their instruments are working properly, protecting the chain of custody, and clearing their backlogs. But by far the task they worry about the most is testifying. The professional, personal, and social implications of their testimony create anxiety for most forensic scientists. Their apprehensive talk in the hallways made it seem as though a specter hovered over the lab, haunting criminalists with the possibility that they would need to appear in court and have their feet held to the fire.

Forensic scientists struggle when confronted with the different norms of science and law, and the adversarial nature of these courtroom interactions leads them to resent lawyers and feel ambivalent about testifying. More important, their identification as scientists (and with science) makes them highly sensitive to the technical accuracy of their analysis, which often conflicts with legal principles and courtroom practices. This is compounded by their marginal status within the community of criminal justice, which leads criminalists to feel isolated on the stand.

Some analysts find the uncertainty about waiting to be the toughest part. As Allison, a DNA analyst, suggested, "It's just the fact that you are on edge until you get it done with." She went on to explain how it felt like "anticipation before a test. You're just ready to take the test, you've studied, you're ready to go and then you have to hold that all day and then even the next day." After all that, she added, you still may not actually be called to the stand. Many forensic scientists are afflicted with physical manifestations of their nerves: stomachaches or shivers or sweaty armpits during the wait outside the courtroom.

Joanna, a young toxicologist who often testifies to drug effects in the body, described her feelings before testifying: "I call my colleagues up and I ask, 'What is this? What do I say about this?' I know nothing, I draw a blank. I'm sick to my stomach." She went on to explain how, after the initial confusion and anxiety, she's "very comfortable" on the stand. But even this can change, she added: "Sometimes there's just so much to talk about that I'll start talking and I actually forget what the hell I'm talking about and go, 'Okay just stop talking. Just stop.'" Similarly, a DNA analyst reported his worry that he "always blurts things out" on the stand. Robin, a narcotics analyst, recalled a time when she had to ask for a pen in order to spell some technical terms: "I'm a really bad speller but I'm especially bad when I'm under pressure. I went so far beyond bad spelling, I had the judge laughing. I try not to spell or do even simple math on the stand because I've found that I just lose the ability."

Part of criminalists' anxiety stems from the personal discomfort many feel at speaking in public. A typical forensic scientist is more comfortable behind a lab bench than in front of an audience. During a hallway conversation, Ellie, a DNA analyst, complained to her colleague Terri about an upcoming testimony appearance, "I think the testifying part will never be easy." Terri replied, "Except for Andy. It is his favorite part, but remember, he also teaches LSAT classes." Having already seen a lot of dread and uneasiness in the lab about testifying, I said, "It seems like it isn't the favorite part for anybody else." "Definitely not mine!" Ellie said emphatically. Terri added, "We all got into this work because we wanted to be in the lab, not in front of people talking or teaching. So it isn't what we want to do." Similarly, talking about a recent court appearance, a very seasoned DNA analyst noted, "This is my least favorite part of the job. I don't like being the center of attention, having all eyes on me. I'm a science person."

But this anxiety over courtroom performance merely overlays the true core of tension in the work of forensic scientists. Rather, it's criminalists' need to balance their scientific commitments with legal and public expectations—that is, the "culture of anticipation" discussed in the previous chapters—that I believe makes criminalists anxious. Forensic scientists are well prepared in terms of their technical expertise, but they feel the pressure of being in the spotlight, where their credibility will be questioned. They may have to perform mathematical calculations on the spot, or answer questions about the scientific literature. The boundary work they perform on the stand is fraught with their commitment to scientific truth in the face of adversarial scrutiny.[7] And, in the courtroom, their credibility and their technical expertise aren't simply being evaluated, but employed by both prosecuting and defending attorneys as a tool for determining whether the criminal justice system will punish someone.

These tensions are evident in a story that Tim related about an experience he had while testifying in a comparative evidence case. Tim had been a criminalist for ten years before becoming supervisor of the lab's chemistry unit. His role required him to technically review thousands of narcotics cases a year performed by his colleagues, in addition to doing his own casework. In this particular case, he performed a comparative analysis of shoeprints. A door had been kicked in, and the collapsed structure had been photographed and analyzed to obtain an estimate of the size of the shoe. The prosecutor did not like the conclusions Tim drew from his analysis of the photographs. When asked by the prosecutor for a second opinion, Tim recommended Joe, a former teacher of his. Joe also analyzed the photographs of the door, and, while Tim concluded the shoe size was 10½ to 11½, Joe concluded the shoe was size 11 to 12. There was some overlap in their interpretations, but Joe and Tim had derived different conclusions from their expertise. As Tim explained:

> Joe made certain assumptions. I made certain assumptions. And he and I were totally fine with it. We were discussing our individual reports and from a science perspective, we agreed that it was a range. Our ranges overlapped. It was probably in that overlap area, but there was no guarantee. It could have been out. It could have been in the bell curves. We were fine with this, but the prosecution and the defense both wanted different answers. So the defense called me, because their client's foot fell outside that range [Tim's range]. The prosecution called Joe, because they wanted to get Joe's opinion because the suspect's foot fell in Joe's range but outside mine.

The prosecutor had gotten what he wanted: a different expert had produced the result that fit his argument. It was true that Tim, his own laboratory's criminalist, found otherwise. But that, it turned out, was something the prosecutor could deal with. Tim reported how, in court:

> When the defense called me, here's the DA, from our office who I supposedly work for, trying to impugn my testimony. He put me up as incompetent and took conversations he and I had that were not part of the case and brought them up on the witness stand. "So, is the reason you're not telling the truth here, because you're afraid for your job?"

Tim was astonished. What could justify such behavior? And yet:

> Afterward, he was fine. He was like, "Let's grab a cup of coffee." I couldn't think of a sufficiently rude thing to say to him right then. I was

going down my entire list of sailor words that I could come up with, and I couldn't think of anything sufficient.

This is a telling example of the dangers and difficulties that criminalists faced in navigating very different social worlds. From Tim's perspective:

> Attorneys don't think like we do. I have known people who will say anything to win an argument regardless of the cost of winning that argument. So the attorneys think different. For them, it's all about winning. And it's just winning now. They don't care about long-term consequences. They don't care about people's careers. It's all about winning this case right here, right now. And criminalists are not that way. The truth for us is going to be true tomorrow, and the next day, and the next day.

Tim's story foregrounds how the norms and practices of discovering legal proof differ from those of uncovering and representing scientific truth.[8] In his words, "attorneys don't think like we do."

———

Testifying is the most immediate, personal, and charged demonstration of the different ways that lawyers and scientists find truth: the one, through adversarial argument, the other, through scientific technique and representation. As such, testifying is particularly difficult for criminalists, as captive experts subjected to aggressive questioning and seeming ignorance—or even willful disregard—of scientific fact and explanation.

Forensic scientists feel that lawyers make a game of science, and treat criminalists as pawns in this game. Tom, a firearms examiner, complained, "It can be frustrating that your product, your work product, may be misrepresented. A lot of times, you're sitting up there, and you kind of feel a little bit like a puppet, because you're waiting for the next question." Robin, a narcotics analyst, similarly felt "wary about what they're trying to pull. . . . Sometimes they play games, not a lot, but it's a play." Because forensic scientists take science seriously, they are disturbed by what they perceive as attorneys' lack of respect for the truth and dignity of science.

Moreover, the tone of this game seems hostile and intimidating. The legal system is inherently adversarial, with prosecutors and defense attorneys facing off on different sides of an argument. Each attorney is trying to make a particular point by using the testimony of expert witnesses (as Tim's story illustrates, these witnesses might include other criminalists working for the prosecutor). The antagonistic nature of the proceedings fits comfortably into the world of lawyering, but remains highly uncomfortable for forensic scientists. Many criminalists, like Tim, feel that the attorneys do not care what the truth is, that their job is to win cases at all costs, and that they are therefore not to be trusted.

One DNA analyst, miserable about the way her testimony had gone, came in to her supervisor's office to vent about the defense attorney's questioning. "You would not believe this guy! He totally schmoozed me beforehand, and then hit me with these questions. It was horrible the way he asked questions. . . . 'You didn't test for body fluids; you didn't test for urine.' We don't even have tests for them!" Others feel physically threatened in the courtroom by attorneys, who stand while the witnesses are seated in front of them: "[The attorney] was kind of a big guy, 6'4", standing over me aggressively, accusing me of not answering the question." Sometimes there are multiple lawyers asking questions in succession, as Holly, the comparative evidence supervisor, noted in her description of one appearance: "It was a grueling three days. I was challenged frequently. There were twelve lawyers there so I was a little intimidated." As a scientific expert, criminalists feel out of place on the stand, especially when addressed so sharply.

But it is not just being attacked that, for analysts, demonstrates the difficulties of bridging these very different worlds. Sometimes, analysts on the stand find the behavior of attorneys simply baffling. I mentioned to Terri and Ellie that I had been impressed by their colleague whom we observed in court the day before: although some of the questions the attorneys asked made little sense to any of us, she maintained her composure. Ellie commented, "I always answer the question I think they should have asked, and then they can ask again if I didn't get it right." Terri added:

> I was up there once for forty-five minutes. The defense attorney was asking me the same question over and over. The DA objected the first time, but then let it go on. Afterward, she told me that she was letting it go on because the defense attorney was making himself look bad. Because the jury understood what I was saying, but he didn't. I don't know, after I while I felt like I was slouching over, saying, "Like I just said," or "As I just told you," over and over.

Ellie, said, annoyed, "What did he think, that you'd give in? Maybe they are trying to tire us out so we'll just agree." Terri agreed, "Yeah, we said the same thing ten million times, now we're going to agree so we can get out of there?" Ellie added, "Like anybody would do that, even though it is really stressful." "And tiring," Terri chimed in. While Terri and Ellie know that the lawyers are making points for the purpose of an adversarial challenge, they dislike being on the receiving end of questions that do not make sense. And even if an analyst knew that the prosecutor had a reason for letting the defense attorney berate her, the experience would not have been any less "stressful" or "tiring."

Firearms examiners were also surprised by what attorneys asked, as I saw when I went to court with Patrick, a firearms trainee. We watched Adam, a firearms examiner, become puzzled by a question from the DA. During cross-examination, Adam described for the defense attorney how he searched a database of gun manufacturers as part of his analysis. Adam produced a list of twenty-seven manufacturers, each of whom produced a .25 caliber bullet with the characteristics he found on the bullet that was discovered at the crime scene. Then, the defense attorney asked Adam to list these twenty-seven manufacturers, one by one—insinuating that each of these might have produced a firearm that could have fired the bullet in question. "It could be any one of those twenty-seven?" the defense attorney kept asking. A few minutes later, the DA got up to redirect and asked Adam, in an apparent attempt to illustrate how a list of twenty-seven manufacturer matches was actually narrow: "How many gun manufacturers are there?" Adam said, "What do you mean?" The attorney clarified, "In the database?" Adam replied, "I don't have that information specifically . . . but thousands."

On our walk back to the laboratory, Adam said to Patrick and me, "See, they can ask any random question when you are on the stand. 'How many gun manufacturers are there?!?' You have to be prepared for anything. You never know what they will ask." When analysts described "not knowing" what they would be asked, it was with a sense that the questions were coming from a different world.

———

This world's members do not just have a different attitude to knowledge. When testifying, forensic scientists also must contend with attorneys' *lack* of knowledge: specifically, their ignorance of scientific techniques and practices. Many prosecutors and defense attorneys do not have a deep understanding of the science and math underlying forensic science. Sometimes, criminalists scoff at them as merely "English majors!" Because of their lack of knowledge, attorneys do not ask appropriate questions about the evidence, nor do they understand the processes by which criminalists achieve their results. Chris, a DNA analyst, commented that sometimes when he met with attorneys, their knowledge lagged far behind the lab's current techniques. "I'd say, 'Okay, look, that question's silly. I don't even know about this technology, because it's so old that I wasn't born yet. I read about it one time in a book.'"

While testifying, forensic scientists find it difficult to answer uninformed questions accurately. This is a particularly common complaint in the DNA unit; here, analysts learn they have to ask for a restatement of the attorney's question. Maureen, an experienced DNA analyst, told me about the first testimony she gave in MCCL's jurisdiction, about a screening she had performed. Afterward, she remained in the courtroom to watch her supervisor testify. "Brenna was testifying on the DNA [results]. And she was asked a question by the defense attorney which was just totally unintelligible. And she said, 'I'm sorry. I don't understand the question.' And he said, 'That's okay, neither do I,' and he just moved on."

When their results and techniques are incorrectly interpreted, analysts are at best flummoxed, if not frustrated. Meredith described a case in which she was called by the defense attorney and asked to testify about her conclusions in a gunshot residue (GSR) analysis:

> I testified on a negative result, which is silly because I can't make any conclusion on a negative result because the absence of physical evidence does not mean that someone was not involved. That was kind of strange.
>
> It was a vehicle that was involved in a drive-by. So I had to assume if the window was open and how fast was the car going. I mean, if you're shooting outside of a car, the car is moving, you're going to most likely lose all of your GSR because they're all going to fly away depending on how long you have your hand out. There are all these variables.

For Meredith, it is an important scientific fact that GSR particles are not sticky and easily blow away, and, as a result, the absence of such particles on a suspect's hands do not provide valuable information about whether or not the suspect has fired a gun. But, in this case, the defense attorney wanted her to testify anyway—specifically, to testify about the negative result. Clearly, the attorney thought this was significant, and that the judge or jury would too. Meredith explained:

> I think the defense wanted me to lead them in the direction that because there was no GSR in this vehicle, that this vehicle was not used in the commission of the crime, which is not the case. It is a possibility, but I cannot say that it was this vehicle for sure or for sure not.

The defense attorney's assumptions did not make sense to Meredith scientifically. But she answered the questions as best as she could.

Attorneys can use their position of power to try and drive the conversation toward unsupported conclusions, a practice that criminalists resist. While Meredith seemed bemused, others are frustrated by testifying in these situations, as another criminalist described:

I went to see Al testify a few months ago. And they put up pictures of a crime scene. They kept trying to get him to make some determinations from these photos. . . . It was bullet holes in a truck or something and they were trying to get him to determine angle of entry. . . . Just stuff that you wouldn't commit to if you had an ounce of sense unless you had personally examined the vehicle.

That is, the attorney demanded that Al, while testifying on the stand, make snap expert judgments, in a manner that was far from the prescribed norms maintained within a forensic lab. The attorney "kept going at Al, and he kept saying, 'I'm not going to make determinations from photos,' and I think he finally got to the point where he was like, 'Dude, I have to examine this vehicle myself in order to testify to that!'" The standard practice of firearms examiners prohibits drawing conclusions about ballistics from images, and Al did not appreciate being repeatedly asked to do so.

Carolyn, a DNA supervisor who often spoke about wanting to help make science clear to attorneys, had similar experiences on the stand. The results of DNA profiling contain statistical representations and precise technical descriptions of biological evidence. Often, attorneys do not fully understand what these representations imply about the physical evidence itself. Carolyn described one experience where she had to correct the DA about the implications of her results so that neither of them misrepresented what the evidence showed:

I said in my report that I had detected two male specific profiles. . . . And she said, "So you detected two different types of semen in the rectum," and I said, "That's not the case. I don't know where the male DNA came from. It could have come from seminal fluid. It could have come from saliva. It could have come from possibly excessive touching or something like that."

What Carolyn said was that she found male DNA; what the attorney heard, or wanted to hear, was that Carolyn had found the DNA in semen. It's a big leap to make, and one that Carolyn would not accept.

Yet the attorney "kept trying to put those words into my mouth, and so I had to constantly get her back on track and say, 'Do you mean to say this,' or 'No, that wasn't what I detected, but I did detect this.'" Carolyn had to not just know her science, but how to convey the science in open court.

In many cases, such as the one Carolyn described, district attorneys in making their arguments unknowingly misrepresent the results presented by the forensic scientists. Forensic scientists strongly identify with scientific methods, the process of careful and meticulous analysis of data to disprove a hypothesis, so they take offense when they perceive others to be careless, or not thorough, in their interpretations and presentations. Even more problematic, in the view of forensic scientists, are the occasions where attorneys disregard their results. Matt, a narcotics analyst, was appalled by the pretrial activity in one case. He got a call from the DA, who was reviewing a particular report that Matt had produced. The report, according to Matt, "says right there, in big words, 'One item: No controlled substances detected.'" But the attorney seemed to want to press ahead, informing Matt that a police officer would contact him the next day. Matt replied, "But I didn't find any controlled substances in this case." According to Matt:

> The lawyer says, "Really?" I say, "No." He goes, "Well, I thought for sure that it said 'cocaine.'" I'm like "Noooo." So, he looks at the report. He goes, "Oh, yeah, it doesn't say 'cocaine.' All right, I'll call you back."
>
> So, then he hangs up and the next day I get a call from another DA [about] the same case. She says, "I'm looking at this report and it says no controlled substance detected. Are you sure?" I say, "Yeah. I'm sure."
>
> She goes, "Well, it was a high-speed chase, and this woman admitted that it was cocaine, and the cops had a presumptive positive on it." I say, "I can't say what anybody else said. I *can* say what the cops bagged [and submitted to the lab]. I didn't find any controlled substances in it."

For the attorneys to repeatedly question the science was bad, of course. But this wasn't what upset Matt the most: "They were going into a preliminary trial. This was a part of the evidence. The prosecution didn't read it. The cops didn't read it. The defense didn't read it. The judge didn't read it. Nobody read it."

Some forensic scientists complain that this disregard is not only unintentionally careless, but sometimes willful. In other words, while some attorneys do not take the time to read the reports carefully, others selectively choose or twist results to serve their particular argument. In Tim's shoeprint case, the criminalists involved were comfortable with their overlapping, but not identical, assessments of the suspect's shoe size, believing these fell within a reasonable range. However, the attorneys used each assessment for opposing arguments about the defendant. As Robin, a narcotics analyst, remarked, "So, you do the work accurately and hope that they don't take that and run with it in a direction or crazy theory that's really not what it means." For forensic scientists, attorneys' use of their work was often problematic and frustrating.

———

Testifying is made all the worse for forensic scientists because of their merely partial membership in the criminal justice community. Their own scientific community is quite different: criminalists are not sworn officers or lawyers; they have vastly different educational backgrounds and training. Their laboratory is in a separate building with restricted access and they interact infrequently with the members of the criminal justice world. When they do interact, their marginal status is reinforced (as illustrated in chapter 4) by attorneys making them wait, not returning their e-mails, or not meeting with them in advance of testifying. As a result, they feel sidelined and disrespected.

Taylor, an experienced toxicologist and narcotics analyst, described to me one memorable negative experience. He was on the stand in a methamphetamine case, testifying about the drugs he analyzed and their potential effects on the body. Taylor was concerned that he hadn't had much discussion with the prosecutor before trial. After being asked a few questions by the prosecutor, Taylor said, "I got raked over the coals" by the defense attorney during the cross-examination. He explained:

> I was on the stand for probably a good two hours on cross, just getting asked all these things that were way off topic. The judge was asleep, the defense was just going at it, and the prosecutor had his head down and just looked, saw me just waffling there, just trying to squirm out of it, as we kept going down this road that this defense attorney was taking us on. We were just so off topic. . . . That was the defining moment when I realized that when I'm in a courtroom I'm my only advocate. There are no other advocates in there for the evidence except for me.

Here, Taylor not only felt like his expertise was being misunderstood or misused. He felt as though the prosecutor had abandoned him in court. Taylor fell back on his beliefs as a scientist and his devotion to evidence: "Everybody in there has their own agenda and I'm the only one that has an agenda for the evidence, that just tries to clarify what the evidence means, what it doesn't mean, and what the limitations of it are."

But for Taylor, the indignity didn't stop there. His suspicions were correct: the prosecutor, in a sense, had left him to the mercy of the defense attorney.

> I found out later that about an hour before I went on the stand, the prosecutor had two of the defendants roll on the mastermind. So, during my entire testimony, while I was getting raked over the coals, [the prosecutor] was writing up the plea agreement while I sat there and waffled and just got absolutely dissed. I thought I got embarrassed.

The prosecutor, according to Taylor, was not paying attention while his expertise was being questioned. Along the way, Taylor was put into a position that many criminalists dread:

> We were going down an avenue of my expertise that was limited and when you start to get to the edge of your limited expertise it becomes really difficult to define what you do know, what you don't know. But

they love to try to take you to the edge right away and then they'll try to get you to step over.

I was talking about fatigue, I was talking about the use of methamphetamine for appetite suppression and for weight loss and for ADHD and it just went on and on and on. I know some about it, I don't know the totality of it, so it was limited but the defense kept pushing as to, "Well, do you know this? How about this?"

While the prosecutor was busy elsewhere, the defense attorney was undermining the credibility of the forensic scientist, by trying to catch him stating something inaccurate. Taylor felt that it could, and should, have gone differently:

I think if, on pretrial, we had gone through that, the prosecutor would have known better. And the prosecutor should have stopped it; the judge should have stopped it! It was way off topic, it wasn't anything to do with the direct, [and] procedurally they can't ask me anything that wasn't asked on direct, but they went ahead and asked me anyway. So, the judge was asleep at the wheel, the prosecutor was asleep at the wheel and the defense had total control in that period of time.

Taylor's story illustrates many of the complaints that forensic scientists have about attorneys' behavior: they do not consult analysts ahead of time, they aggressively question, and they leave criminalists feeling defenseless. As one DNA analyst put it, "When you are on the stand, nobody is your friend." Feeling alone on the stand is certainly difficult. But, for criminalists, there were still worse things to fear from the way attorneys treated them while testifying. By undermining, or failing to support, forensic scientists on the stand, attorneys might do harm to careers, or even to an entire lab.

The attack on Tim's shoeprint testimony could possibly have professional consequences for him. These implications were obvious to the members of MCCL, but seemingly ignored by the DA who questioned him. Willow, a member of Tim's chemistry unit, was in the gallery at the time of Tim's testimony. She left the courtroom furious. After Tim testified for the defense, she said, "the DA totally raked him over the coals.

He was such a fucking asshole to him. Talk about stabbing yourself in the back for the future."

By discrediting Tim's testimony about the size of the shoeprint, the DA not only questioned the validity of the evidence; he also cast doubt on Tim's professional expertise. Because analyst testimony is legally discoverable in future cases, Willow thought this could cause potential problems in the future—for Tim's reputation, for his ability to successfully testify, and for the very same DA calling on him for another case. "Now if he wants Tim to testify for anything, [the defense] can say, 'Well, isn't it true that you called him all of these things and said he was incompetent in all this stuff? But now that you like his answer, you're going to say he's an expert?'" Such thoughts seemed not to have crossed the attorney's mind, even though they might not only threaten the career of a colleague, but possibly his own future cases.

Sometimes, attorneys not only discredit individual forensic scientists and their conclusions, but go so far as to discredit the techniques of the crime laboratory itself. In a case in Suburban County, an independent forensic DNA defense expert had asked Willow for help with using likelihood ratios in statistical analyses of partial DNA profiles on behalf of a defendant. Likelihood ratios were the standard in the forensic biology community for interpreting partial profiles. The defense expert informally asked Willow's opinion of her planned analysis of the case. She also told Willow that the DA in Suburban County had responded with his intention to block the use of this technique, saying, "We are going to have an admissibility hearing to prove that likelihood ratios aren't good science and they shouldn't be admitted."

DNA analysts at MCCL regularly use likelihood ratios, and Willow thought Suburban County's crime laboratory had also started using them as well, so she was troubled to hear about the DA's response.

I've watched DAs do [this] to analysts at Metropolitan County also. They get so focused on an individual case that they're willing to do anything to win that one case, and they don't realize the implications. That's now going to screw up every case in the future. And I think this DA is thinking, "Ugh, stupid defense. Let's just shut the defense down by saying, you know, these are wrong," without realizing that [their own lab is] doing likelihood ratios. So, then the defense will be able to say [in future cases], "Well, wasn't there this case where you challenged the admissibility of these, and said that these numbers weren't accurate? So, why should we believe your numbers now? Because you're doing the same thing." I find DAs don't care. They don't look ahead. They're so worried about their own case right here, right now, that they don't look at the implications.

As this example illustrates, criminalists perceive that, sometimes, legal advocacy in the pursuit of winning a case undermines the work of forensic science. Attorneys may see discrediting evidence only narrowly, in the context of a particular case, but, for forensic scientists, such attorney actions diminish the credibility of individuals' expertise, as well as weaken the laboratory's ability to convincingly present science in future court cases.

The specter of testimony, then, comes from the hardly unwarranted fears of criminalists, who employ the scientific ethos of the laboratory, but whose results are evaluated *outside* of the laboratory: that is, within the criminal justice system. While wanting to be true to their scientific results, forensic scientists are well aware that they are simultaneously expected to anticipate the needs of criminal justice.

BECOMING THE VOICE
OF THE EVIDENCE

Forensic scientists anticipate that they will be challenged in the courtroom and are anxious about what will happen on the stand, particularly given the high stakes of their testimony. Therefore, in response to the friction between the social worlds of science, law, and the public arena, these criminalists approach and manage the attacks on their expertise by becoming the "voice of the evidence."

First, criminalists take ownership of their results in the laboratory through interactions with their colleagues, which gives them the confidence to assert their expertise. Then, in the courtroom, they balance the need to appear as credible with the need to simplify the science for their audience. Becoming the voice of the evidence helps analysts prepare for and respond to the struggle over knowledge and expertise, a contest inherent in their position at the boundary of science and law.

———

Criminalists create confidence, for themselves and others, through community. In the process of analyzing evidence in the lab, analysts participate in a communal practice of applied science. No criminalist works alone: informally, they get support, advice, help, and confirmation from their colleagues, all before they sign off on a case report, while formally, they check one another's work—a standard part of the lab's technical review process.

Criminalists, as shown in chapter 2, look for affirmation from their scientific community, both within and outside of the lab. In the forensic biology unit, technical reviewing is a painstaking process: examining the electropherograms and instrument documentation to confirm the original analyst's calls of every allele. As DNA analyst Terri said, "You are ultimately accountable for your calls, but you can ask people for help, what they think the interpretation should be." All units at MCCL have similar formal processes, and criminalists frequently ask one another for advice. While working in the chemistry unit, analysts often chatted across their benches about their cases. One afternoon, Meredith complained to Robin about the results of an SEM test for a GSR case. "I've never found anything so low," she said. "The suspect said he washed his hands beforehand." Robin suggested that the police may have fingerprinted him, and Meredith repeated, "It is strange, I've never seen such an absence of particles." Robin, reassuring Meredith, pointed out, "If you aren't comfortable with the results, you can always rerun it."

As they talk at their benches and review one another's work, criminalists also discover the various ways that their colleagues might interpret something. As Chris, a DNA analyst, told me about reviewing the casework of other criminalists: "I have noticed that some people reach in their conclusions, and others are a lot more conservative." This awareness reinforced the role of individual confidence, both in science and on the stand. As Chris continued: "I don't push people if they say they really aren't comfortable saying something. Because they have to go to court and say it, so it is up to them." I asked him, "Where are you on this dimension [of conservativeness]?" and he said, "Somewhere in the middle. It depends on the case. . . . Then when the supervisor reviews [the case] she might say, 'I don't know. Are you sure?' and as long as I can explain my reasoning on the stand, I'm okay."

By talking together about their own cases, and reviewing others' work, criminalists develop an understanding of what interpretations are acceptable in their community.[9] These discussions give forensic scientists confidence, when they are making assertions in reports and on the stand, that they have the force of the community's expertise behind them. Developing this assurance is particularly important because once they sign the report or step up to testify in court, analysts are on their own. Their community may be figuratively behind them, but criminalists are held individually accountable for their conclusions.

———

Remaining internally assured about one's expertise is important. But being able to project this expertise outward is just as critical. When criminalists take the stand, they know that they will have to offer compelling evidence of their own expertise and credibility. At the same time, they know that they must simplify the science in order to communicate clearly to the attorneys, judge, and jury.

Usually, the first few questions they answer on the stand give criminalists an opportunity to provide evidence of their own expertise: they explain their educational credentials and describe their work. As Carly, a DNA analyst, told me, "As far as the direct examination, it is pretty standard: 'What is your name? Where do you work? How long have you worked there? What is your education, training, background? What did you do in this case?'" But criminalists also anticipate that attorneys might try to undermine their expertise and credibility, particularly during cross-examination. As Allison explained, "I've been to different [training] classes and one of the teachers actually contracts out as a defense expert. And she said, 'I will look for things you haven't written down that could possibly change your results or be a way for me to discredit certain things about your results or your interpretations.'" Criminalists experience a multitude of challenges to their expertise and their work, including claims of contamination, flawed procedures, poor documentation, and incomplete knowledge of the literature.

As Taylor commented in his description of his toxicology testimony, attorneys will push criminalists to the limits of their expertise, "and try to get you to step over." Jonah, an experienced DNA analyst, was also pushed by an attorney in one case, who asked, "Did you contaminate something?" After Jonah explained the procedures that they took in the forensic biology lab to try to avoid contamination, the attorney pressed further, asking, "Does contamination occur in your lab?"

"This is a curveball," Jonah told me, "because contamination can occur, and does occur, I would say, in pretty much every laboratory. It's part of the nature of the beast. I mean we're working with such sensitive technology. That's why we have a lot of the measures we do in place to catch that."

In addition, with respect to complicated techniques, attorneys often raise questions about following procedures. As Eden, a DNA supervisor, described a case: "That testimony was challenging in that it was very long. I was on the stand for two to three days. And the prosecutor had about an hour's worth of questions to demonstrate that the procedures we use are generally accepted: we followed our procedures, the results were reliable." But even so:

> The defense attorney went through the minutia of what we do from beginning to end, and tried to find any way to muddy the waters and make it seem like what we do isn't credible, or somehow it's flawed. And it was humorous to me, because his questions were so off the rocker. But the judge, who doesn't know anything about DNA, was very confused. And so you have to be articulate enough and knowledgeable enough in order to answer every little question."

Eden listed about ten different types of questions that the defense attorney asked about the steps taken in the capillary electrophoresis. She continued, "It's just very tiring. If you know your stuff, you'll be fine, but getting through the day is just exhausting."

Attorneys also undermined criminalists' credibility by questioning their knowledge of the relevant scientific literature. As Jason, a toxicologist, explained,

> You get questions on the stand. "Are you familiar with this article, with this person's research?" If you are going to sound like an expert, you better know the literature. I've heard stories of defense attorneys holding up articles and asking, "Have you read this article?" And then when the criminalist asks to see it, it turns out to be an article on something else entirely. It is just a prop!

Billie, a seasoned chemist, described her experience of a similar tactic on the stand:

> The defense attorney said, "Have you read this article?" And I'm like, "As a matter of fact I just read it last night." He said, "Well, are you aware that it says 'blah, blah, blah'?" And it *didn't* say "blah, blah, blah." That was the opposite of what the point of the article was. He was claiming there was a quote in this article that said this. So I said, "You know I don't remember it saying that anywhere." And that was all and he let it go.

Billie called the defense attorney's bluff, but sometimes criminalists are not so lucky. As Jason described:

> The defense's favorite thing is to mention a specific article, ask if you've read it, and when you've read it. By the time you are a forensic alcohol specialist, you've read hundreds of articles. So you aren't going to remember when you've read it. And if they get you to admit that you can't remember, they think they've got you.

With questions about their techniques, practices, and knowledge of the literature, attorneys attempt to make analysts seem inexpert and unprofessional. One DNA analyst, Maureen, spoke about how her typical testifying experiences contrasted with the time she was asked informed questions about her expertise. She said:

> The last time I testified, there was a defense expert sitting next to the defense attorney, and she had contested some of the interpretation of my results. I think of it probably as the best time [I've testified], because it was the time I was challenged by somebody who knew what I was doing. It's so nice, because then you can actually be asked questions and you can actually think about it and give a coherent answer and defend your position. I think that was maybe the most exhilarating testimony for me—having somebody there who understood what I was doing, and who had legitimate concerns.

Maureen was proud of her ability to engage with an expert who understood the science, and she contrasted the "legitimate concerns" of this expert with the usual questions of attorneys. Criminalists generally expect uninformed questions yet are ready to display their expertise.

Another tactic forensic scientists use to assert expertise on the stand is to bound their knowledge: presenting themselves as experts only in a narrow range of forensic science. Analysts must be formally trained and qualified as proficient in particular analytical procedures to speak as an expert in them. Therefore, when they are asked on the stand to give an opinion about a piece of evidence for which they have not been formally qualified, analysts engage in what I call "expertise hedging."

For example, in the DNA unit, because they do not perform a conclusive test to determine that the blood in a sample is human, in describing the sample (whether in print or on the stand) they will not use the term "blood." When I observed his testimony for a homicide case, Chris described the evidence he had found on the glasses of a homicide victim, and the DA asked him if he noticed anything unusual on them. He responded, "There were red-brown stains on both lenses and on the frame itself." The DA asked, "Did you do a presumptive test for blood?" Chris answered, "The presumptive tests reacted with the red-brown stains." Here, Chris affirmed that he did a presumptive test after he mentioned the red-brown stain. He would not, however, say that the stains were definitively blood.

In another DNA profiling case described to me, Ellie said in her testimony that she took a sample from the root of a "possible hair," and the defense attorney asked, "You don't know what a hair is?" Ellie said, "When I said I was not a hair expert, the jury was looking at me like, 'Are you serious, you can't say it is a hair?'" This hedging was occasionally comical, as Eden described in a different case involving hairs:

> There was a hair I found on the victim's shirt, and it was almost twelve inches long and so I called it a head hair. And [the defense attorney] said, "Well, is it true you're not a hair expert?" and I said, "That's true, I'm not." The attorney said, "How do you know it wasn't a pubic hair?" And I answered, "In my own experience," and I'm thinking to myself, "In my own laboratory experience," but I said, "In my own experience, I've never seen a pubic hair that long." And I had everybody cracking up. I didn't mean it to come across that way, but it did. And even the defendant was laughing.

It may have been funny, but it was a defense against exposing herself to more pointed attacks.

Willow, a comparative evidence analyst, described one of her testimony experiences as "almost like the game Taboo, where you aren't allowed to say specific words." She had pieced together some fragments of cloth that had been used to bind a victim in a hotel room where two of the pillows were missing pillowcases. Some pieces appeared to have been cut with a scissors or knife while others were more frayed as if they had been torn. During Willow's testimony, in her words,

> The defense objected, saying, "She is not an expert in tearing versus cutting cloth." They asked, "Do you have any sort of expertise in cloth?" And I said, "Well, I've been sewing my own clothes since I was seven, but I have no formal training in rips versus tears, or versus cuts." So, they said, "Then you are not allowed to use the word 'tear' or 'cut' or 'rip' through any of this."
>
> Then I had to try to explain clearly to a jury without using those words. I said things like, "This sharp and jagged edge matched up to this one . . . and this frayed edge, matched up to this other frayed

edge." And it was very difficult to be clear without using the very obvious words, you know. And any person looking at this can tell this difference between what's cut and what's ripped, you didn't really need expertise for that.

While criminalists feel these hedges sometimes seem silly, using them to clarify and delineate their expertise helps defend them from attorneys' attempts to undermine their credibility.

Criminalists also feel their credibility depends on displaying neutrality in their testimony. This concern extends beyond their commitment to scientific neutrality: they worry specifically about being charged with bias by the defense attorneys. Many analysts encounter the question "Who do you work for?" during cross-examination. As Meredith, a criminalist in the chemistry unit, told me:

> At the end of my most recent testimony, after I went through all the different variables [that affected whether gunshot residue was found on a defendant's hands], there was the jab. "Who do you work for? Do you work for the DA?" Because we are a DA-funded crime lab. I have already been asked this twice in court [and she had only testified twice since coming to MCCL]. I guess they are trying to put some doubt into the jury's mind about who we work for . . .
>
> We are unbiased, but we [also] have to make that appearance. I think it does look kind of fishy because people know how money dictates things, but that's where your personal integrity and ethics, and the standards we are held to by our accreditation board comes into play.

Meredith's concern is shared by other MCCL criminalists, who believe they are perceived as biased. Andy simultaneously acknowledged this concern while asserting his belief in the neutrality of criminalists' work: "One nice thing [about DNA profiling] is that it doesn't matter what I find. We don't have a dog in the fight. Yes, we are officially part of the district attorney's office but it doesn't matter to me if I don't find the suspect's DNA." Several criminalists acknowledged that the laboratory's tie to the district attorney's office, which controls the laboratory budget, makes it challenging to appear neutral.

Perceptions of bias in crime laboratories because of their link to the criminal justice system was a particularly acute problem at the time of my study, since the National Academy of Sciences report on the status of forensic science had been recently published. One of its main recommendations was that crime laboratories in the United States should be independent of law enforcement agencies.[10] Criminalists respond to this concern by distancing themselves from their affiliation with the criminal justice system. Although they answer "yes" when asked if they work for the DA's office, criminalists specify their personal and professional distance by fully describing the organizational hierarchy. Meredith continued:

> I say I don't work for the district attorney, I work for my supervisor, Tim, who works for the lab director and then the lab director works for the DA. We try to make it seem like Neal is our top dog and he is not a part of the DA's office. He's our laboratory director and I don't think any chain of command would go all the way up to the DA . . . [the lab] is so far down.

Meredith's framing of the distance, in contrast to public perception, is rooted in the reality of her daily experience of the organization: she perceives a lack of direct connection to the DA's office, because she almost never speaks to anyone from that office.

By displaying their credentials, bounding their expertise, and asserting neutrality, criminalists bolster their scientific credibility on the stand and defend their expertise from being undermined by attorneys. But communicating expertise isn't enough. At the same time, criminalists are cautious not to overwhelm their audiences with science. Multiple criminalists mentioned to me that "the juries in Metropolitan County have an average of an eighth-grade education," and "we are lucky that they are more educated here than in many places." Attending to the average jury's level of education, criminalists simplify their testimony by trying to use as little jargon as possible, employing visual aids and analogies to help the audience understand the science and keeping their answers short.

Using scientific jargon on the stand is a problem for criminalists for several reasons, as summarized by Maureen, a veteran DNA analyst:

> I try not to use jargon. First, because you have to spell it. I think I learned the first time I testified that anytime I used an unfamiliar term, I'd have to spell it out loud. And so the third time I testified, I was asked when I got on the stand, "What does DNA stand for?" I wanted to throttle the attorney, because that meant I had to spell deoxyribonucleic acid on the stand.

Jargon can be off-putting, Maureen noted: even for "very bright" attorneys who "have always felt that they know what's going on." Suddenly, when confronted with science, they realize "it's a separate world. And I try to always remember they have no idea what I'm talking about, because they don't do this day in and day out." Willow agreed, describing how a colleague asked her advice about how to represent her work on the stand. "She asked, 'Do you say 'infrared spectrograph' or 'spectrogram'?' and I told her, 'I say 'the graph from the computer.' That's what they'll understand.'"

Taylor developed an informal persona on the stand that he felt helped him be more direct. As he described,

> I can sense watching other criminalists that they are very scared to elaborate or qualify. Many are scared to talk in normal speech, talk like a normal person. I mean, they get up there and they are so nervous and they use a lot of technical terms and they are not really clear. They use very formal language when they speak because the attorneys are using very formal language, right? But when you are trying to get across to a jury, one of the things I learned a long time ago was to relax on the stand, get comfortable on the stand and talk like a normal human being on the stand.

Keeping jargon to a minimum is something criminalists are trained to do, as described in chapter 4, so they anticipate simplifying their language on the stand.

Criminalists often deploy analogies to help illustrate a scientific process in a simpler way. One analogy that DNA analysts frequently use is "Xerox copying" to represent the polymerase chain reaction that multiplies the copies of DNA fragments in a sample. Criminalists were accustomed to making these comparisons for laypeople and even explained their work to me this way when they sensed confusion on my part. For example, when Jason was teaching me about the standard curve used in toxicological analyses, he offered an analogy for how the gas chromatograph measures peak heights. He said,

> This is just a more practical way of thinking about it. I like to think about stupid analogies for a jury. So, imagine a sidewalk on a cloudy day. When the sidewalk is light, there are no clouds, and when it is dark, there are thick clouds. When the sidewalk is in-between [light and dark], without looking up, you know there is a medium cloud up there.

This analogy did not actually help me very much in understanding the standard curve, which represents another aspect of the difficult balance that analysts need to navigate while testifying. As Chris, a DNA analyst, said,

> Some people totally get it right away, and some people, you see that it's not working. I've found that analogies are helpful, but sometimes, I just really hate coming up with an analogy, because it's like, "Is this going to work for them? Do they understand this one? Do you know what a Xerox machine is?" Everybody kind of knows what a copy machine is, but sometimes you give the analogy, and it doesn't work.
>
> And then on the converse side, too, you don't want to give them an analogy that's, you know, so layman that they're like, "Really, please!" You get the guy who goes like this [rolling his eyes], "Oh, geez." So you've got to find that happy medium of where you're not insulting the jury, but you're not going so far over their head that they're going, "Dude, I am lost. I am going to take a nap now."

The "happy medium" that Chris refers to is the balance that criminalists anticipate will help them appear to be credible, yet not too abstruse, experts.

Criminalists also stress that they try to answer only the questions they are directly asked, because this is what the legal system expects of them. Robin, a narcotics analyst, described the training she received in a laboratory on the East Coast: "We were essentially told to answer the question, don't elaborate. Just, basically, don't go off on a tangent. If it's a yes or no question just answer yes or no. You don't need to expand unless they ask you." She found this funny in a particular case when the DA asked her, "So cocaine is a narcotic?" and she said, "Legally, yes," and stopped there, because she does not expand unless asked. "Of course," she told me, "cocaine is not an actual narcotic, it is a stimulant, the complete opposite of a narcotic. But when I said yes, that's all he cared about! It isn't correct from a technical standpoint, but it is correct under the law."

Criminalists are also trained to simplify information through visual aids. In the comparative evidence unit, criminalists compare evidence from a crime scene with reference samples of fingerprints or toolmarks. When they find correspondences in the evidence, they take careful digital images and enlarge the images for use on the stand. As Paul, a fingerprint examiner, told me about his preparation for prior testimony, "I made chart enlargements of fingerprint matches, so I would have the unknown print and the identified print in court and I would explain the charts. Those actually made my testimony easier because I had a visual aid to help express what I was talking about versus an abstract idea."

Similarly, Doug, a document examiner, described the advantages of visual aids in his testimony, as he showed me some he had used in the past:

The nice thing about [testifying for] documents is that you can prepare something similar to this little chart. So what I did, I broke down the questioned writing, some of the letters and words that this person had written. And then they actually sat her down and had her write the same text so I was able to compare some similar letters and features, which is nice, because you just go through it with the jury and it ends up being a little demonstration to them as to why you came up with your conclusion.

Analysts in the DNA unit also capture high-resolution images of evidence as they process it. As described in chapter 1, when Ellie screened a dress for possible biological stains, she hooked up a camera to her laptop to download the images. She told me, "I want big pictures for court. You need to talk about them so it is helpful to see them. This is an important part of the job, because what is the point of doing all these tests on the evidence if you can't convince the jury?" Because Ellie did not find biological materials on the dress, she never used these images in court. However, she anticipated needing them in order to provide evidence that would be compelling to the jury.

ANTICIPATING AND TESTIFYING

Testifying, therefore, is an exemplar case of how the culture of anticipation in the laboratory colors the work of criminalists. It is an intense example of the endpoint of anticipating and navigating multiple social worlds. Testifying is the most salient time at which the worlds of science and criminal justice overlap: the courtroom is where the criminalists and their evidence directly encounter representatives of both the law and the public.

While the need to balance scientific and legal concerns in testifying is shared by the entire field of forensic science, the members of each discipline have different experiences in the courtroom. Of the tiny number of criminalists' courtroom appearances of MCCL (less than one hundred per year), two-thirds were for toxicology and narcotics cases. And criminalists reported that the only discipline in which testifying was common was toxicology. DNA analysts might go to court once a year; similarly, firearms examiners rarely testify in court. Al and Adam, examiners with decades of experience in the field, had spent more time in the courtroom. But Tom had been handling firearms cases at MCCL for almost four years before he first testified, near the end of my fieldwork.

In contrast, toxicologists are called to testify in DUI cases frequently. Because there were only a few toxicologists at MCCL who were qualified to testify on the effects of drugs in the body, as one DNA analyst said, comparing their court experiences, these toxicologists "go all the time. Sometimes they have more than one court appearance in a day!" Toxicologists are called to court often because "DUI is big business. For some attorneys it is a lot of what they do." As a consequence, it is very demanding to testify in toxicology, as many of the toxicologists (and other criminalists) reported to me, because the defense attorneys are well trained and well paid. Defense attorneys, due to their deep knowledge of the ways of challenging a DUI charge, know more about the science involved in toxicological analysis.

This was evident in the proceedings of an adjudicated DUI case I attended at a high school with Joanna, who was one of the toxicologists who frequently testified to the effects of drugs and alcohol. On cross-examination, the defense attorney asked her a series of questions about alcohol burn off and rising blood alcohol level. Then she asked Joanna to do calculations for the defendant's specific body weight and gender and analyze how these affected her symptoms of impairment. Afterward, I asked Joanna how testifying in this case differed from proceedings in the courtroom, and she said, "Today, they are going relatively easy on me." According to analysts at MCCL, this level of knowledge about scientific technique and intensity of questioning is not characteristic of defense attorneys in other areas, such as homicide. Because the defense attorneys have extensive experience in DUI cases, toxicologists are accustomed to regularly facing scientifically well-informed questions and challenges on the stand.

In contrast, the scientific practices of narcotics analysis do not receive close scrutiny in the courtroom. Narcotics analysts are not called to the stand very often, partially due to a law in the state that allows police officers to testify to their results if the attorneys agree. When they do testify in controlled substance cases, their expertise is not challenged by attorneys. One analyst told me:

> The thing about controlled substances is, nobody, none of the lawyers, care how we got our conclusion. The defense doesn't care and the prosecution doesn't care. Maybe the judge cares, but he doesn't get to ask. They just don't care at all, because the question of

whether it is the drug or it isn't, that's never the part of controversy. I think I'm at about 3,200 analyses so far, I've testified six or seven times and I've never been challenged as to the science. Ever.

As he went on to say, the scientific makeup of the drug is "not the question, the question is whether or not it is a usable dose . . . enough to get high."

While they have different experiences in the courtroom, criminalists are all aware of the tensions that testimony presents for their work. They are conscious of their allegiance to the neutrality and objectivity of science and at the same time anticipate the requirements of these other worlds. Criminalists act to protect what is at stake for them as scientists, asserting their expertise and neutrality, and they balance this with a need to simplify by avoiding jargon, speaking simply, and using visual aids to enable attorneys, judges, and juries to follow their arguments. By doing so, criminalists hope to make a compelling presentation of their truth and successfully speak for the evidence.

As these examples of testifying suggest, for criminalists the reality of being in a captive occupation really hits home during these moments. Despite all of their preparation and anticipation, when giving testimony, criminalists do not have control of their own expertise. The attorneys are in a position of power: they lead the questioning, and they can manipulate the findings. While criminalists are not quite the puppets they perceive themselves to be, their voices are directed by the attorneys, who are outsiders to science. All forensic scientists feel a similar need to be the voice of the evidence, and they are prepared to do so by the culture of anticipation in the lab. What it takes to serve as this voice, however, has changed over time, as science and technology in forensic science has evolved. The rise of DNA profiling has altered the perceptions of forensic evidence in the legal and public realms; in turn, this shift has changed what it means to offer scientific support for evidence. I turn to the implications of these changes for the different areas of forensic science in the next chapter.

Chapter 6

DNA ENVY

Responding to Shifting Scientific and Legal Standards

Forensic scientists, like many expert workers, experience shifts in the technology used in their work—changes that have effects on their expertise. In the last thirty years, technical and scientific advances have significantly altered the methods and distribution of the work within crime laboratories. Most dramatically, advances in biology (such as polymerase chain reaction techniques) have made it possible to analyze and interpret DNA evidence. In so doing, DNA profiling has become an established investigative tool. After surviving court challenges—and being held up as rigorous and scientifically valid by National Academy of Sciences reports in 1992 and 1996[1]—the DNA methods used in forensic biology have become the gold standard of forensic science practice.[2]

The supposed scientific unassailability of DNA evidence is not only pervasive in the public realm, but, surprisingly, also in the worlds of law and criminal justice.[3] These changes complicate the anticipatory culture of forensic scientists. Not only must different disciplines anticipate the questions of the legal and public worlds; they must also address the constant demand to "be more like DNA."

Since the ascent of DNA profiling, onlookers have questioned whether the other, traditional forensic sciences are as valid scientifically. In 2005, Congress authorized an independent committee, formed by the National Academy of Sciences, to conduct a study of the forensic sciences. The broad charge to this committee of scientific, legal, and forensic experts was to assess the state of forensic science: identify the community's needs, recommend ideas for maximizing its uses, improve and enlarge its staffing, promote best practices and guidelines, and surface any additional issues.[4] At the time, legal commentators advised that "traditional forensic sciences need look no further than their newest sister discipline, DNA typing, for guidance on how to put the science into forensic identification science."[5]

The National Academy of Sciences released its report in 2009, at the start of my fieldwork at MCCL, delineating the problems the committee found with forensic science and laying out recommendations for solving them. Notably, the NAS report warned of the "limited foundation in scientific theory or analysis" for much of forensic science, with the exception of DNA analysis.[6] The report garnered significant media attention, including front page coverage in the *New York Times* and a full session on Science Friday on NPR. Since the report's release, a number of news outlets have called out forensic science as "junk science."[7]

In the wake of increasing scientific and public opinion that DNA profiling is the only valid forensic science, members of other forensic science disciplines feel pressure to change their analyzing, reporting, and testifying practices so as to emulate DNA profiling. The NAS report drew close attention among forensic scientists; some professional associations in the field issued written responses, including the American Academy of Forensic Sciences (AAFS), the general professional association covering forensic sciences as a whole; and the American Society of Crime Lab Directors (ASCLD), the main association for laboratories. Both of these organizations professed support for the report's recommendations, including accrediting all laboratories, certifying all criminalists, and standardizing terminology. In addition, ASCLD suggested that laboratory directors and managers "prepare their staff" for questions in the courtroom related to the NAS report. Directors and managers were encouraged to "identify and take the steps necessary to prove the existence of valid, reliable science and interpretations behind the forensic analysis."[8] At MCCL, the laboratory director immediately e-mailed the initial executive summary to all criminalists, followed by an announcement at the next all-staff meeting that everyone should read the full report.

While all forensic scientists do their work in the public eye, each discipline has encountered the comparison to DNA profiling in different ways. Some disciplines, like firearms examination, have come under significant public and legal attack, while the scientific bases of others, such as narcotics analysis, are ignored by the media and the courts. The overarching process of analyzing evidence is similar across disciplines, but the underlying science, techniques, and work practices differ. As a consequence, some resist the pressure while others embrace the call to be more like DNA. In this chapter, I explore the reactions of specific disciplines of forensic science to the rise of DNA profiling and show how the different ways in which they inhabit the worlds of science, law, and the public sphere influence their responses.

DNA PROFILING AS THE GOLD STANDARD OF FORENSIC EVIDENCE

During the so-called "DNA Wars" of the early 1990s, DNA profiling survived a rigorous vetting in the courts, as well as scrutiny in the scientific and mainstream press. In these venues, the practices of forensic biology were challenged in terms of scientific technique, administrative care, and statistical accuracy.[9] The resolution of these controversies raised DNA profiling to the gold standard against which other forms of evidence are compared.[10]

While DNA evidence was being challenged and ultimately upheld as admissible in the court system, the discipline of forensic biology established practices for representing evidence in ways that appeared credible and legitimate. The graphs, tables, and statistical claims made by DNA analysts produce an impression of scientific objectivity that other forensic disciplines lack, to varying degrees. They anticipate the needs of the criminal justice community, as well as the public—but, in so doing, they also open the door for skeptics from both of these worlds to critique other forensic sciences.

Translating the natural world into such representations is, generally speaking, much of the work of science itself.[11] When creating documents and displays, scientists simplify the messy natural world, select particular aspects to represent, and turn these aspects into mathematical and graphical presentations.[12] Scientists use these to convince other scientists and interested publics of the validity of their results and the clout of science.[13] Such representations are particularly powerful in courtroom settings, where expert witnesses use visual authority to frame evidence and convince juries.[14]

In forensic science, DNA analysts invest time and effort into turning their analyses into visual representations that will be compelling in court. The techniques and methods used in the DNA unit are instrumental and standardized. Once analysts create a profile through capillary electrophoresis, they view and interpret the electropherograms and convert these into tables of alleles from each sample. Analysts also produce comparative statistics of the likelihood of the profile appearing at random in a demographically similar local population. In addition to these representations, the legal parties involved in a case can review the documentation (e.g., raw data and graphs) from the capillary electrophoresis instrument. These become visible and verifiable scientific evidence.

———

Although DNA profiling is held up as the gold standard, DNA analysis is complex, uncertain, and fallible,[15] as are all sciences.[16] The tables and graphs in the reports suggest a tidy and impersonal outcome, but the process of producing a standard DNA profile requires analysts to complete multiple rounds of interpretation. This subjective, though expert, judgment is vital to producing results, although invisible in the finished representations. And while forensic scientists recognize the messiness and personal judgment inherent in DNA profiling, others may not. Within the worlds of criminal justice and the public sphere, DNA is the infallible standard of forensic evidence that other forensic disciplines feel pressure to emulate. Therefore, it is the alleged objectivity of DNA profiling—in the eyes of outsiders—that influences the development and perceptions of expertise of all forensic scientists.

Consequently, a pervasive feeling of what I would call "DNA envy" has grown within the professional world of forensic science. Within

MCCL, criminalists covet the resources commanded by the "DNA princesses" of the forensic biology unit: they gripe that more equipment, funding, grants, and staff are available for DNA than other disciplines. In another laboratory I visited, a supervisor reported some competition between the firearms examination and forensic biology units. Here, a firearms examiner joked that the forensic biology unit was "like mold, growing and coming to take over their space." A trace examiner suggested, "There is a lot of funding for DNA, and I am not trying to belittle what they do. It is a godsend, and you can solve a lot with DNA, but when there isn't DNA evidence, you need these other methods. We are constantly trying to sell ourselves, even to lab directors."

This resentment also manifests within forensic science professional associations. A group of trace evidence examiners, who analyze evidence such as gunshot residue, fibers, glass, and hairs that might link a suspect to a crime scene, were trying to form a new national professional association after the release of the NAS report. This group, acting on their belief that DNA profiling received more than its fair share of attention and resources, issued a flyer to laboratories that opened, "Since the wide scale application of DNA has taken hold of the forensic sciences, trace evidence examinations have taken a back seat."

In addition to feelings of envy, the comparisons encourage members of other forensic sciences to feel that their analytic and reporting practices should be (or at least look) more like DNA profiling. But DNA profiling is not an abstract standard to which other disciplines are compared. Each attempt to compare other disciplines to DNA is made in a particular context and, consequently, takes on significance for different forensic sciences at different moments, within specific circumstances. Moreover, each discipline interprets how they compare to DNA by using their own understandings of what is possible and preferable for their own expert work.

Within MCCL, specifically, criminalists interpreted these comparisons within their own forensic science expertise: their epistemology, technique, and values.[17] These comparisons took shape by drawing on different aspects of the work of each group. Therefore, toxicologists, firearms examiners and narcotics analysts had distinct responses and were more or less willing to change their practices.

FIREARMS UNDER FIRE

Even prior to the publication of the NAS report, firearms examiners knew that others questioned the scientific bases of their work. In fact, examiners had already changed their practices in the past, so as to maintain credibility in the field. Firearms examiners at MCCL are aware that their identifications in the courtroom need to be highly visible and scientifically verifiable.

During their examinations, when methodically comparing microscopic images of multiple points on bullets (or cartridge casings) found at a crime scene to those from a particular weapon, they are therefore careful to make the evidence of their judgments visible to nonexperts. To do so, they insert digital images from the microscope throughout their report, and they enlarge these when testifying in court. This documentation is critical for making the similarities in their identifications evident. For verification purposes, they also review each other's work through the microscope as they perform examinations, and reviewers sign off on every page of their colleagues' notes.

A year before the release of the NAS report, a separate National Academies committee prefigured its findings. This 2008 report, which analyzed whether a "national ballistics database" was a good idea, concluded that "the fundamental assumptions of uniqueness and reproducibility of firearms-related toolmarks"—that is, the norms relied on by forensic scientists to compare guns—"[have] not yet been fully demonstrated."[18] Therefore, firearms examiners were not taken fully by surprise at the criticism of their scientific foundations.

When the NAS report was released in 2009, the public most pointedly criticized comparative evidence techniques, such as those used in firearms identification. This, of course, increased attention on how firearms examinations lack rigorous scientific methods. The first chapter of the report contains the section "Questionable or Questioned Science," which begins: "Many forensic tests—such as those used to infer the source of toolmarks or bite marks—have never been exposed to stringent scientific scrutiny. Most of these techniques were developed in crime laboratories to aid in the investigation of evidence from a particular crime scene, and researching their limitations and foundations was never a top priority." The report found that many of the techniques employed by forensic scientists were developed ad hoc, from unscientific foundations, and it explicitly labeled firearms examination as problematic. Rather than having been developed in research facilities and then exported to forensic laboratories, the report explains, crime labs innovated their techniques through trial and error. Not a bad system, necessarily, but less rigorously scientific than we might expect: "There is some logic behind the application of these techniques; practitioners worked hard to improve their methods, and results from other evidence have combined with these tests to give forensic scientists a degree of confidence in their probative value. . . . However, although the precise error rates of these forensic tests are still unknown, comparison of their results with DNA testing in the same cases has revealed that some of these analyses, as currently performed, produce erroneous results."[19] The report praised the practitioners of firearms examination for their efforts while sounding an ominous note about the accuracy of their analyses.

Comparing firearms examination to DNA profiling occurred throughout the social worlds of forensic science. The scientific criticism represented in the NAS report was picked up by the media, creating new public scrutiny on established techniques. The fallout from the report also yielded broad court challenges to the admissibility of firearms evidence. These criticisms created evaluative pressure on firearms examination. The press predominantly expressed concern that there was no scientific basis for a "match" of the evidence in some areas of forensic sciences, especially in the case of the pattern matching fields, such as firearms and fingerprint analysis.[20] A *New York Times* article headed "Plugging Holes in the Science of Forensics" noted: "The most damning conclusion [of the report] was that many forensic disciplines— including analysis of fingerprints, bite marks and the striations and indentations left by a pry bar or a gun's firing mechanism—were not grounded in the kind of rigorous, peer-reviewed research that is the hallmark of classic science."[21] The concerns raised in the media echoed those of court cases, in which defense attorneys increasingly sought to exclude firearms testimony from consideration. At a statewide criminalists' meeting, a firearms examiner (who was a board member of the scientific working group for firearms examiners) noted an increasing number of attorneys and academics who were attempting to bar the admission of firearms evidence during the pretrial phase of proceedings.[22] Thus, while new claims of the discipline's lack of scientific basis reverberated through the field of forensic science, another threat emerged: the credibility and legitimacy of the entire discipline of firearms examination was being scrutinized in courtrooms.[23]

These public and legal attacks worried the professional community of firearms examiners, which responded in both defensive and pragmatic ways. The Association of Firearm and Tool Mark Examiners (AFTE) issued a public response to the report, refuting select points of criticism and noting that the NAS committee "did not address the relevant scientific literature . . . or acknowledge existing or ongoing research" to achieve statistical foundations for toolmark identification.[24] At the same time, AFTE's letter endorsed some of the report's conclusions, promising future study of the recommendations by the association's research committee.[25]

Examiners presenting at professional meetings had similar responses. At a statewide criminalists meeting I attended, some firearms examiners critiqued the critics, citing their lack of training as firearms examiners.[26] One speaker presented photos of academic critics, listing their affiliations and singling out how they had participated in pretrial courtroom admissibility challenges (e.g., Professor Stern at Eastern State University "was the first one to come out against us"). Since the release of the NAS report, he said, it is more difficult to testify, "especially when it is you going up against a report with twenty PhDs on it." Another firearms examiner described feeling so nervous about an upcoming court appearance that he accidentally left his laptop in a hotel lobby. The report amplified the specter of testifying for these examiners, making it more unpleasant and provoking more anxiety.

Others used these external critiques to call for an examination of practice to better understand the potential bias of examiners. Noting that he had not been barred from testifying as an expert witness after the report's publication, one firearms examiner presented what he learned from his experience with defense attorneys questioning the legitimacy of firearms evidence in court. Before discussing how examiners might guard against bias in their identifications, he pointed out,

> It is easy for us to point fingers at these critics and say, "They don't know how to do firearms examination." But they are basing their critiques on our own testimony, and it is up to us to be more convincing. . . . Sometimes motivation for change comes from the outside. They are giving us a good kick in the pants to motivate us.

Professional representatives of firearms examination defended the field pragmatically in both public and private spheres.

Despite critics coming into courts and academics filing affidavits, firearms identification overwhelmingly remained admissible in court as evidence. Yet firearms examiners continued to be concerned. In rising tones of frustration, one examiner at the statewide meeting pronounced: "We can't be like DNA, no matter how much they want us to be, it is just impossible!" Moreover, members of other units at MCCL recognized the pressure being brought to bear on firearms. One narcotics analyst told me that for firearms examiners, the critics seemed to be accusing: "Why can't you be more like DNA?? We *like* DNA!"

Even though the scrutiny brought to bear from the outside was significant, the firearms examiners inside MCCL did not respond to these pressures by changing their practices. The MCCL firearms unit is a close-knit community of practitioners who place great value on their expertise and believe in the holistic craft of firearms identification. They use their subjective understandings of families of objects and specific markings to make judgments. Science studies scholars label this type of expertise, which entails significant interpretation on the part of a trained scientist, "judgmental objectivity."[27] This value was made clear by the firearms examiners at MCCL when they talked about a recently developed method of identification called CMS. This method, by requiring examiners to count "consecutively matching striae" at particular points on a cartridge casing, offers a system by which examiners can quantify the marks they observe in a consistent manner. The threshold number of how many marks, or striae, are significant is based on a statistical analysis of "best-known nonmatches" from guns from the same manufacturer.[28] CMS identification depends on a set of simple guidelines, such as "you need two groups of three consecutive striae within the firing pin impression," that serve as a threshold for an examiner to identify a match.

The MCCL firearm examiners recognize that the numbers provided by CMS appeal to laypeople outside the laboratory. As Tom said, "Some people like CMS, because numbers are easy to understand. They are universal. Everyone knows what you mean." And yet, at MCCL, none of the three qualified examiners use CMS regularly to identify a match. Although they are all trained in CMS and conversant with its rules, they do not believe these rules are as conservative as their own judgments. Members of the firearms unit speak of CMS somewhat derisively. In a conversation I had with two experienced examiners about the technique, Tom labeled CMS as "more of a tool that I might use when I'm on the fence, when my criteria is borderline. I'm actually more conservative than CMS. I don't go to it immediately." In an interview, he expanded on this point:

> I believe I usually find a lot more than the CMS number in my identifications. [CMS] numbers are actually lower, if you were to count. Their requirements are actually probably less than my requirements. And on a marginal case where you're close to making your ID, if you're not sure if you should be finding more, you could go back and maybe apply this counting method to what you already have found to see if you already passed what somebody else might have called an ID.

Adam agreed and described how examiners in other labs used CMS for testifying: "Some people physically write on their notes. They'll mark up a group of seven [striae], write next to it in a silver pen on the image, 'times seven.' They think this makes them more objective than me." For Adam, simply counting the number of marks, despite the number's convincing appearance on a firearms comparison report, didn't guarantee objectivity. Firearms examination, for Adam, "is a subjective discipline. It is the totality of the mark I am looking at. . . . There are a million factors that create the image, and it comes down to the subjective opinion of the examiner."

In the statewide meeting of forensic scientists I attended, the MCCL examiners challenged the firearms examiner who was presenting his ideas about bias and CMS. They called into question CMS's ability to "outperform" or improve on the subjective expertise of firearms examiners. They asked whether CMS might itself introduce bias and questioned whether CMS could solve an age-old dilemma: "What if two examiners have a different count in their comparison?" And the presenter generally agreed with their underlying assumption of the necessary subjectivity in firearms examination, remarking, "CMS is nothing more than a numeric description of what I observe, so it is subject to the same subjectivity." MCCL's firearms examiners value their pattern recognition abilities, subjective training, and experience, and they chafe at the notion that identification can be objectified through standardized guidelines.

The way that firearms examiners respond to being compared with DNA profiling goes beyond their valuing of holism and subjectivity and draws significantly from the techniques and epistemology of firearms examination itself. Firearms examiners' form of inquiry—comparative microscopy—is quite different from the instrumental graphs and statistical analysis used in forensic biology. The firearms examiners at MCCL did not believe the underlying science of DNA analysis was analogous to their own. I asked Tom and Patrick what it meant to be more like DNA. Patrick said, "One thing is statistics. They want us to be like DNA, but it is different though, because you can't look at every bullet." That is, DNA profiles don't simply compare the DNA of a defendant, for example, to that found at a crime scene. DNA analysis uses population statistics to generate a likelihood of a match; it includes a statistical calculation of profiles within a demographically similar sample of the local population to generate a measure of how rare or common the noncoding alleles in the DNA profile are in this population. The end result is that the individual comparison is bolstered by a wider context. To be more like DNA, according to Patrick, would require having knowledge about every bullet fired, so as to provide a similar population-level context for an individual bullet comparison. Such knowledge would be, of course, impossible to obtain or maintain. Moreover, to rely on a statistical or numerical calculation would depart significantly from MCCL's values of holistic and subjective assessments of identification.

Tom added, "They want it more objective, but we don't give our results in numbers. Firearms is not objective, not definitive like in narcotics." Patrick said, "We can't report a 70- percent match on a bullet, it is or it isn't," and Tom elaborated:

> Some people are trying to make it objective, like counting consecutive numbers of striae. But that doesn't really work. . . . Through training, you see so many images, you get an understanding of the best known nonmatch. From reading and experience, you build your own internal threshold. But there's a big stigma because we can't put numbers on it. For outsiders, they think, "How do you know that? You aren't telling me it's 70 percent!!"

Here Tom notes that through the course of training and on-the-job experience, a firearms examiner ends up having many, many images in their head, which allows them to create a better comparison than a simple count. And he feels that one's "internal threshold" for how many and what kind of marks are significant is more accurate than a standardized tool like CMS. But without that outward facing ability to report a simple statistic, such as a "70-percent" match, the subjective expertise sounds insufficient.

The expertise of firearms examiners at MCCL was therefore threatened by comparisons to DNA profiling and discounted by the exhortation to be "more like DNA." The vulnerability of the position of firearms, in comparison with DNA profiling, was pointedly conveyed to me at one moment during my fieldwork in the firearms unit. The laboratory director, citing case backlogs, decided to transfer criminalists across units and swapped a firearms examiner with a narcotics analyst. The firearms examiners, who had a significant case backlog, felt this would be detrimental to their work, since the new criminalist would be unable to work on cases until she had completed two years of training. In contrast, at the time the DNA unit had ample resources and analysts to clear their entire case backlog. The firearms examiners appealed to the union to prevent this transfer but their efforts to keep their group intact failed. In their anger, they asked me to leave their unit and stop observing their work, suggesting that I go "study the supervisors" instead. The firearms examiners' feelings of resentment and powerlessness about their position in the laboratory spilled over, and they took them out on me, one person over whom they had some control.

TOXICOLOGY'S GOLDEN OPPORTUNITY

Unlike firearms examiners, who were threatened by and resentful of comparisons to DNA profiling, toxicologists embraced this comparison. Toxicologists are considered by some to be the "button pushers" of the crime laboratory, since their work within the field of forensic science is the most routine. They require the least amount of training to do casework; therefore, at MCCL, the unit is the starting point for many rookie criminalists.

Toxicologists use instruments to detect and identify drugs and poisons in body fluids, tissues, and organs. Their analyses, which employ specific instruments and protocols in a standardized manner and often examine multiple samples at once, report whether the dose in the sample of blood or urine is above the state's cutoff for intoxication. The toxicology reports offer elements of visibility and verifiability comparable to DNA profiling, but in a much simpler fashion. Toxicologists always test two samples from the same suspect and report these results, the second providing verification of the results of the first. The machine sets a cutoff point, which visibly demonstrates where the sample fell in terms of the legal standard. At MCCL, toxicologists' logs and instrument output were all available for the legal parties involved in cases, providing additional visibility of how results are created. Consequently, the expertise of toxicologists was not threatened by comparisons to DNA profiling; instead, these comparisons resulted in toxicologists striving to enhance their expertise.

The discipline of toxicology drew no direct scientific or public attention in relation to DNA profiling. The 2009 NAS report barely mentioned toxicology and did not criticize toxicological analysis at all. However, the report drew critical attention to laboratory error in forensic science in general and, in particular, to uncertainty of measurement. The report noted, "The assessment of the accuracy of the conclusions from forensic analyses and the estimation of relevant error rates are key components of the mission of forensic science."[29] This attracted the interest of enterprising defense attorneys working on DUI cases, who began to capitalize on the NAS statements about measurement error. One attorney used the report to win DUI cases in other states by employing a specific, technical tactic: showing that crime laboratories had omitted estimates of measurement uncertainty in their reports. Such estimates are a standard of other scientific disciplines, and, by calling for laboratory reports to explicitly display sources and estimates of measurement uncertainty, the NAS report's publication offered this attorney an argument to attack the accuracy of DUI tests.[30] Given his success, the defense attorney began training and encouraging other defense attorneys and experts across the country to win DUI cases in the same manner, bolstered by the NAS findings. A specific case arose in MCCL's jurisdiction: a defense attorney planned to challenge the lab's toxicology results on this basis, as well as call an engineering expert from one of these other states to testify. This local and immediate challenge to toxicologists' testimony in an upcoming court appearance in Metropolitan County propelled the toxicologists to consider changing their practices.

Prior to the release of the 2009 NAS report, MCCL had been adjusting their practices and protocols to conform to ISO17025 (ISO): a set of general laboratory standards recommended by the American Society of Crime Laboratory Directors (ASCLD) for future accreditation. The toxicology unit was revising their protocols in accordance with ISO, and one requirement was creating a three-year plan to "apply procedures for estimating uncertainty of measurement." Therefore, when they heard about a potential challenge to their testimony on the basis of uncertainty measurement, the toxicology unit was already planning to change their protocols and revise their reports. Instead of waiting the three years allowed by the accreditation process, the toxicologists decided to implement their plan immediately. So they put together the statistical analysis to prepare for testifying in this particular case.

Toxicologists at MCCL embraced the challenge to be more like DNA profiling, as it fit well with the characteristics of their expertise. Toxicology, like DNA profiling, is instrumentally mediated. But, unlike DNA profiles, which require multiple interpretations by analysts to produce a judgment, toxicological outputs of BAC require little to no interpretation. In toxicology, the reports are short and standardized, the interpretation minimal. Toxicology cases entail what science studies scholars label "mechanical" judgment, in which instruments provide the objective results.[31] Moreover, the values of the unit require that a good toxicologist meticulously log information, keeping track not only of the sample, but of the processes and the materials used. As the "OCD unit," their goal is to reduce all errors as much as they possibly can, and reducing measurement error aligns with this value.

While the reports they used did not yet include the standard of measurement uncertainty called for in the NAS report, toxicologists at MCCL were already concerned about tracking uncertainty of measurement. The blood alcohol analysis (BAC) protocol in use required that they trace the instruments, reagents, and standards used in a laboratory log. The state law required that BAC measurements had a confidence interval of $+/-5$ percent (which matched the ASCLD requirement), so the lab had been reporting results at the 95-percent confidence level. With their intention to meet ISO's requirements, the toxicology unit was prepared, on the basis of the protocols they had already been using, to accurately report the uncertainty of their measurements.

Jason, an experienced toxicologist who was spearheading these changes, spoke about these issues at a training session held for the criminal justice community. He highlighted the compatibility of what the toxicology unit at MCCL was already doing with the new standards called for in the NAS report:

> I've heard lots of defense attorneys say that labs are scrambling to put in uncertainty due to the NAS report. This is not true, we were already doing it . . . uncertainty of measurement is not just spurred by NAS, it is called out in many documents in scientific fields, it is scientifically known.

He explained that MCCL's current uncertainty measurement was based on historical data, which the lab had already been collecting since they updated their protocol over five years ago:

> So the instrument is the same instrument we've been using for five years, and our method hasn't changed. . . . We average out our quality control data, and we not only use that historical data, but go through every step of the procedure and assess it for uncertainty. If you use glassware, or pipettes, every piece of equipment, the reagents, all are assessed for uncertainty. We quantify them, normalize them, and then combine and express them together.

In their presentation to the criminal justice community, the toxicologists were visibly proud of their new practice of reporting measurement uncertainty. They were now able to report a measure of BAC with a confidence level of 99 percent—a narrower interval than their earlier analysis.

The characteristics of toxicologists' expertise, therefore, made them open to being more like DNA. Their form of inquiry is chemical instrumentation, a technique that includes careful attention to detail in analyzing many similar samples simultaneously, which instills values of error-free, obsessively organized processing. Toxicologists are very comfortable with the scientific bases of their analyses. They have a strong conviction that their machine-based judgments are accurate, so they are not as worried about their assessments of results. Instead, they are concerned with making sure the evidence samples match the many logs they keep. Given their attention to detail and their love of accuracy, measuring and reporting the uncertainty in their analytic process feels natural; it is compatible with their values.

Also, toxicologists viewed this change as an opportunity to exercise their expertise. In fact, the process of changing their protocols provided variety and challenge in their work and resulted in putting MCCL on the cutting edge of statewide practice. As Jason joked with some defense attorneys at the end of his presentation, "You all have great questions. I don't want to see you in court! I'll e-mail you with the jurisdictions that haven't done uncertainty measurement yet. Metropolitan County is kind of leading the state. So try your luck, bring it!" Their pride at developing a leading edge protocol also reflected the increased autonomy that the project demanded from the analysts, which was a welcome contrast to the repetitive practices of their daily work.

NARCOTICS, EAST AND WEST

Like toxicology, narcotics analysis was seen by the scientific community, the public and the courts as legitimate. Narcotics also escaped negative mention in the 2009 NAS report. However, the release of the report triggered renewed attention to a professional debate over technique among narcotics analysts nationwide.

In the narcotics discipline, laboratories in the eastern and western United States favored different techniques: in the east, GC/MS (gas chromatography/mass spectrometry) was the method of first choice for identifying controlled substances; in the west, however, microcrystallography was used more frequently. Although the narcotics community agreed that both methods were scientifically valid, GC/MS had the advantage of instrumentation logs and graphical outputs that some perceived as more compatible with the standards of DNA profiling. This internal professional debate over the relative legitimacy of their own analytical techniques drew the attention of the narcotics analysts at MCCL, as they were worried their laboratory practices might be outlawed by the professional community.

At MCCL, narcotics analysts use crystal tests for many of their cases, resorting to GC/MS analysis only for the "unknowns" they cannot recognize by sight or smell, or for other drugs that cannot be confirmed through crystal testing. In their jurisdiction, the law requires a short turnaround time for narcotics cases; moreover, how suspects are specifically charged depends on identifying the controlled substance they were carrying when arrested and how much of it they had. This places pressure on narcotics analysts to finish the analyses on their samples rapidly and accurately. The most common substance analyzed in the unit is methamphetamine, which can often be confirmed in ten to fifteen minutes with crystal testing.

With crystal testing, analysts record what the crystals under the microscope look like, both by drawing them and describing what they see.[32] Matt, as described in chapter 1, reported seeing "clothespins" and "rabbit ears" in the two crystal tests he performed on a sample he identified as methamphetamine, and he drew both sets of images in his notes on the case. Crystal tests, then, employ chemical reactions, but depend on the subjective image matching expertise of an analyst. In contrast, the GC/MS and other instrumental tests in narcotics analysis rely on standardized, instrumental assessments, which report a chemical match with a known substance. Therefore, narcotics analysts, in science studies terminology, use both "trained judgment" and "mechanical objectivity" to identify controlled substances.[33] With microcrystallography tests, narcotics analysts report visual assessments, while GC/MS reports from instruments contain standardized logs of output.

As in all the presentations of evidence at MCCL, an important aspect of producing drug evidence was making the results compelling in the courtroom. Unlike the drawings and descriptions analysts make of the fleeting and impermanent crystal tests, GC/MS instruments produce documentation and raw data that is visible after the analysis is completed. Verification was also an important practice in the narcotics unit. Because crystal tests provide "less certainty" than the chemical profile produced by the GC/MS instrument, the guidelines of the scientific working group (SWG-DRUG) already required that two tests be performed on each sample, using different reagents. Current practice, therefore, was to provide verification of the results of the first crystal test with a second, different crystal test. One of Matt's two methamphetamine tests used gold chloride, while the other used phosphoric acid and iodoplatinate.

With the publication of the NAS report, the debate within the professional community of narcotics analysis intensified. Their online SWG-DRUG board was filled with comments about whether and how changes were likely to be made to the guidelines for analysis. In the narcotics unit at MCCL, there were some discussions within SWG-DRUG about requiring that a second analyst visually review the crystals. This would be time consuming, because crystals form very rapidly, so a second analyst would have to perform a duplicate set of crystal tests from scratch, doubling the time the analysis took.[34] However, it would add another dimension of verifiability to the results. Another idea was to add digital imaging, as used in firearms examination. Analysts at MCCL, recognizing that their drawings were not as compelling to outside audiences as images, had been debating whether the lab should purchase digital cameras for their microscopes. This was not an inexpensive option, although, as one of the analysts pointed out, it would be a lot cheaper than purchasing additional GC/MS instruments for all of the analysts.

The MCCL analysts were primarily concerned that the debate might result in the prohibition of crystal tests entirely. This fear was because eastern analysts preferred instrumentation, and they were thought to be overrepresented on the board of their scientific working group. Jodi, a veteran narcotics analyst, explained that crystal tests are "the oldest identification method for drugs; it has been around since the 1800s. And it is very definitive, and quick and easy to do." She valued the test and didn't want to see it phased out. However, she feared "we'll probably have to move to the GC/MS tests, that's mostly what they do back east. But that takes a lot longer to analyze, and we wouldn't get our results back immediately. Now, we do the crystal tests and it is much quicker." Billie elaborated on this problem as she described a workshop she attended about a recent hearing that challenged the use of crystal testing:

"It depends on the kinds of cases you have. Here in Metropolitan County, we couldn't keep up with the caseload if we didn't do crystals. We only have two instruments, and the runs take a long time, so we couldn't keep up."

At MCCL, a good narcotics analyst was one who could make quick, accurate identifications. But the analysts also valued the use of personal judgment on tough cases. Therefore, the prospect of changing to instrumentation for their identifications worried them, because of the loss in autonomy, variety, and control over the work that it implied. They saw the work of analyzing controlled substances through GC/MS as simple and requiring less judgment. Taylor, a narcotics analyst, pointed out this distinction: "On the East Coast, the instruments are there and ready to go, just dilute and shoot. Any schmo from the street can do it, just let them on the instrument. With crystal tests, we have to validate [the procedure] and train people to do crystals." Such training entailed coursework in which novices worked side by side with experienced analysts on specially equipped microscopes, learning to identify the crystalline forms properly. Potential changes to their current practice threatened the analysts' sense of craft training and judgment. As Billie noted:

> I like crystal tests partly because I'm a chemist. I like chemistry and I can get behind the chemical part of the crystal tests. The other part is . . . I don't want to do the same thing twelve billion times in a day. I like to do different things. So if I have different tools in my arsenal I'm happier. I know other people would prefer just to take all their drugs, put it in methanol, throw it on the GC and be done with it. But I'm not one of those people, because it would bore me to death. I would hate that.

Narcotics analysts at MCCL resisted turning their work into the standardized "boring" practices they felt comparisons to DNA profiling implied.

In narcotics, analysts had a choice: they could adopt practices that moved them toward "being like DNA" in instrumentation, visibility, and verifiability, or they could not. But, even though adopting instrumental techniques would bring them more in line with the gold standard of DNA profiling, the analysts at MCCL resisted these changes, because they strongly valued autonomy and variety in their work. Additionally, the challenge to be more like DNA came from an internal debate within their professional association, and so far there was no direct or immediate need to make change. Therefore, they held on to their practices.

DNA PROFILING AND CHANGE IN FORENSIC SCIENCE

For forensic science as a whole, DNA profiling epitomized modern, efficient progress,[35] an advance that was accepted by the courts and the broader scientific community, as well as in the public sphere. Forensic scientists' responses to this change are telling, because, returning to the concerns of chapters 2 and 3, they highlight some of the ways in which both science and law matter to analysts. The practices that analysts use to turn the products of their work into evidence also make science meaningful and convincing in a courtroom.

Firearms examiners spent much of their time creating images to support their judgments in court. As Tom mentioned to me, "I've become an excellent photographer since starting this job." In toxicology, Jason noted that, although "we know all about uncertainty in science already," the laboratory was responding to legal pressures to provide measures of this uncertainty. The importance of legal concerns was also evident in the narcotics crystal test debate, which turned not at all on the science of the analysis: the field agreed that both sets of practices constituted "good science." Instead, the discussion of narcotics analysts in MCCL focused on whether and how to change their practices so that the science appeared more visible and verifiable to members of other social worlds, while still maintaining their quick turnaround time.

The ways in which firearms examiners, toxicologists, and narcotics analysts discussed and changed their practices demonstrates how external conceptions of "objective"" scientific evidence were drawn into lab practice, influencing conceptions and representations of expertise. The disciplines of forensic science not only developed under different historical circumstances, but varied in their scientific techniques, which were perceived as more or less objective. As noted earlier, the debate among narcotics analysts was one of evolving scientific practice. External publics saw the GC/MS procedure as more objective and modern than crystal testing. When a narcotics lab in California came under media scrutiny for drug theft and poor management, the news reports labeled the crystal tests performed in this lab as "outdated tests" that produced "telltale crystal patterns" in contrast to the "sophisticated drug analysis instruments" the lab should have been using.[36]

This news story invokes competing images of forensic analysis as craft or science: "telltale patterns" are opposed to "sophisticated instruments." While all the patterns of forensic analysis require analysts to interpret them (including DNA profiling), instrumentation, by objectifying the results, is perceived as requiring less personal judgment and less susceptibility to bias.[37] With DNA reports, the mediator between the evidence and the jury is removed by the analysts' graphical representations of the results: the tables and the probabilities take the person out of the judgment. The same is true in toxicology, where the analysis is fully instrumental and the reports could be made more probabilistic with the addition of measurement error. This is less true of narcotics reports, in which the analysts draw the crystal patterns freehand and give them descriptive labels. And it is even less true in firearms examinations, in which the examiners tout their holistic judgment of the mark.

The difference in degrees and types of interpretation of the forensic sciences is not only a perception of the public; it is also rooted in the technical differences of forms of analysis noted by criminalists themselves. While all of the subdisciplines of forensic science require the criminalists' interpretation in order to make judgments about the evidence, these judgments reflect varying levels of scientific objectivity in terms of both technique and perception. Tim, the chemistry unit supervisor, responded to my question about scientific criticisms of forensic science by saying:

There are differences. Having somebody put a mysterious off-white powder onto an instrument, say the IR [infrared spectrometer], and it comes back as cocaine base. A thousand people could test that same sample, and they sure as heck better all get cocaine base. There's no room for negotiation. There's no room for doubt, or interpretation, or even discussion. Versus, I'm going to put it at the other end of the spectrum, bite mark interpretation, which I think most genuine forensic scientists are a little hesitant about, but there is still a forensic Odontology section of the American Academy. Our lab director thinks questioned documents [which uses comparative analysis of handwriting] is voodoo?!? Wow. Bite marks, way out there. Earology? There are some folks in California working on that!

Tim highlighted that forensic science has always operated on a spectrum. Some serious scientists had worked on accurately identifying the bite marks of teeth and the shape of ears. On the other hand, cocaine was always, chemically, cocaine. Yet he elaborated on how even seemingly objective measurements had subjective elements:

So, how many points does it take for a fingerprint? How many matching, consecutive matching, for firearms to match? How many similarities in questioned documents? How many points on a shoe, until you can say that shoe and only that shoe? These are different parts of forensics than DNA, which has a classic sort of a "Hey, we can put numbers on it." But, I think even the DNA folks make certain assumptions. And the biggest task for them is deciding which way to count the statistics; I mean that has a certain subjectivity to it, in its own right. So while DNA is the gold standard in forensic science, I'm not convinced that all of those statistics are as accurate as they would like you to believe.

I think they will never be equal. They can't be. The idea that somebody can do toxicology and say there's five milligrams per liter, or something like that, I mean that's sort of a hard science, the same thing with chemistry. But then, you get into something like hairs. Wow. Do I believe in hair comparison? Yeah, as long as it's taken in context. I think all of these things need to be taken in context.

Differences in the degree of interpretation created different perceptions of scientific objectivity across the subdisciplines, which can be seen in the three examples in this chapter.[38] In the media and the larger scientific community (as represented by the NAS report), the discipline of firearms was perceived as one of the least objective and least scientific, with attendant concerns about bias and error. These differences echo the distinction between mechanical objectivity and trained judgment in science studies: Should judgments be made by an impartial person (or machine) that follows rules or by a trained expert?[39] In the case of forensic science, our criminal justice system seems to prefer rule following.[40]

Given this legal and public preference, all of the members of the forensic science community could see the value of presenting evidence that looked "more like DNA" evidence. What it meant to be more like DNA manifested differently in the case of each of the other occupations: for firearms, DNA profiling was an overarching objective statistical practice; in toxicology, comparisons were made specifically to error measurement practices; and, for narcotics, the certainty of the instrumental output of DNA profiles motivated comparisons to instrumental chemistry. However, within all the units at MCCL, there was a sense of inevitability around these issues. In fact, analysts believed that the entire field of forensic science was moving in the direction of increased scientific objectivity as defined by DNA profiling practices. This is not to claim, however, that the particular epistemological characteristics of DNA analysis explains the evolution of forensic science practice. In the past, other evidentiary analyses were considered the gold standard of forensics—most notably, fingerprint analysis.[41] Even dust from the crime scene captured the imagination of practitioners of forensic science in the era of the invention of the vacuum and was explored as a possible source of evidence.[42] DNA analysis is merely the current favorite, offering a set of scientific and legal standards that can be compared to the practices of other forensic sciences in terms of their technical, epistemological, and moral characteristics.

The comparison across these three discipline's responses to the rise of DNA profiling highlights how criminalists' participation in the social worlds of forensic science, criminal justice, and the public sphere impact the work of the crime laboratory. In all three cases, we see how criminalists' interactions with scientific communities, courtrooms, and the media relay interpretations of DNA profiling to members of the occupation. Their different interactions within these worlds serve as the impetus for the changing manifestations of expertise in forensic science.[43]

CONCLUSION

The criminalists at the Metropolitan County Crime Laboratory are expert workers inhabiting a complex system of intertwined social worlds. As such, exploring their daily work illuminates the challenges facing all expert workers. Being an expert calls for frequent boundary work, because expertise requires representation and translation in order to be made useful to nonexperts.[1] Criminalists must produce different forms of explanation within each of these worlds. Within forensic science—their home community—they demonstrate particular forms of scientific understanding, follow established standards of rigor, and adhere to protocols that lay out specific methodologies and practices. Criminalists are most at home in this world of applied science, as it is the one they elected to join, and the community in which they have trained and established their regular routines.

But what is scientifically appropriate inside the world of forensic science is incomprehensible to the inhabitants of the world of criminal justice. Common understandings about the messiness of science—concepts that they can rely on inside the world of forensic science—are anathema to attorneys. Therefore, in order to make claims that are compelling to law enforcement, attorneys, and judges, criminalists cannot simply stay with the science. Instead, they must adapt to the law's adversarial norms, where a bright line needs to be drawn as to whether a suspect is guilty or innocent. They must translate scientific expertise to inform pressing legal questions.

Connecting science to the world of criminal justice requires anticipation and negotiation. To stay true to the science and also do their job well, forensic scientists need to know when and how they can push back on the impractical or wasteful requests of investigators, like those who show up at the laboratory with hundreds of beer cans to be analyzed. They must figure out how to articulate their findings in ways that are usable by attorneys, while preserving the scientific facts as they understand them. Criminalists are a captive occupation; their output is used solely in the service of criminal justice, and the members of this world make demands and create constraints on the work of criminalists.

Also, criminalists need to translate their work for the broader public. When thinking about this world, criminalists primarily want to ensure that the evidence makes sense to a lay audience: the people they expect to be on a jury evaluating their findings. This world requires both claims to legitimacy and simplification of the science. It is not easy, for instance, to explain to a layperson what DNA is while avoiding the embarrassment of making a mistake in spelling out deoxyribonucleic acid. Moreover, the direct scrutiny by the jury creates the high stakes that criminalists feel: the role of their assessments in jurors' determination of guilt or innocence has crucial consequences.

As a result, criminalists' expertise exhibits different forms in different places. Forensic scientists don't just master the science; they develop finesse in translating the science into the arenas of both criminal justice and the public in order to write convincing reports and successfully testify. Moreover, forensic scientists use their expertise when these other worlds impinge on them: they learn to negotiate when attorneys or police make requests and to address the public with care. Thus, criminalists become expert at lighting digital images, explaining how to bag evidence so that it does not deteriorate in transit, and maintaining composure under questioning while looking jurors in the eye. Multilayered expectations of translation across social worlds create an extraordinarily high bar for criminalists' work.

WHAT IS EXPERT WORK?

Studying criminalists shows how crucial it is to examine the nature of experts' social worlds and the dynamics of their interrelationships. Criminalists have to find ways to bridge gaps in perceptions and expectations across these worlds, in addition to their main task of drawing scientific conclusions about evidence. They do this by reaching out to educate the public and the members of the criminal justice community, especially district attorneys, who have structural power over them and whose understanding (or lack thereof) can have significant implications for criminalists. The culture of anticipation in the laboratory provides criminalists with communal resources to figure out how to translate their work, given the characteristics of their diverse audiences, which helps them manage this difficult task. To work effectively, all expert workers, just like the criminalists at MCCL, must figure out which social worlds matter, who is judging them, and who has the power to undermine their authority.

Thinking about the translation challenges of criminalists uncovers critical questions for understanding the work of all experts. Who are the audiences for a given class of expert workers? What are the characteristics and structures of the social worlds they inhabit? How do these worlds differ in their knowledge, power, and investment in the outcomes that flow from expert work? What characterizes the dynamics of the interactions that expert workers have within and across these worlds? How is the output of experts used by others, and how severe are the consequences of mistranslation within a particular world? Understanding these factors that influence the way experts work enables us to appropriately trust and value their expertise.

Forensic science illustrates an extreme case of a captive expert occupation. Because they are captive, criminalists' work output always must address the world of criminal justice. Moreover, as they communicate in the courtroom, they also face the scrutiny of the public. Because the interests, needs, and understandings of these worlds differ, criminalists have a particularly narrow path to walk while on the stand. Not only could a misstep lead to a failure to adequately represent the science, but it could mean falling prey to an attorney's machinations or losing the jury as their eyes glaze over in boredom.

Other types of experts are increasingly scrutinized outside of their core social worlds. While doctors in hospitals have been subject to review by insurance companies for decades, in recent years, with the proliferation of online "best of" listings and ratings websites, public assessment of their work has intensified.[2] The social media landscape contributes to this effect as well: when President Trump tweets about cold winter weather belying climate change, it garners additional attention from the public, the media, and the government that climatologists must consider.[3] Translating at the boundaries of social worlds is already difficult, and it becomes more so when the social constraints on experts multiply. The science underlying expertise can be lost during these translations, and concerns of other worlds may be overemphasized.

Given that more and more expert work is now done in organizations,[4] the position of experts with respect to members of other social worlds has become increasingly critical. Expert work was once primarily the province of professionals, who selected, trained, and monitored their own community members.[5] In contrast to the autonomous private practices of the past, twenty-first-century experts—such as doctors, lawyers, and accountants—are increasingly subsumed in organizations where they are managed by nonexperts.[6] This means their expertise is captured within a system where they may not approve or be in control of how their knowledge is applied.

Put another way, expertise once meant independence, authority, and legitimacy. Today, expertise can secure certain benefits—professional security, financial stability—but it does not always lead to autonomy over the output of one's work, or even influence. The story of forensic scientists makes this clear: on the stand, an analyst likely knows more about DNA profiling or narcotics analysis than anyone in the room. Yet not only do criminalists exert little influence on the legal conversation; they may well suffer professional setbacks for even a slight error. What would it mean if the same was true for the work of attorneys or doctors? When expert work is captive to nonexpert systems of evaluation, outsiders impinge on the control of the professional. And the trend toward captive expertise is increasingly the norm.

Can Captive Criminalists Produce Good Science?

When experts do not have autonomy over their work, as in the case of captive occupations such as forensic science, it makes the work more difficult. Whether the work of crime laboratories should be supervised by the world of criminal justice has become a pressing national question. Many interested parties have argued that the independence of forensic science suffers when beholden to criminal justice.[7] Having spent a year and a half in a captive crime laboratory, I would agree.

Being a captive occupation has consequences for the form that forensic science work takes, the resources provided to do the job, and the evolution of the field. For example, since forensic science is subordinate to criminal justice, the question of who gets what resources becomes particularly troublesome. We can see the difficult choices a city or county faces in deciding between putting cops on the beat or hiring criminalists, between investing in new police cruisers or purchasing expensive laboratory equipment. The overarching context of the criminal justice system also influences decision-making about crime laboratories. The NAS report recommended the creation of an independent National Institute of Forensic Science to oversee the field and set standards, which would provide crime labs freedom from the oversight of police departments and other agencies. However, the Department of Justice and local police organizations successfully opposed this recommendation, slowing change and maintaining the dependence of crime laboratories.[8]

What may be less obvious are the hazardous implications of this choice when it comes to how evidence—a necessary input into the criminal justice system—is produced. When a narcotics analyst such as Annie Dookhan identifies a controlled substance without completing confirmatory analysis of it in the lab (known as "dry-labbing"), she is obviously not meeting the scientific standards of the work or being accountable to the public. However, the investigation that followed the Dookhan scandal in Massachusetts showed that the narcotics laboratory was understaffed. Audits following a similar case in San Francisco in 2010 where dry-labbing and other malfeasance occurred also uncovered understaffing of the narcotics unit. In these laboratories, there was no possible way to thoroughly analyze the caseload of controlled substances within the turnaround time established by the law, given the number of analysts on staff.[9] Failing to invest in forensic science not only constrains the production of good science, but can lead to poor outcomes for the legal system that result in public skepticism and distrust.

The Implications of Anticipation across Social Worlds

The need for criminalists to translate across other social worlds can have even deeper, more subtle consequences. Criminalists' lower power and status relative to the criminal justice system creates a culture of anticipation in the laboratory. Anticipation, as I have shown, does not necessarily mean coercion or bias. I saw little evidence of these at MCCL. The criminalists were dedicated to the norms of science and saw their neutrality as paramount; their protocols elaborated carefully prescribed steps to avoid biased results. Moreover, as described in chapter 3, I heard of only one case of attempted "coercion," which (according to colleagues) resulted in an attorney getting an earful rather than a change in the evidence report to support his argument. Instead, what anticipation looked like at MCCL was early and frequent considerations about the probative nature of their tasks, thoughtful and protracted planning of language that would communicate both science and justice, and perennial hope for educating attorneys, judges, and members of law enforcement about science.

Anticipation, therefore, has both positive and negative implications for expert work. In other domains, particularly medicine, we can see the dilemma this creates. Preventive medicine is in many ways about anticipation: doctors anticipate the course of disease and worry about possible consequences for patients. On the positive side, excisional biopsies, genetic testing, and other preventive tactics enable patients to prevent small medical problems or indicators from spiraling into terrible health consequences. At the same time, anticipation in the form of overzealous patients and the threat of possible malpractice suits can lead to unnecessary procedures, expensive diagnostic tests, and the overprescription of antibiotics.[10] Thus, it is important to think about how anticipatory tactics and strategies can be harnessed toward positive outcomes.

How might the structures and practices of crime laboratories change in order to ensure that anticipation is oriented in a positive direction? First, although the proposed system of independent crime laboratories has proven unlikely to be implemented,[11] any plans to distance crime laboratories from the criminal justice system should carefully account for the implications of the culture of anticipation in these labs. In a completely independent crime laboratory, criminalists might not fully understand the nature of their tasks from a legal and public perspective and might provide conclusions that make less sense in the context of criminal justice. It also would be difficult for criminalists to analyze the evidence without some knowledge of the details of the crime, particularly in the case of DNA profiling.

Rather than removing laboratories from the oversight of criminal justice agencies, it might instead be useful to consider smaller, more pragmatic steps. The goal is to make sure that the culture of anticipation that exists in crime labs remains faithful to the science, useful for criminal justice, and accountable to the public. For instance, the technical review process is a step that laboratories already take to see to it that more than one criminalist examines the output and conclusions, so as to confirm that they meet scientific standards. A similar legal review process should be put into place for the attorneys in the case, who are using evidence from the crime laboratory. If attorneys were required to sign off on the laboratory report as well as criminalists, they might feel more accountable to better understanding the conclusions. Or, to ensure discussion of the report with criminalists, jurisdictions should require attorneys to have at least a fifteen-minute premeeting with the criminalist any time they call a member of the crime lab to the stand.

Exploring structural solutions to the problem of captivity, an alternative plan might be to make forensic scientists independent officers of the court. Such a structural shift would establish them as equals rather than lower-status captives of the criminal justice system. It makes sense for criminalists to be in contact with members of law enforcement in order to analyze evidence while a crime is being investigated. However, at the point at which a suspect is charged, criminalists could report their findings not to law enforcement agencies, but to the court. This would make certain that all of their findings are equally and simultaneously available to the prosecution and the defense, which would help to balance accountability as well as reduce any appearance of bias. While it is not clear that any of these ideas would be feasible within the current criminal justice system, they are ways to give more weight to criminalists' expertise within the worlds of law and criminal justice.

Do Criminalists Have Good Jobs?

I have painted a somewhat dire picture of the work of criminalists—captive to the whims of law enforcement, let out from behind the locked doors of the laboratory only to sit in the hot seat in the courtroom. There is no question that theirs is a stressful job. However, criminalist jobs are sought after, and not only because *CSI* and *NCIS* make them seem sexy.

Forensic science appeals because it offers challenging work. The organizations in which scientific experts work have status hierarchies, often based on educational attainment. An alternative source of employment for experts like criminalists, who hold bachelor's degrees in science, are science or hospital laboratories. In these labs, however, technicians are at the bottom of the status ladder, many rungs below MDs and PhDs.[12] Being a hospital or biotechnology technician requires routinized work under the supervision of higher-status experts. When I talked with criminalists at MCCL about their career trajectories, they described the jobs available in these other types of laboratories as mere "button-pushing." In contrast, criminalist jobs are "good science" jobs with respect to both material employment characteristics—income, job security—and the characteristics of the work itself. The craft aspect of the work is a big draw for science graduates; developing expertise is challenging, and using that expertise is motivating.[13] The chance to conduct autonomous analyses and think about new protocols appeals to criminalists.

Moreover, the latitude to perform this advanced work is directly related to the growth of expertise. Studies of professional expertise show that it develops through hands-on practice under the collective tutelage of skilled colleagues.[14] Setting up instruments, developing protocols, and making and correcting mistakes all deepen experts' understanding of their processes, tools, and the material constraints of their analyses. And, by performing these collaborative tasks, they enhance their expertise, which makes them better equipped to judge outputs and make good decisions about evidence, as well as translate that work for others. Some commentators have suggested that forensic science should enhance its research culture through increased funding for research and the hiring of more PhD scientists in crime laboratories.[15] Given the interests and values of the criminalists at MCCL, I believe an enhanced research culture would be welcomed by many forensic scientists. But laboratories hiring more PhD scientists should be careful not to reduce the challenge and skill-enhancing tasks that are currently valued by practicing criminalists. If we reduce forensic scientists to button-pushers unable to carry out the craft of criminalistics, we dilute the expertise of people we expect to issue expert judgments.

WHAT WILL TECHNOLOGY DO TO EXPERTS?

The challenges to the work of experts in the modern world proliferate when we consider that technical and scientific knowledge do not stand still. In the midst of the digital era, we have even more of a need to understand how technological change affects expert workers. Scholars and pundits alike have become fascinated by questions of how digital technologies will change work, but their answers are mostly speculative and not very grounded in what expert workers actually do. The work that criminalists do reflects what it means to be an expert in a job where knowledge is evolving and contested, standards are uncertain, and technologies are intensifying.

Understanding how organizational forces and social worlds have influenced the evolution of forensic science work helps us to temper overblown fears about the algorithmic takeover of the professional workplace. We see that expertise in forensic science is not easily replaced: the institutions in which these experts work require their translations in order to make sense of their findings about evidence. At the same time, my study of criminalists highlights that we must remain cautious about the notions of objectivity that such algorithms raise. Ideas of mechanical expertise taking over for human judgment are quite visible in the ways that the algorithm revolution has been playing out with respect to the future of work. What scholars tell us is that artificial intelligence and data science technologies have made dramatic strides in their capability to parse and visualize information, predict outcomes, and help produce products and services. These digital advances are changing the way we do business, and that change is one to be feared: such advances, we are told, will displace humans in some jobs while changing tasks for a whole lot of us. The novelty in this latest industrial revolution is that, unlike the craftsmen put out of work in the past, professional and knowledge workers are going to bear the brunt of the impact of artificial intelligence technologies. The superior information processing and decision-making capabilities of these technologies will hijack the cognitive and evaluative functions of experts.[16]

The literature on the future of work in the digital era has largely focused on implications for business strategies or for workers who need to augment their skills, rather than on experts' worlds of work. It therefore presents a somewhat atomistic and forbidding picture of a future in which the workers must focus on improving the types of "soft" communicative and cognitive skills that the "smart machines" lack.[17] Instead, what I've shown in this examination of criminalists' work is that these experts work in dialogue with their instruments and techniques, and their embodied and community understandings are needed for interpretation and translation.

Moreover, by focusing on what strategy-makers or individual workers might do to "reskill" organizations in the face of digital technologies, these recommendations fail to acknowledge a repeated dynamic in the history of technological change: experts tend to resist. On the one hand, evolving technology can be a source of occupational change.[18] In the case of accounting, for example, incorporating tax laws into computer programs paved the way for the rise of nonprofessional tax preparers, who lack the expertise of CPAs but can be hired on a temporary basis for low pay.[19] On the other hand, we know that organizations and professionals do not adopt technologies in a predictable fashion, because social dynamics interfere.[20] The ways that organizations approach and implement new technologies matter, as do the ways that workers respond. Many have the expertise and authority to ignore and criticize the technological tools that their organizations deploy. The firearms examiners at MCCL resisted any changes to their practices. Similarly, judges, when supplied with algorithmic risk-assessment tools to make bail decisions, often do not even look at the recommendations from the algorithm.[21] Workers do not have to be Luddites to slow technological incursions into their work.

Also missing in accounts about the impending extinction of experts is the role of institutional and organizational structures and practices in technological change. The example of DNA profiling in forensic science, which represented a significant technological advance in the analysis of biological evidence, makes clear that organizations and institutions exert a significant influence on how changes in work will unfold. While DNA profiling created more useful and scientifically advanced identification practices in forensic biology, these changes had limited effects on the rest of the field. The responses within the field of forensic science followed different trajectories and depended on interpretations of the similarities drawn between DNA profiling and the work within each discipline. While the media and the government used comparisons to DNA profiling to highlight what they saw as broad problems in forensic science, the courts interpreted the potential for change much more narrowly: they supported maintaining the status quo with respect to the admissibility of firearms comparisons, but pursued advances in the measurement of error in toxicology.

Institutions and organizations can be a countervailing force on the displacement of experts by technology. As my examination of the impact of DNA profiling in forensic science demonstrates, workplace change comes not simply from the advent of new technologies, but derives from the social and cultural practices of the social worlds in which experts are embedded. The effects of algorithmic technologies on work, therefore, need to be considered within the context of the workplaces and occupations that might adopt them. As economic historian Louis Hyman points out, the path of change in the workplace is not driven inexorably by technology, but is the consequence of decisions made by organizations and governments.[22] It behooves us, therefore, to be thoughtful about these decisions.

Are Technologies (or Experts) Objective?

An aspect of these decisions that deserves closer consideration is our societal perceptions about the objectivity of technology. Believing that machines are more rational, and thus superior to human judgment, is problematic for our assessments of expert work. In the case of forensic science, the rise of DNA profiling as the gold standard of evidence points to the ways in which rationalized, objective knowledge is increasingly valued.[23] This is true, even though DNA profiling, like other forms of forensic science, is messy and requires analysts to use significant judgment to interpret the output and translate it for others to use.

But this human interpretation is not visible to or understood by the members of other social worlds: attorneys, judges, juries, the public. Ways of knowing in science are in fact varied, but, in these worlds, DNA profiling represents a particular standard. To outside audiences (such as the media), the graphs and tables of DNA profiles are seen as very objective while comparative microscopy and wet chemistry are seen as subjective. People associate numbers with a sense of accuracy and validity, whereas human judgment is thought to be subject to bias and error.[24] This perception of the superiority of machines and numbers and a lack of appreciation of the nature of expert work combine to encourage organizations to adopt technologies that displace experts, without understanding the limitations of using technologies.

We encounter this process of rationalization in which human judgment is made suspect in many other expert domains, especially in medicine, where doctors now use standardized protocols based on evidence-based medicine and draw upon (or ignore) pop-up recommendations from computer systems in examination rooms and at the bedside.[25] Many organizations adopt algorithms with the notion that they will be more objective than humans (and also less expensive), without calculating what is lost from context. As algorithms are being increasingly used in decision-making, in domains ranging from determining promotions in companies to setting bail in courtrooms, it is becoming clear that they are not as objective as organizations hoped.[26] Moreover, they can introduce new biases in ways that are less visible or understandable than the biases of humans.[27]

As I have shown, human judgment is an inherent part of producing and translating expertise, and this is what is being pushed aside in the algorithmic revolution. The key to human expertise is interpretation. At MCCL, even in the most objective statistical analysis of computer output, the criminalists' interpretation of the findings in the context of the scientific process is core to making effective judgments. DNA analysts spend as much time thinking and talking together about blips on electropherograms and statistical calculations in spreadsheets as firearms examiners spend in communal judgment of the striae they see under the comparison microscope. This judgment requires embodied experience, which influences their perception of the possibilities of what to do next. Therefore, it is impossible to separate the results from the process by which they produced expertise. Sociologist Angele Christin, in her study of the use of algorithmic risk assessment tools in bail determination, quotes a judge about his use of such tools: "I don't look at the numbers. There are things you can't quantify."[28] In the course of making decisions, judges interpret the individual's situation and the case details in context. His words sound remarkably similar to the way Tim described expert judgment in cases at MCCL: coming to any conclusions about forensic evidence requires interpreting the details within the context of the case and the experts' knowledge.

At MCCL, these understandings are rooted in cultural communities of work, developed over years of examinations and discussions of case evidence in the company of skilled colleagues.[29] And the judgments criminalists make are not rote: they are often complex and always highly consequential. In forcing human judgment into numerical or statistical formats, or pushing it aside in favor of an algorithm, we are eliminating critical understandings of the ways that expertise is produced. We ignore this problem at our peril. Some recent algorithmic decision-making disasters bring this problem to light. Amazon's algorithmic hiring tool, trained on its primarily male technical staff, immediately began discriminating against women candidates; in the healthcare domain, IBM

Watson's oncology treatment recommendations were notably subpar.[30] Given these issues, we are starting to acknowledge the problems that come from dismissing the judgment and expertise of humans. A leading AI researcher, describing IBM Watson's problems, agreed that "no AI built so far can match a human doctor's comprehension and insight."[31] So the question remains: How do experts stay relevant in a world that devalues their expertise and authority?

THE BOUNDARY WORK OF EXPERTS

All expert workers disseminate their expertise within complex organizational systems—doctors, engineers, and climatologists as well as forensic scientists. Thus, we can learn from the challenges forensic scientists face and the strategies they use as they communicate across the boundaries of criminal justice. Like other expert workers, forensic scientists do not have formal authority, but they want members of other social worlds to respect and use their expertise. To successfully navigate these multiple worlds, their boundary work has to address two main problems. One is the problem of intelligibility: How can you make sure that members of other groups understand the knowledge you are sharing? The other is the problem of legitimacy: How do you get others to value your expertise if you are lower in status and negotiating from a captive position?

Of course, in experts' daily work, the problems of intelligibility and legitimacy are inseparable and need to be managed simultaneously. Take the example of criminalists' hedging their expertise while testifying in the courtroom. Criminalists carefully delimit the arenas in which they have expert authority; they only claim to be expert in analyses for which they are trained and have been found qualified. Rather than over-claiming expertise, they bound it, sometimes to jurors' amusement. Doing so calls attention to where their expertise actually lies, enhancing their credibility on the stand and their presentation as legitimate experts in the areas where their knowledge matters. Careful boundary work in the courtroom and the laboratory enables criminalists to successfully maintain their legitimacy and relevance as expert witnesses.

However, the need for translation extends beyond the courtroom. In the complex organizational structures in which experts are embedded, formal channels of influence are not enough. For criminalists, boundary work is much broader than a brief explanation of their analysis on the stand. They view all moments of interaction with other worlds as opportunities to educate. They try to meet informally with attorneys before cases go to trial. They open their laboratory to tours and reach out to investigators and attorneys to explain their work in training sessions. This increases intelligibility, but is complicated by the problems of status and legitimacy: attorneys and police never attend as frequently as criminalists would like.

Moreover, doing boundary work in such consequential situations requires a backbone. In the criminal justice system, members of other worlds do not always share criminalists' goals; they make statements and requests that criminalists find confusing and problematic. Working in a system where criminalists have little formal authority means that when they are asked to do work that does not meet their scientific standards, they need to push back.

When technologies evolve, expert workers respond by drawing on their occupational values, techniques, and practices. When the legitimacy of their knowledge is contested, workers try to anticipate these challenges. Boundary work of this nature is the best way that experts can maintain relevance, legitimacy, and status in a dramatically changing world. This approach is both more accurate and more realistic than the distant prescriptions that the literature has provided to date to help us navigate the rise of the robots and other prophecies of the coming era.

The position of forensic scientists means negotiating how scientific knowledge is construed in the criminal justice system and the court of public opinion. For other experts and professionals, these negotiations will not look identical, but they should exhibit similar contours. Physicians encountering new digital tools and techniques are likely to respond differently, depending on specialty and the origin of their authority. Radiologists may ignore the AI indicators on their screens, believing the technology conflicts with their expertise and wastes their time;[32]

family practitioners, in contrast, may embrace algorithms that help them diagnose the stream of patients sitting in their exam rooms. Navigating technological change and challenges to legitimacy requires negotiation of how forms of expertise are used across boundaries.

Exploring the dynamics of the social worlds surrounding expert work is critical in order to understand how this work will change. The evolution of expert work goes beyond job displacement and skill development to the occupational values, boundary work, and interactive strategies of experts. What criminalists do is more than simply translate science into courtrooms. They demonstrate all the ways that dedicated, skilled experts can weave diverse threads of knowledge across social worlds to solve real problems.

CASE NOTES ON AN ETHNOGRAPHY OF A CRIME LAB

The appendix in an ethnography is the backstage document that reflects what I did during my fieldwork and analysis, much like a criminalist's case notes. As such, it is the part of the book that most appeals (in the multiple senses of the term) to the members of my own social world—other ethnographers. In the appendix, ethnographers assert their credibility while explaining the details of the study that support their knowledge claims.

Authors may adopt a variety of narrative tones in their methods appendices, including both realist and confessional.[1] The realist tale presents a set of "facts" about what happened to the ethnographer in the field and is a staple of organizational ethnography. I've written quite a few realist methods sections for management journals, and, as all of us who write them know, they are what we might politely call a "gloss." Much of what really happens—all of our interesting meandering thoughts, the dead-end coding, the uncertainty—are left out in an effort to hew to stylized objective practices while citing the canonical texts ("I was there, I observed people for a suitably long time and in the prescribed manner, and then my coding proceeded neatly, piling up in a hierarchy of abstraction until I ended up here").

In books, the tone of the ethnographic appendix often takes on more of a whiff—or even a reek—of a confessional tale. What exciting things happened while the ethnographer was doing fieldwork, and where were his moments of struggle? What was the ethnographer's place in the field, and how did she navigate it? What are the aspects of the author's biography that predispose her to asking this set of questions about this particular organization or type of work? Whereas the realist tale offers credibility, the confessional tale contains the juicy tidbits that build solidarity among ethnographers.

I struggled with my authorial voice during the writing of this appendix. Nothing very dramatic happened to me in the field: the details of how the research unfolded are relatively typical for an organizational ethnography, and I don't have any secrets to confess. My book buddies, upon reading an initial draft, told me that my "confessions" were not juicy at all. Instead, reading me sounded more like having coffee with me. This, then, is really a conversational tale. In my ethnographic projects, my main goal is to offer interesting stories that give readers a feel for the inside of a social scene. These stories should resonate for my informants; I want them to say, "Uh-huh, I'm not surprised by this, it looks familiar." Thus, I was delighted (and relieved) after sending the first draft of the manuscript to a few members of MCCL, to hear from one that I "held up a mirror" for him on the work of his group. Similarly, in this conversational tale, I hope ethnographers recognize themselves in my stories.

INTO THE CRIME LABORATORY

When I was an undergraduate, my apprenticeship as an ethnographer was a study of laboratory technicians at a university biotechnology facility. Since then, my research has focused more on technical and knowledge work than science, running the gamut from semiconductor equipment manufacturers to consultants, programmers to film production crews. My primary concern is how work is accomplished in organizations, which leads me to analyze relationships across different occupational groups. I thought that crime laboratories would be an ideal place to study these relationships, while also enabling me to satisfy my continuing curiosity about applied science.

Crime laboratories, however, are a very particular form of applied science workplace; the way they are organized is complicated by their location within the criminal justice system. As is typical in ethnographic research, I got entangled in these organizational complications the moment I tried to gain access to a lab. Because my interest was in the science rather than in criminal investigation, I initiated the research in the fall of 2004 by inviting a former lab director to coffee, hoping for context on the field of forensic science and some assistance in beginning a project. He offered to introduce me to colleagues who were currently heading laboratories. These three directors gave me tours of their labs, each lasting about two hours. On my first laboratory visit, one director and I walked into the chemistry unit to find a fume hood nearly overflowing with marijuana. She was unfazed, remarking that because the smell of some kinds of controlled substances often can be overwhelming, criminalists contain them in fume hoods. At that moment, I was certain I wanted to learn more about this work.

My interest and expertise in issues of coordination and organization seemed to appeal to the directors, who told me stories about the problems of poor communication across their organizations. All three of them asked me to write a proposal for the project and then left me anxiously awaiting their permission. In the meantime, I audited a crime scene investigation course that was part of a university forensic science master's program. The course was useful as background, although by the point I finished it I realized that I would not be going out to crime scenes as part of my fieldwork. Through discussions with the lab directors I learned that criminalists rarely go to crime scenes themselves, since police departments and sheriffs' offices often have internal evidence technician units. Also, it turns out that I am very squeamish: just the photographs of crime scenes I saw in the class disturbed me.

My experience with the laboratories while trying to negotiate access taught me about the status of forensic science within the justice system. Each one I visited reported to a different law enforcement agency. Laboratory budgets are controlled by these agencies, and the lab directors described feeling like the "stepchild" of their organizations, short-staffed and underfunded. Reinforcing this impression of marginality, the laboratories I visited were buried in windowless basements of municipal buildings and in far-flung warehouses. In all cases, the agency heads to whom the lab directors reported were not scientists, and the directors felt they did not appreciate the value—or the values—of science. If the choice is to put more officers on the street or buy a new GC/MS instrument, they asked, what do you think the police chief or sheriff is going to choose?

It became clear through these interactions that the lab directors felt politically insecure in their role within the criminal justice system. All eventually told me that I could not do an ethnography of their lab, either because their agency head said no, or they were unwilling to ask. For example, after several months of putting me off because the lab was "too busy," one lab director finally told me that he was not only worried I'd take up the criminalists' limited time, but that he also wasn't sure whom the new police chief was going to be, and so he couldn't risk making a request like this. Of course, it could be that all three directors used a political refusal as a way to evade responsibility for the decision and deflect further discussion of my project. However, I suspect that they were initially sincere in their interest, but my project seemed too risky for them to push forward with their law enforcement superiors.

These refusals took place over an academic year, at the end of which I was a year away from going up for tenure. Although the tours had piqued my interest considerably, and I was very disappointed, I decided to shelve the idea, concentrate on other work, and think about a new ethnographic project after my tenure case had been decided. Then, in the fall of 2008, my initial contact unexpectedly reached out to me. The organizers of an annual meeting of crime laboratory managers wanted to include a session about lab management, and he remembered my interest in crime labs and recommended me as a speaker on this topic. I agreed and waived the offered speaking fee in return for permission to attend the entire meeting as an observer. After giving a talk about managing technical work, I met a number of laboratory directors and supervisors. The talk and my contact's introductions provided me with credibility (or at least made me appear harmless), and one or two of the directors expressed interest in having me observe at their lab.

Thus, four years after I began, the project was reborn! After a meeting at MCCL, the director, deputy director, and several supervisors approved my ethnography, contingent upon the successful completion of a background check. I was fingerprinted, and my dean and my neighbors were called and questioned about me. I began my observations in February 2009 in the forensic biology unit, since one of the supervisors there was interested in the questions I raised about coordination in the lab.

———

I studied the four applied science units inside MCCL: forensic biology (DNA), chemistry, toxicology, and comparative evidence. Members of these units were similar in their age range (pretty evenly distributed across their mid-twenties to early fifties) and their educational background (all had bachelor's degrees in biology or chemistry and some had master's degrees in those sciences or a related field). However, the gender composition of the units varied, with mostly women in the forensic biology unit, almost all men in comparative evidence, and an equal split in toxicology and chemistry.

The forensic biology unit comprised eighteen criminalists, including three supervisors, and was responsible for screening evidence for biological fluids and performing DNA profiling on those samples. It also managed and monitored the county's contributions to the Combined DNA Index System (CODIS) database of unknown profiles and profiles of known felons, which is used, for instance, to develop cold hits. The chemistry unit's main work was to identify controlled substances (also known as narcotics) and was made up of eight criminalists, including the supervisor, who reviewed all of the narcotics cases. The remaining criminalists analyzed physical drug evidence and also performed comparative and trace evidence analysis. This included analysis of shoeprints, duct tape, gunshot residue, fire debris, pepper spray, and dye packs.

The toxicology unit was made up of nine toxicologists, including one supervisor, and was responsible for analysis of drugs in the body. The DUI program for the county was also under this unit's purview; it managed all the breath alcohol instruments in the police agencies, and some members of the group were also certified to testify in court about alcohol and drug effects on the body. Finally, the comparative evidence unit, made up of seven criminalists and a supervisor, was divided into two subunits: a three-person latent fingerprint processing unit and a four-person firearms and toolmarks unit. The print unit did not perform fingerprint identification, but processed items for latent prints and took digital photographs that were sent to requesting agencies for identification. The firearms unit performed function testing of firearms, firearms identification, and distance determinations, and it managed the IBIS database of unknown bullets and cartridge casings.

I spent three to six months in each unit doing participant observation three days a week. I observed every analyst in each unit, many for multiple days, as well as every supervisor, as they all went about their regular duties in the lab. As someone who describes work practices in detail, my preference in the field is to take a crack at doing the work myself, both in order to understand it better and to be (somewhat) useful to my informants. I could not do this at MCCL due to concerns about maintaining the sanctity of the chain of custody of the evidence. Although I had access to most areas of the lab except the evidence lockers, I was not allowed to handle any of the case evidence, which kept any useful participation to a minimum. However, in several of the units I had opportunities to practice some forms of analysis. In the forensic biology unit the criminalists were eager to teach me how to develop a DNA profile, and, given that I could not touch case evidence, I ran my own buccal (cheek) swab through the entire profiling sequence. They were proud that I turned out to be a very precise pipetter, although it took me a lot longer to finish a plate than anyone in the unit. In the comparative evidence unit, a fingerprint examiner taught me how to process my own indented writing, and I test-fired guns with the firearms examiners both in the lab and at the sheriff's range. During the course of my regular visits to the laboratory, I also attended unit, supervisor, and all-staff meetings, as well as eight training sessions given by lab members to agency populations, defense attorneys, and the district attorney's office.

After the fieldwork at MCCL, I visited a county crime laboratory in an eastern state, where I interviewed the deputy director and spent a day observing the work of the forensic biology, comparative evidence, and controlled substances units. My time in this lab reassured me that while all crime laboratories have differences, their work is similar. Finally, to understand work sociologically, I think it helps to understand both the institutions within which occupational members are embedded, and their daily life in organizations.[2] I therefore attended professional meetings: in addition to the one that introduced me to the field of forensic science, I also went to a three-day statewide criminalists' meeting, and a one-day local criminalists' continuing education meeting.

I am using pseudonyms for MCCL and my informants, and, additionally, I have disguised some details about particular criminalists. People open their work lives to me, allowing me to follow them around all day long and pester them with questions. I have always provided confidentiality to my informants so that they feel comfortable sharing their work and their views; in return I feel an obligation not to put their jobs or relationships in jeopardy because of something I inadvertently reveal in my analysis. In the case of forensic scientists, I felt it was particularly important to try to protect their identity. During my fieldwork, I did not observe anything about which I felt ethically uncomfortable. However, it is clear that attorneys can create problems for criminalists in court even out of perfectly normal laboratory behavior.

EXPECTATIONS (AND FIELDWORK) DISRUPTED

While in the field, the things that surprise you and run counter to expectations provide fodder for developing an understanding of the social scene. As I entered the world of forensic science, my encounter with the everyday reality of a crime laboratory proved, not so surprisingly, that you can't believe everything you see on TV. Criminalists at MCCL scoffed at the *CSI* TV franchise (and others), noting that in their laboratories you don't find beautiful, well-coiffed people quickly whipping up unaccountably precise results from rare, strange bits of evidence. I had enough prior experience to realize that painstaking, time-consuming bench work is de rigeur for any type of laboratory science. However, the documentation requirements and the fraught relationship with the world of criminal justice came as more of a surprise.

At MCCL, my expectations of what the work would be were initially influenced by the talk I overheard in the laboratories and hallways. Criminalists complained anxiously about court appearances from the moment I arrived. Given this, I assumed that I would be attending court with criminalists all the time. In my second week, I started handing out my card and asking people to call me if they were going to be heading to court to testify. Nobody ever called. It soon became clear, as chapter 5 describes, that while criminalists constantly complain, worry, and tell stories about testifying, they rarely go to court. In the course of a year and a half, I observed two DNA analysts, a firearms examiner, and a toxicologist testify (the last in an adjudicated session at a high school rather than in court). Also, I attended a day of courtroom testimony training at a statewide criminalists meeting, as well as mock court inside the laboratory.

This disparity in the amount of time spent worrying about court versus actually testifying was indicative of the way that expectations of criminal justice shaped the process of creating evidence, through what I eventually conceptualized as a culture of anticipation in the laboratory. Given how strongly criminalists felt about testifying, it seemed important for me to get a deeper understanding of what happened to criminalists in court. Since I could not do so through observation, I turned to interviews to access some of their experiences. Near the end of the fieldwork, I interviewed over thirty criminalists, including a subset of members of each unit, as well as every supervisor and the director and deputy director of the lab. These semistructured interviews began with career histories, lasted about an hour on average, and were recorded and transcribed. In these interviews, I asked criminalists to take me through good, negative, average, and/or memorable experiences of testifying in court. This enriched my data collection by including additional narratives of testifying, which clarified criminalists' meaning-making around their court appearances. In addition, I used this time to probe criminalists' feelings about the National Academy of Sciences report and how they felt it had changed laboratory practices, as well as encouraging them to tell me about other scientific changes in their particular discipline.

About a year into my fieldwork, while I was observing in the firearms unit, there was a personnel shakeup at the lab. I had been hesitant about my entrée into firearms, because while I was studying other units in the lab, when criminalists asked me what I'd seen so far, they always concluded the conversation in whispers, with eyebrows raised: "Oh, but have you been to the firearms lab yet?" And, on my first day in firearms, I was warned, "These guys don't want you in here. They don't understand why you need to watch them doing casework." However, by the time of this shakeup I had been observing in firearms for over a month. Each of the examiners had tutored me at the shooting range. Al had started advising me about possible gun purchases. While listening to Nine Inch Nails and Ministry in the lab, Tom and Adam and I had reminisced about the mosh pits of our youth. I felt as though I was settling in and that they were less resistant to my being there.

Then the lab director announced in a monthly all-staff meeting that he would be moving people to different units to cover some case backlogs. Tom got word that they were moving him into the narcotics unit, and the firearms guys were ready for battle. While Tom's case completion numbers were low in the prior year, he had not gotten a negative performance review. Rather than as a reflection on his performance, the group interpreted the move as a way for the lab director, "who thinks we are a rogue group," to "show us he has power over us." They all talked about the role that Tom was hired for—could the director switch him to another unit when he was hired as a firearms examiner? They believed that although their supervisor was not in favor of the move, there was "not much she could do." Tom decided to have a conversation with the union representative to see if they would help him fight the move.

The union said they could not. In the firearms lab, I became a visible reminder of the perfidious managers of the laboratory, and my position as an observer was suddenly precarious. The next morning I went to the firearms unit, and Tom said he was too busy wrapping up his cases for the impending move, so he couldn't take the time for me to observe. Al was nowhere to be found. When I asked Adam if I could spend the day with him, he stared me down and replied, "Nothing personal, but I don't want you watching me do my work. You've already seen what we do here. . . . Why don't you go hover over Holly and see how the supervisors are handling this? Or the lab director?"

It is a terrible feeling to be ejected from a field site, even partially. At past field sites, I had encountered people's reluctance to be observed, but this was outright hostility. The supervisor encouraged me to continue to observe the unit, but I suggested it might be better to wait and see how the firearms examiners felt after I spent a while with the toxicologists. In the end, I did not return to the firearms unit. However, being kicked out was invaluable in highlighting the vulnerability felt by the firearms examiners; they were not in a position to challenge the lab director's decision and would be in a worse position to get their casework done given Tom's transfer. Their group was being torn apart, while the DNA unit had enough resources and criminalists to clear their entire backlog of cases. Given this situation, I was the person on whom they could take out their frustration, regardless of any mutual love of eighties industrial music.

Ironically, firearms examiners in forensic science are close kin to ethnographers in business schools. The values they hold resonate with my ethnographic sensibilities: subjectivity, holism, and a conviction that numbers are not the best way to reflect the world. I too am resentful when colleagues who manipulate numbers suggest that it would be better to "test" my findings in some way. Or when they say, "Can you provide empirical data to support that?" The parallels resonated for me repeatedly as I thought about the work of forensic scientists. I cannot (and would not) count the number of times I have insisted to students and junior colleagues, "You do not need to make your work look more objective by providing the number of hours you have been in the field, or the number of pages in your field notes, or a falsely representative set of first, second, and third order codes in a table." The multiple ways of representing truth in the field of management are not all equally valued, just as is the case in forensic science. My empathy for criminalists' position is echoed in the concerns of this book.

ACKNOWLEDGMENTS

This is my first book, so I have a lot of acknowledging to do. While I take sole responsibility for the final product, I truly appreciate everyone who has helped me develop it. First, the project owes its life to the director of the Metropolitan County Crime Laboratory, who took the risk of opening his organization to an ethnographer. And, although I cannot thank them by name, I am very grateful to all of the criminalists at MCCL for their enthusiasm (and forbearance) in teaching me about their work.

My time in graduate school at Stanford University has cast a long shadow over my intellectual life. Much of what I believe about the world of work and organizations I learned while working with Steve Barley. Bob Sutton rescued me when I was a flailing first-year student and reminded me to always pay attention in the field to what people complain about. Julian Orr taught me that everybody's work has value, and also that an espresso and a chat in the afternoon are very conducive to thinking.

My colleagues from the Industrial Engineering Department have remained my academic compatriots and close friends. Kim Elsbach's mentorship shepherded me through my junior faculty years and the Qualitative Conference she founded is a source of wonderful community. Mark Zbaracki is the most thoughtful person I know, and he allows me to be cranky when he blows up everything I think I am writing about. My first phone call for help and advice is always to Gerardo Okhuysen; most recently he offered me an academic home at the University of California, Irvine during the summer of the first draft. Andy Hargadon and his family gave me a literal home through many years of teaching at the University of California, Davis. During fieldwork overnights, Jeannie Kahwajy and I shared dinner, wine, and fascinating conversations. And Siobhan O'Mahony, my academic sibling across multiple institutions, is really more like an actual sibling at this point.

My California writing group has been an opportunity to gather with some of these friends annually for a sanity-saving retreat: Mark, Gerardo, Siobhan, Melissa Mazmanian, Christine Beckman, and Michel Anteby have read iterations of parts of the book from Asilomar to Nantucket and back. One writing group is not enough, so I also depend on monthly meetings with my virtual book group of Nahoko Kameo and Tim Hallett. Daisy Chung, Angèle Christin, and Natalya Vinokurova have also waded through more than one chapter on my behalf. I am grateful to Nancy Rothbard for being a sounding board, especially when I was down to the wire on the copy editing. And I thank Simon Cole for sharing his knowledge of (the sociology of) forensic science throughout the project.

The UC Davis Graduate School of Management is the least political (and thus most comfortable) department in which I have ever worked, and my colleagues there were a great source of support for this project, as well as many others. My work life has been tremendously enriched by my friendships with Greta Hsu and Gina Dokko. Rodney Lacey's famous popcorn kept me going on many an evening. Mario Biagioli organized a fabulous forensic science workshop at his Center for Science and Innovation Studies, which kickstarted much of my thinking about the project.

My colleagues in New York have helped make New York University a generative environment for me. Our Qualitative Interpretive Ladies who Lunch (QUILL) group—Maria Binz-Scharf, Natalia Levina, Hila Lifshitz-Assaf, and Anne-Laure Fayard—had regular working lunches that expanded to become the Qualitative Paper Workshop. We have grown into a community of qualitative organizations scholars from multiple departments and schools who support each other's work (and eat a lot of Taim). I am lucky to have colleagues like Anne-Laure, who is always willing to take a look at anything on short notice, and Callen Anthony, who joined me on several productive impromptu writing weekends. On my walks with Danielle Warren, we rarely discuss the book, but we talk about everything else. My graduate and postgraduate students are a source of inspiration: Esther Leibel, Jennifer Nelson, Kevin Lee, Tina Wu, Sonya Pyo, Tamar Gross, and Sarah Lebovitz. My colleagues in the management department have provided helpful feedback at several brown bags. Iddo Tavory and Paul DiMaggio keep me connected to sociology.

I had a sabbatical right after the fieldwork that offered a great opportunity to think about the project (and travel). Thank you to Steve Barley and Stanford's Center for Work, Technology and Organization; Anca Metiu at ESSEC; David Stark and the Center on Organizational Innovation at Columbia University's Department of Sociology; and Anne-Laure Fayard at NYU Tandon School of Engineering for generously hosting me during that year.

This book would not exist if it were not for several amazing editors. Meagan Levinson and her team at Princeton University Press have been great. Margo Beth Fleming pushed me to figure out what I wanted to say, kept reminding me that I wanted to say it, and greatly improved the proposal. Ben Platt jumped in to help transform my organization theorist's prose into something readable, and his enthusiasm for the book kept me going on the occasions when I felt I was writing into a void.

Finally, thanks and love to my family. My parents and grandparents always made me feel I could do no wrong. This turns out to be an excellent defense mechanism against academic criticism and rejection. My sisters always make me laugh—yet another good defense mechanism. My aunt Ronni encourages me to let go a little and spend more time on the beach. Scott listened to about a million early versions of what the book might be and guided me to the one that worked best for me. And Vaughan, who has lived his entire life with my book in the background, has been very patiently waiting for me to finish writing. I will happily give my weekends back to him now.

NOTES

PREFACE

1. Unless otherwise noted, the names of all of the forensic scientists in the book are pseudonyms.

2. Forrest, 2018; Pegues, 2018.

3. Watkins, 2019.

4. Jacobs, 2013; Smith, 2014.

5. Smith, 2013.

6. Trager, 2017.

7. Smith, 2012.

8. Schuppe, 2017.

9. Lichtblau, 2006.

10. Starr, 2016: 1135.

11. Both the Mayfield and the Knox cases featured not only cross-national disagreements over interpretations of forensic evidence, but also contentious legal debates about overzealous prosecution (Kington 2011; Fields, 2011; Lichtblau, 2006).

INTRODUCTION. WELCOME TO THE CRIME LAB

1. National Research Council, 2009.

2. Susskind and Susskind, 2016.

3. Hess and Ludwig, 2017; Frank, Roehring, and Pring, 2017; McAfee and Brynjolfsson, 2017; Davenport and Kirby, 2016; Frey and Osborne, 2016; Susskind and Susskind, 2015; Brynjolfsson and McAfee, 2012.

4. Frey and Osborne (2016), for example, use the Bureau of Labor Statistics O*Net classification of occupations to calculate which tasks within each occupation are likely to be taken over by new digital technologies.

5. Lave and Wenger (1991) demonstrate how expertise develops in multiple occupational communities through a process that they call "legitimate peripheral participation." For rich descriptions of such apprenticeships, see Becker et al. (1961) on doctors, Bucciarelli (1994) on engineers, and Schon (1983) on architects.

6. For the learning-by-doing processes of biologists, see Keller (1984) and Myers (2008). Barley and Bechky (1994) describe this process of learning for laboratory technicians, and Orr (1996) depicts the hands-on learning of copier technicians.

7. Abbott (1988) argues that diagnosis, the process of figuring out how to solve the problems faced by others, is not only a vital characteristic of experts, but is also an important means for professionals to gain and maintain jurisdiction over a set of tasks.

8. Latour, 1987; Fujimura, 1988.

9. Henderson (1991) demonstrates how engineers organize, mobilize resources, and get political support for their designs through the use of drawings and prototypes. Bechky (2003a) shows that engineers can more effectively communicate with assemblers through concrete machines rather than abstract drawings; drawings, on the other hand, were more effective as a tool to consolidate their legitimacy in the organization (Bechky 2003b).

10. Heath and Luff, 1998.

11. For instance, Wynne (1996) shows how the participation of nuclear experts and sheep farmers in the post-Chernobyl controversy were rooted in different perceptions of uncertainty and control that came from their experiences in different social worlds. Bechky (2003a, b) demonstrates the underlying differences in the worlds of engineers, technicians, and assemblers, even working within the same organization.

12. Davenport and Landler (2019) document the Trump administration's changes to the methodologies underlying the National Climate Assessment, such as shortening the timelines of the impact measures so that climate change appears less of a problem.

13. Science studies scholars have been investigating the relationships between science and the public sphere since the postwar period. In a recent paper on climate science in the Indian national context, Mahony (2014) describes the coproduction of national and territorial politics and scientific knowledge about the Himalayan glaciers. For a concentrated dose of science studies scholars' perspectives, see the symposium in *Social Studies of Science* (Jasanoff, 2003; Rip, 2003; Wynne, 2003) responding to Collins and Evans's (2002) call for a third wave of science studies that focuses on the role of expertise and experience in public scientific debate.

CHAPTER 1. FORENSIC SCIENTISTS AT THE LAB BENCH: TAMING, QUESTIONING, AND FRAMING THE EVIDENCE

1. Scholars distinguish between the work of basic science and that of applied science. Moreover, lab workers without PhDs are not considered scientists; they are called technicians (Shapin 1989). One of the things that surprised me as I talked about this research is the number of academics who objected to me calling the criminalists "scientists." It does seem to me, however, that a bachelor's degree education in a science invests its graduates with a scientific identity and a distinct understanding of science.

2. Latour and Woolgar, 1979; Barley and Bechky, 1994.

3. Merton's (1973 [1942]) norms of science—especially notions of distinterestedness and organized skepticism—cropped up often in our conversations about what forensic scientists did, especially in my first days in each unit when analysts were describing their findings.

4. At some other laboratories in the United States, forensic biology units have a hierarchy and a division of labor that includes analysts labeled "technicians" who perform screening and/or analysis, while senior analysts interpret and report the results of DNA profiling.

5. As Latour and Woolgar (1979: 32) note, the work of scientists is to construct order out of the chaos of multiple perceptions of the world. Taming the evidence is the first step on the path to constructing this order in forensic science labs.

6. Barley and Bechky (1994) describe the sources of error in science laboratories in terms of types of mistakes, malfunctions, and engimas, and the ways in which technicians avert trouble through routines of documentation, redundancies, habitual cleanliness, and vigilance. These routines were also typical at MCCL.

7. These are standard bench practices undertaken to avert or find sources of errors, as Barley and Bechky (1994) describe. See also Lynch, 1985.

8. Jordan and Lynch (1998) describe how biologists neaten their work through a similar interpretation and representation process.

9. A "best-known nonmatch" is described in the theory of firearms identification as the *best agreement demonstrated between toolmarks known to have been produced by different tools* (Biasotti and Murdock 1984; Miller and Mclean 1998). It is based on an examination of the striations of two bullets or casings that have been fired from a gun from the same manufacturer, but not the same gun. Typically they will fire bullets from sequentially manufactured guns from the same manufacturer—in other words, the barrels have been made and the guns assembled at almost exactly the same point in time. In order to make an identification, examiners look at striations made by multiple parts of the gun (e.g., firing pin, barrel), and expect more striations to match than in a best-known nonmatch with which they are familiar.

10. Goddard, 1980.

11. In the chemistry unit, the bulk of the casework is narcotics analysis. However, members of the unit also perform trace evidence analysis on a small number of cases annually (less than one hundred total). Two of the criminalists are proficient in GSR (gunshot residue) analysis, in which they receive evidence from the hands of suspects who were thought to have fired a gun. These are analyzed using an scanning electron microscope. One analyst performs fire debris analysis. A few analysts are in training to do casework on additional forms of trace evidence: dye packs, hair, and glass.

12. Following Keller's (1983) description of geneticist Barbara McClintock's "feeling for the organism," science studies scholars have demonstrated how scientists use their senses to develop a "feel" for their materials. For instance, Myers (2008) shows the importance of the embodied, visual, and spatial feel that molecular biologists have for their computer models of molecules. Forensic scientists develop this same kind of sensory feel for the evidence.

13. The narcotics analysts use several other techniques for particular controlled substances. To identify cocaine base, they employ infrared spectroscopy; for marijuana, a microscopic exam is performed after the color test.

14. Some people have acetone in their blood or urine from underlying physical causes such as diabetes or hypoglycemia. Acetone can be falsely identified as alcohol, so the instrument must be able to distinguish between them.

15. Less frequently, toxicologists screen and confirm using methods and samples that are more complicated. For instance, some controlled substances cannot be screened in the EIA directly, such as GBH, and require elution to separate out the substance. At MCCL, toxicologists also are responsible for testing coroner's samples, which are usually messier (because they

are taken postmortem). These are analyzed in a LC-MS/MS (liquid chromatography with tandem mass spectrometry) instrument, which can detect and identify up to 170 different drugs.

CHAPTER 2. THE SOCIAL WORLDS OF FORENSIC SCIENCE: SCIENCE, CRIMINAL JUSTICE, AND THE PUBLIC SPHERE

1. I will use the term "social worlds" throughout to refer to the different social realms in which criminalists participate as a part of their work. Sociologists have used the concept of social worlds to describe the realms of activity in which people participate together, share resources and commitments, and engage in collective action (Strauss, 1978; Clarke, 1991; Fujimura, 1988). In organizational theory, it is more common to see such realms conceptualized as an organizational field, a set of organizations sharing a common meaning system that interact frequently and fatefully with one another more often than with other organizations (DiMaggio and Powell 1983; Scott 1995). Because I am interested in the interactions of *individuals*, which happen within and across organizations and institutions, I think "social worlds" is the more fitting concept.

2. Scholars long ago debunked the image of the lone genius scientist or inventor. Science is a communal activity that entails building on the work of others. This has been demonstrated both at the level of the scientific field (Kuhn 1962) in terms of working within an "invisible college" to develop scientific ideas (De Solla Price 1963), and also in the day-to-day practices of working together at the bench (Barley and Bechky, 1994; Shapin, 1989; Latour, 1987; Latour and Woolgar, 1979).

3. Mergel, Lazer, and Binz-Scharf (2008) demonstrate the importance of forensic scientists' social network ties for their learning.

4. Merton, 1973 [1942].

5. Latour and Woolgar 1979; Barley and Bechky 1994. Of course, as science studies scholars have shown, the practices and the espoused norms of science differ.

6. I later learned that I could also refer to criminalists with the informal designation analyst (for narcotics and DNA analysts) or examiner (for the firearms and fingerprint units).

7. Barley (1996) would characterize forensic scientists as "buffer" technicians, translating the empirical world into representations used by another occupation (see also Barley and Bechky 1994). However, many of the buffer technicians in science and medicine studied by Barley and colleagues (Scarselletta, 1997; Barley and Bechky 1994; Nelsen and Barley 1997) reported to PhD or MD professionals, and were not interested in professionalizing (Barley, Bechky, and Nelsen 2016). Forensic scientists are actively involved in professional activities and are supervised by other criminalists, unlike other buffer technicians.

8. As Barley and Bechky (1994) describe, in university laboratories supervisors often remarked on the expertise of the technicians, although their skills were not formally acknowledged or rewarded by their organizations.

9. Jasanoff (2005) notes that while some see the adversarial character of the law as antithetical to the truth-seeking of science, careful comparisons find some congruence in the two activities.

10. Deutsch, 2014.

11. Peters, 2009.

12. Peters, 2009.

13. Giddens (1990) argues that science, as an expert system, retains an attitude of respect from the public for its technical expertise, but that laypeople are also inherently skeptical when considering that expertise. Public trust in the authority of science is a subject of some investigation among science studies scholars, and arguments and forms of measurement vary. Recently, Gauchat (2012) examined survey data that showed that the public's confidence in science remains favorable, except among particular subsets of the population such as highly educated conservatives.

14. National Research Council, 2009.

15. National Research Council, 2009.

16. National Research Council, 2009: 7.

17. Moore, 2009.

18. Flatow, 2009.

19. As Cole and Dioso-Villa (2007) point out, media reports of the *CSI* effect far outstrip any evidence of an actual effect. Surveys and jury-simulation studies have not found evidence of different expectations between *CSI*-watchers and nonwatchers, and some scholars suspect that it is the actual advance in forensic investigative techniques that have raised expectations. See also Podlas, 2006; and Shelton, Kim, and Barak, 2006.

CHAPTER 3. A CULTURE OF ANTICIPATION: THE CONSEQUENCES OF CONFLICTING EXPECTATIONS

1. Latour's *Science in Action* (1987) is the classic discussion of how scientists use representations to appeal to others' interests and enroll them in their discoveries and projects.

2. Gieryn (1983) describes the rhetorical boundary work that scientists do to demarcate themselves from others in order to advance their authority, deny resources to pseudoscientists, and protect the autonomy of their work. Practical work can also enable autonomy for experts, as Huising (2015) shows in the case of university health and safety scientists, whose participation in low-status tasks in laboratories convinced other scientists to let them maintain control over their work.

3. Barley, 2015.

4. I use the label "captive occupation" to describe criminalists because the occupation is structurally embedded in the world of another: their work is dependent on the criminal justice world and their output is destined for the sole use of a higher-status and unlike occupation (attorneys). In contrast to other occupations that are subordinate to groups with higher-status task jurisdictions (Abbott 1988), such as nurses and doctors, forensic science does not exist outside of the domain of criminal justice. Being captive also differentiates criminalists from other technician occupations with comparable education levels. For instance, laboratory technicians working in industry, academia, and hospitals have bachelor's or master's degrees in science, as do criminalists, but their work is primarily evaluated by people with scientific backgrounds who share their social world (Barley and Bechky 1994; Barley 1996; Barley, Bechky, and

Nelsen 2016). Another interesting contrast is with medical examiners, who work within similar social worlds as criminalists but are not part of a captive occupation. As Timmermans (2006) shows, medical examiners are not subordinate to these other worlds in the way that criminalists are: as medical doctors, their high status shapes their work. Medical examiners have legal authority to made death determinations, and they interact frequently with other doctors on cases, whom they consider equals and allies.

5. Timmermans (2006: 114) describes similar practices among medical examiners, who "mentally rehearsed their defense of a suicide determination in court before filling in the death certificate."

6. Melendez-Diaz v. Massachusetts (2009) ruled that blanket narcotics report certificates (that simply named the controlled substance found and its reported weight) violated defendants' Sixth Amendment rights.

7. Testifying was also a rare occurrence for criminalists, as I detail in chapter 5. Given that criminalists rarely testified and that attorneys only occasionally held a pretrial meeting with them, I did not have much opportunity to observe these infrequent interactions.

8. A reference sample is one that is taken directly from the individual. The sample typically comes from a buccal (cheek) swab if the person is available to swab, and sometimes it comes from other biological materials such as blood or tissue.

9. Although this was the only time I heard about anyone being pressured to change their reports at the MCCL, pressures from the district attorney or other members of law enforcement are reported to be a problem in crime laboratories. This concern is raised not only in the popular press (i.e., J. Smith, 2014; T. Smith, 2012; Giannelli, 2010; Mills and Possley 2001), but also in academic commentary (S. Thompson, 2015) and the NAS report (2009). The NAS Report (2009: 24–25) states, "The best science is conducted in a scientific setting as opposed to a law enforcement setting. Because forensic scientists often are driven in their work by a need to answer a particular question related to the issues of a particular case, they sometimes face pressure to sacrifice appropriate methodology for the sake of expediency."

CHAPTER 4. CREATING A CULTURE OF ANTICIPATION IN THE CRIME LABORATORY

1. As Schwartz (1974) argues, waiting is an indicator of status. Control of time is an essential property of power, and the distribution of waiting time coincides with the distribution of power.

2. Schwartz (1974: 853) suggests that in public service provision, organizations such as courts routinely "overschedule" to ensure the highest status person in the system—the judge—is not forced to wait at all.

3. The discussions I saw among criminalists resembled Orr's (1996) descriptions of copier technicians sharing "war stories" when they get together and talk about machine problems. Like the copier techs, these stories allow criminalists to support one another, better understand the problems that are likely to arise, and share ideas for solutions that might work in the future.

4. I did not have access to Peter's report, so I cannot evaluate what he wrote.

CHAPTER 5. THE SPECTER OF TESTIFYING: FORENSIC SCIENTISTS AS THE VOICE OF THE EVIDENCE

1. Courtroom testimony provides what Giddens (1990) labels an access point into an expert system. As a place where laypeople encounter experts face to face, interactions at access points are a source of vulnerability to the system and can result in an increase in either trust or skepticism. Criminalists acutely feel the importance of these interactions.

2. As Kohler-Hausman (2018: 110) notes, given the volume of cases and lack of resources in courts, fewer cases are brought to trial as legal actors perceive other forms of social control to satisfy their goals.

3. As in other workspaces, these coworkers get to know each other by socializing, both inside and outside the courtroom (Van Cleve, 2017).

4. Van Cleve (2017) describes how dominance and power are routinely conveyed in Chicago criminal courts: professionals carrying case files can skip lines outside the building, armed officers inside the courtroom prevent nonprofessionals from stepping forward to ask questions, and judges berate defendants and their families.

5. Schuster and Frieden, 2006.

6. Alexander and Zauzmer, 2015.

7. As noted earlier, scientists accrue authority, resources, and autonomy through boundary work and their representational and rhetorical activities across social worlds (Gieryn, 1983). Scholars have also elaborated how knowledge is developed through boundary work within science (Fujimura, 1988), focusing on how social structures and interactions have epistemological consequences. In the organizational theory literature, analyses of boundary work also tend to focus on how situated practices enable the sharing of knowledge in organizations (Carlile, 2002; Bechky, 2003a). Here, rather than examining knowledge development through boundary work, I will be examining the emotional consequences that boundary work creates for criminalists, and how they manage it in practice.

8. Here I use the term "truth" as my informants use it: they view the scientific results that emerge from their analyses as truth (within a margin of error).

9. In addition to what we know about the role of communities in structuring science work (DeSolla Price 1963; Latour 1987), scholars of occupations also suggest that communities are a strong force for developing common understandings and common values (Van Maanen and Barley, 1984). By participating in these communities of practice, members "acquire a particular community's subjective viewpoint" (Brown and Duguid, 1991: 45), developing shared perspectives about the substantive work, or what Schon (1983: 271) calls "the art of the practice."

10. While many people in the field of forensic science agree with this recommendation, nobody that I encountered—academics, government officials, laboratory directors, criminalists—believed it to be a realistic possibility. Not only would it be costly; it would mean creating a new federal agency to oversee crime laboratories, which would require tremendous political will. Indeed, the commission formed by President Obama to consider the implementation of these recommendations was disbanded by Jeff Sessions at the start of the Trump administration (Hsu, 2017).

CHAPTER 6. DNA ENVY: RESPONDING TO SHIFTING SCIENTIFIC AND LEGAL STANDARDS

1. National Research Council, 1992, 1996.

2. Lynch, Cole, McNally and Jordan, 2008.

3. For example, Toobin, 2007; Saks and Koehler, 2005.

4. National Research Council, 2009: 1–2.

5. Saks and Koehler, 2005: 895.

6. National Research Council, 2009: 133.

7. For example, Stern 2014; Edwards and Mnookin, 2016.

8. American Society of Crime Laboratory Directors, 2009: 3.

9. Lynch, Cole, McNally, and Jordan (2008) detail across multiple chapters of their book the ways in which DNA profiling was attacked in court with respect to its techniques meeting established scientific standards, the likelihood of laboratory error, the administrative chain of custody, and the problem of statistical techniques of probabilistic estimation.

10. The concerns about technique, care, and accuracy in DNA profiling were taken up by governmental bodies of science in the United States in two NAS reports; prominent scientists were also embroiled in the controversy in the science press (Lander and Budowle, 1994; Hartl, 1994; Lewontin, 1994). The ways in which these controversies were overcome, as Lynch et al. (2008) thoroughly document, rested on the social construction of these technical concerns. However, when the dust cleared, DNA profiling had emerged as an unassailable form of evidence, and, as Lynch et al. (2008: 255) note, "the acceptance of such evidence has become so strong, it has become a basis for doubting all other forms of criminal evidence." In their analysis of DNA profiling and opposition to the death penalty, Aronson and Cole (2009) further argue that the certainty accorded to DNA evidence in public discourse makes it possible to challenge the law's truth-making authority and its use in this way has strengthened the "myth" of science as a producer of epistemic certainty.

11. Latour and Woolgar,1979; Lynch, 1988, Lynch and Woolgar, 1990; Coopmans, Vertesi, Lynch, and Woolgar, 2014.

12. As Lynch (1988: 218) notes, scientists "work methodically to expose, work with and perfect the specimen's surface appearances to be congruent with graphic representation and mathematic analysis." This scientific translation role is often fulfilled by laboratory technicians and other non-PhD holding scientists (Barley and Bechky, 1994; Shapin, 1989).

13. Latour and Woolgar, 1979; Latour, 1987; Fujimura, 1988; Gieryn, 1983.

14. Jasanoff, 1998; Goodwin, 1994. Goodwin (1994) shows how the use of coding schemes, material representations, and discursive frameworks in courtroom testimony transformed the vicious beating of Rodney King into a series of rational escalations and deescalations of force in response to an aggressor.

15. Murphy's (2015) analysis of DNA evidence unpacks many of these issues with DNA profiling.

16. For examples of the complex messiness of science, see Latour and Woolgar (1979); Collins (1985); and Traweek (1992).

17. Galison (1999) calls the intertwining of the characteristics of epistemology, technique and morals the "comportment" of scientists. In his analysis, he argues that comportment varies

depending on historical circumstances. Here, I describe the techniques, values, and ways of knowing of forensic scientists to demonstrate how they responded in varying ways to comparisons to DNA profiling.

18. National Research Council, 2008: 3.

19. National Research Council, 2009: 42.

20. See, for instance, Moore, 2009; Felch and Dolan, 2009; and Fountain, 2009.

21. Fountain, 2009.

22. During the pretrial phase, the Daubert standard is used by a trial judge to make a preliminary assessment of whether an expert's scientific testimony is based on reasoning or methodology that is scientifically valid and can properly be applied to the facts at issue. Under this standard, the factors that may be considered in determining whether the methodology is valid are: (1) whether the theory or technique in question can be and has been tested; (2) whether it has been subjected to peer review and publication; (3) its known or potential error rate; (4) the existence and maintenance of standards controlling its operation; and (5) whether it has attracted widespread acceptance within a relevant scientific community (Legal Information Institute, 2017).

23. It is impossible to know for sure whether challenges to firearms examination increased after the report, because in the United States we lack any systematic databases of court transcripts. However, scholars of law and science who have studied decisions since the NAS report note that courts have not found the report's arguments particularly persuasive and have not denied admissibility to firearms, fingerprint, or other comparative evidence, although two or three appellate decisions have put limits on the degree of certainty that examiners could state about their conclusions (Cooper, 2013; Epstein, 2014; Cole and Edmond, 2015).

24. AFTE Committee for the Advancement of the Science of Firearm and Tool Mark Identification (2009: 207).

25. AFTE Committee for the Advancement of the Science of Firearm and Tool Mark Identification (2009).

26. Lynch et al. (2008) mention a similar response to the initial scientific criticisms of DNA profiling. Scientific practices are transferred tacitly through experience and often cannot be duplicated in protocols (see also Barley and Bechky, 1994; Jordan and Lynch, 1998; Latour and Woolgar, 1979), and therefore practitioners of specific techniques resent nonpractitioners, even other PhD scientists, criticizing technique without experiencing practice.

27. Historians of science Lorraine Daston and Peter Galison have traced the history of scientific objectivity through an examination of scientific atlases; when objectivity arose as an epistemic virtue, it was considered "to be knowledge that bears no trace of the knower—knowledge unmarked by prejudice or skill, fantasy or judgment, wishing or striving" (2007: 17). Galison (1999) notes shifts over time, from depictions of genius prior to the industrial revolution, to machine objectivity during the factory era, in which mechanical output was the source of judgment, and, later, to judgmental objectivity that relies on the conditioned judgments of a trained expert. The firearms examiners, with their holistic values and intensive training to see striae, resemble these latter scientists with their "practiced eye" and "art of judgment."

28. A "best-known nonmatch" is described in the theory of firearms identification as the best agreement demonstrated between toolmarks known to have been produced by different tools. It is based on an examination (or a count in the case of CMS) of the striations of two bullets or

casings that have been fired from a gun from the same manufacturer, but not the same gun (Biasotti and Murdock, 1984; Miller and McLean, 1998).

29. National Research Council, 2009: 106.

30. Specifically, the NAS report stated that "all results for every forensic science method should indicate the uncertainty in the measurements that are made, and studies must be conducted that enable the estimation of those values" (National Research Council, 2009: 184). It called for complete and thorough laboratory reports that "describe, at a minimum, methods and materials, procedures, results, and conclusions, and they should identify, as appropriate, the sources of uncertainty in the procedures and conclusions along with estimates of their scale (to indicate the level of confidence in the results)" (National Research Council, 2009: 186).

31. Daston and Galison, 2007.

32. This is particularly relevant given the Supreme Court case Melendez-Diaz v. Massachusetts (2009), which ruled that blanket report certificates without descriptions (used in a different US state) violated defendants' Sixth Amendment rights. In the Massachusetts case, there were no descriptions or images of the controlled substances in these certificates. Narcotics analysts, as well as attorneys in MCCL's jurisdiction, viewed this as an important distinction in their practices.

33. Daston and Galison, 2007.

34. I was unable to see some forms of microcrystals in the lab because I couldn't get my eyes onto the scope before they overcrowded the slide.

35. Smith, 1994.

36. Van Derbeken, 2010.

37. Daston and Galison, 2007. See also Porter, 1996.

38. As Kruse (2016) describes, Swedish forensic scientists, recognizing these differences, "calibrate" their interpretations across fields by discussing the levels of certainty in meetings with criminalists from other units.

39. Daston, 1992; Daston and Galison, 2007; Porter, 1996.

40. Lynch et al. (2008: 245–46}), in their analysis of the legitimation of DNA profiling, make a similar argument about the prevailing preference for mechanical judgment. Espeland and Stevens (2008: 432–33) make the case more broadly about quantification, arguing that it is widespread in society: "So much opportunity and status, and so much power, is now mediated through mechanical objectivity in administration, management, education and finance, that we cannot understand the basic terms of justice if we do not understand quantification."

41. Cole (2001) traces the history of fingerprint identification technologies and their use in law.

42. Burney (2013) describes forensic scientists' fleeting fascination with collecting and analyzing the dust at crime scenes.

43. Building on Hallett and colleagues' work (Hallett, 2010; Hallett and Ventresca, 2006) on inhabited institutions, Leibel, Hallett and Bechky (2018) suggest that it is these social interactions that drive field formation and change in institutional fields generally. For a fuller version of this argument with respect to DNA envy, see Bechky (2019).

CONCLUSION

1. Latour and Woolgar, 1979; Gieryn, 1999.

2. Samydurai, 2016.

3. Worland, 2019.

4. Gorman and Sandefur, 2011.

5. Abbott, 1988; Friedson, 1998, 2013.

6. Scott, Reuf, Mendel and Caronna, 2000; Leicht and Fennel 1997.

7. Rakoff, 219; National Research Council, 2009: 133; Giannelli, 1997; Koppl, 2005.

8. Rakoff, 2019.

9. Silverberg, 2012; Van Derbeken, 2010.

10. Freedman, 2019.

11. The general assessment of commentators suggests a lack of political will to make laboratories independent. Thompson (2015) describes the political motivations behind the resignation of the head of Washington, DC's independent crime laboratory. See also Mnookin et al. (2010). Moreover, in 2013, the Obama administration established the National Commission on Forensic Science to follow up on the NAS report. As a member of this commission noted (Rakoff, 2019), while some of its recommendations were adopted by the federal judiciary, many states ignored or resisted it. The commission was disbanded in the first year of the Trump administration (Hsu, 2017).

12. Barley and Bechky, 1994; Shapin, 1988.

13. Years of research on job satisfaction suggests that the intrinsic motivation that comes from doing a whole job well relates to satisfaction at work (Hackman and Oldham, 1976; Hertzberg, 1964).

14. Lave, 1988; Lave and Wenger, 1991; Orr, 1996. For an example of how skill in surgery suffers dramatically when novices cannot participate in such hands-on practice, see Beane (2019).

15. Mnookin et al., 2010.

16. Brynjolfsson and McAfee, 2014; McAfee and Brynjolfsson, 2017; Frank, Roehrig, and Pring, 2017; Hess and Ludwig, 2017.

17. Hess and Ludwig, 2017; Frank, Roehring, and Pring, 2017; McAfee and Brynjolfsson, 2017; Davenport and Kirby, 2016; Susskind and Susskind, 2015; Brynjolfsson and McAfee, 2012.

18. Abbott (1988) describes, for instance, how railroad occupations such as dispatchers died with the demise of the railroad; Zetka (2003) demonstrates how the gastric medical professions shifted in status as a result of the adoption of the endoscope.

19. Galperin, 2017.

20. Barley, 1986; Orlikowski, 1992.

21. Christin (2017) shows how judges ignored, criticized, and co-opted the algorithmic tools that their workplaces put in place.

22. Hyman, 2018.

23. Espeland, 1998; Porter, 1996.

24. Espeland and Stevens, 2008: 431–32. See also Espeland and Sauder (2007) and Strathern (2000).

25. For medicine, see Timmermans and Berg, 2003. See Christin (2018) on journalists' use of algorithms and metrics. Galperin (2017) describes the rationalization of accounting.

26. O'Neil, 2016; Starr, 2014.

27. Barocas and Selbst, 2016; Burrell, 2016; Harcourt, 2007.

28. Christin, 2017: 9.

29. Lave, 1988.

30. Strickland, 2019; Weissmann, 2018.

31. Strickland, 2019.

32. Lebovitz, Lifshitz-Assaf, and Levina, 2020.

APPENDIX: CASE NOTES ON AN ETHNOGRAPHY OF A CRIME LAB

1. Van Maanen, 1988.

2. Hughes (1994: 76) notes the importance of understanding the occupational field, describing the "study of whole settings in which particular occupations occur, with attention to the shifting boundaries between them and the kind of cooperation required for any of them to perform effectively; to the shifting boundaries between professions and the clienteles they serve; and finally, to the development of new definitions growing out of constant social interaction and change."

REFERENCES

Abbott, Andrew. 1988. *The System of Professions: An Essay on the Division of Expert Labor.* Chicago: University of Chicago Press.

AFTE Committee for the Advancement of the Science of Firearm and Tool Mark Identification. 2009. "The Response of the Association of Firearm and Tool Mark Examiners to the February 2009 National Academy of Science Report 'Strengthening Forensic Science in the United States: A Path Forward.' June 22, 2009." *AFTE Journal* 41 (3): 204–8.

Alexander, Keith L., and Julie Zauzmer. 2015. "Director of DC's Embattled DNA Lab Resigns after Suspension of Testing." *Washington Post*, April 30, 2015. https://www.washingtonpost.com/local/director-of-dcs-embattled-dna-lab-resigns-following-suspension-of-testing/2015/04/30/1c619320-ef80-11e4-8666-a1d756d0218e_story.html.

American Society of Crime Laboratory Directors. 2009. ASCLD's Comments on the Release of the NAS Report on Forensic Science. February 19, 2009. https://www.ascld.org/wp-content/uploads/2014/08/ASCLD-NAS-Comments-090219.pdf.

Aronson, Jay D., and Simon A. Cole. 2009. "Science and the Death Penalty: DNA, Innocence, and the Debate over Capital Punishment in the United States." *Law & Social Inquiry* 34 (3): 603–33.

Barley, Stephen R. 1986. "Technology as an Occasion for Structuring: Technically Induced Change in the Temporal Organization of Radiological Work." *Administrative Science Quarterly* 31:78–108.

———. 1996. "Technicians in the Workplace: Ethnographic Evidence for Bringing Work into Organizational Studies." *Administrative Science Quarterly* 41 (3): 404–41.

———, and Beth A. Bechky. 1994. "In the Backrooms of Science: The Work of Technicians in Science Labs." *Work and Occupations* 21 (1): 85–126.

———, Beth A. Bechky, and Bonalyn J. Nelsen. 2016. "What Do Technicians Mean When They Talk about Professionalism? An Ethnography of Speaking." In *The Structuring of Work in Organizations*, Research in the Sociology of Organizations, 47:125–60. Bingley, UK: Emerald Group.

Barley, William C. 2015. "Anticipatory Work: How the Need to Represent Knowledge across Boundaries Shapes Work Practices Within Them." *Organization Science* 26 (6): 1612–28.

Barocas, Solon, and Andrew D. Selbst. 2016. "Big Data's Disparate Impact Essay." *California Law Review*, 104:671–732.

Beane, Matthew. 2019. "Shadow Learning: Building Robotic Surgical Skill When Approved Means Fail." *Administrative Science Quarterly* 64 (1): 87–123.

Bechky, Beth A. 2003a. "Sharing Meaning Across Occupational Communities: The Transformation of Understanding on a Production Floor." *Organization Science* 14 (3): 312–30.

———. 2003b. "Object Lessons: Workplace Artifacts as Representations of Occupational Jurisdiction." *American Journal of Sociology*, 109:720–52.

———. 2019. "Evaluative Spillovers from Technological Change: The Effects of 'DNA Envy' on Occupational Practices in Forensic Science." *Administrative Science Quarterly*: https://journals.sagepub.com//10.1177/0001839219855329 (accessed June 2, 2020).

Becker, Howard S., Blanche Geer, Everett C. Hughes, and Anselm L. Strauss. 1961. *Boys in White*. Chicago: University of Chicago Press.

Biasotti, A. A., and J. Murdock. 1984. "Criteria for Identification or State of the Art of Firearm and Toolmark Identification." *AFTE Journal* 16 (4): 16–24.

Brown, John Seely, and Paul Duguid. 1991. "Organizational Learning and Communities-of-Practice: Toward a Unified View of Working, Learning, and Innovation." *Organization Science* 2 (1): 40–57.

Bucciarelli, Louis. 1994. *Designing Engineers*. Cambridge, MA: MIT Press.

Brynjolfsson, Erik, and Andrew McAfee. 2012. *Race Against the Machine: How the Digital Revolution Is Accelerating Innovation, Driving Productivity, and Irreversibly Transforming Employment and the Economy*. Research Brief, MIT Center for Digital Business, January 2012. http://digital.mit.edu/research/briefs/brynjolfsson_McAfee_Race_Against_the_Machine.pdf (accessed June 2, 2020).

———. 2014. *The Second Machine Age: Work, Progress, and Prosperity in a Time of Brilliant Technologies*. New York: W. W. Norton.

Burney, Ian. 2013. "Our Environment in Miniature: Dust and the Early Twentieth-Century Forensic Imagination." *Representations* 121 (1): 31–59.

Burrell, Jenna. 2016. "How the Machine 'Thinks': Understanding Opacity in Machine Learning Algorithms." *Big Data & Society* 3 (1): https://journals.sagepub.com/doi/10.1177/2053951715622512 (accessed June 2, 2020).

Carlile, Paul R. 2002. "A Pragmatic View of Knowledge and Boundaries: Boundary Objects in New Product Development." *Organization Science* 13 (4): 442–55.

Christin, Angèle. 2017. "Algorithms in Practice: Comparing Web Journalism and Criminal Justice." *Big Data & Society* 4 (2): 1–14.

———. 2018. "Counting Clicks: Quantification and Variation in Web Journalism in the United States and France." *American Journal of Sociology* 123 (5): 1382–415.

Clarke, Adele. 1991. "Social Worlds/Arenas Theory as Organizational Theory." In *Social Organization and Social Process: Essays in Honor of Anselm Strauss*, edited by Anselm Leonard Strauss and David R. Maines, 119–58. Seattle, WA: Transaction.

Cole, Simon A. 2001. *Suspect Identities: A History of Fingerprinting and Criminal Identification*. Cambridge, MA: Harvard University Press.

———, and Gary Edmond. 2015. "Science without Precedent: The Impact of the National Research Council Report on the Admissibility and Use of Forensic Science Evidence in the United States." *British Journal of American Legal Studies* 4:585–617.

———, and Rachel A. Dioso-Villa. 2007. "*CSI* and Its Effects: Media, Juries, and the Burden of Proof." *New England Law Review* 41:435–69.

Collins, Harry. 1985. *Changing Order*. Beverly Hills, CA: SAGE.

———, and Robert Evans. 2002. "The Third Wave of Science Studies: Studies of Expertise and Experience." *Social Studies of Science* 32 (2): 235–96.

Cooper, Sarah. 2013. "The Collision of Law and Science: American Court Responses to Developments in Forensic Science." *Pace Law Review* 33 (1): 234–301.

Coopmans, Cateline, Janet Vertesi, Michael E. Lynch, and Steve Woolgar. 2014. *Representation in Scientific Practice Revisited*. Cambridge, MA: MIT Press.

Daston, Lorraine. 1992. "Objectivity and the Escape from Perspective." *Social Studies of Science* 22 (4): 597–618.

———, and Peter Galison. 2007. *Objectivity*. New York: Zone Books.

Davenport, Coral, and Mark Landler. 2019. "Trump Administration Hardens Its Attack on Climate Science." *New York Times*, May 27, 2019. https://www.nytimes.com/2019/05/27/us/politics/trump-climate-science.html.

Davenport, Thomas H., and Julia Kirby. 2016. *Only Humans Need Apply: Winners and Losers in the Age of Smart Machines*. New York, NY: HarperBusiness.

De Solla Price, Derek J. 1963. *Little Science Big Science*. 1st ed. New York, NY: Columbia University Press.

Deutsch, Linda. 2014. "OJ Simpson Trial: 'If It Doesn't Fit, You Must Acquit.'" *NBC*, June 11, 2014. http://www.nbclosangeles.com/news/local/OJ-Simpson-20-Years-Later-Glove-Fit-Darden-Dunne-Murder-Trial-of-the-Century-262534821.html.

DiMaggio, Paul J., and Walter W. Powell. 1983. "The Iron Cage Revisited: Institutional Isomorphism and Collective Rationality in Organizational Fields." *American Sociological Review* 48 (2): 147–60.

Edwards, Harry T., and Jennifer L. Mnookin. 2016. "A Wake-up Call on the Junk Science Infesting Our Courtrooms." *Washington Post*, September 20, 2016. https://www.washingtonpost.com/opinions/a-wake-up-call-on-the-junk-science-infesting-our-courtrooms/2016/09/19/85b6eb22-7e90-11e6-8d13-d7c704ef9fd9_story.html.

Epstein, Jules. 2014. "Preferring the Wise Man to Science: The Failure of Courts and Non-Litigation Mechanisms to Demand Validity in Forensic Matching Testimony." *Widener Law Review*, 1:81–118.

Espeland, Wendy Nelson. 1998. *The Struggle for Water: Politics, Rationality, and Identity in the American Southwest*. Chicago: University of Chicago Press.

———. 2008. "A Sociology of Quantification." *European Journal of Sociology / Archives Européennes de Sociologie* 49 (3): 401–36.

———, and Michael Sauder. 2007. "Rankings and Reactivity: How Public Measures Recreate Social Worlds." *American Journal of Sociology* 113 (1): 1–40.

———, and Mitchell L. Stevens. 1998. "Commensuration as a Social Process.'" *Annual Review of Sociology* 24:313–43.

Felch, Jason, and Maura Dolan. 2009. "Report Questions Science, Reliability of Crime Lab Evidence." *Los Angeles Times*, February 19, 2009. https://www.latimes.com/archives/la-xpm-2009-feb-19-na-crime-science19-story.html.

Fields, Kim. 2011. "BSU Professor's Work Helps Set Amanda Knox Free." NCWN, October 3, 2011. https://web.archive.org/web/20120107042453/http://www.nwcn.com/home/?fId=131019638&fPath=%2Fnews%2Flocal&fDomain=10227.

Flatow, Ira. 2009. "Report Finds Forensic Evidence Lacking." National Public Radio, Science Friday, February 27, 2009. https://www.npr.org/templates/transcript/transcript.php?storyId=101242472.

Forrest, Adam. 2018. Cesar Sayoc: How US Authorities Used One Fingerprint to Catch Serial Pipe Bomb Suspect. *Independent*, October 27, 2018. https://www.independent.co.uk/news

/world/americas/cesar-sayoc-arrested-fbi-pipe-bomb-mail-investigation-trump
-fingerprint-dna-maga-a8604166.html.

Fountain, Henry. 2009. "Plugging Holes in the Science of Forensics." *New York Times*, May 11, 2009. https://www.nytimes.com/2009/05/12/science/12fore.html.

Frank, Malcolm, Roehrig, Paul, and Pring, Ben. 2017. *What to Do When Machines Do Everything: How to Get Ahead in a World of AI, Algorithms, Bots, and Big Data.* Hoboken, NJ: John Wiley & Sons.

Freedman, David. 2019. "The Worst Patients in the World." *Atlantic*, July 2019. https://www.theatlantic.com/magazine/archive/2019/07/american-health-care-spending/590623/ (accessed June 2, 2020).

Frey, Carl B., and Osborne, Michael A. 2016. "The Future of Employment: How Susceptible Are Jobs to Computerization?" *Technological Forecasting & Social Change*, 114:254–80.

Freidson, Eliot. 1988. *Professional Powers: A Study of the Institutionalization of Formal Knowledge.* Chicago: University of Chicago Press.

———. 2013. *Professionalism: The Third Logic.* Hoboken, NJ: John Wiley & Sons.

Fujimura, Joan H. 1988. "The Molecular Biological Bandwagon in Cancer Research: Where Social Worlds Meet." *Social Problems* 35 (3): 261–83.

Galison, Peter. 1999. "Objectivity Is Romantic." *American Council of Learned Societies Occasional Paper*, 47:15–43.

Galperin, Roman V. 2017. "Mass Production of Professional Services and Pseudo-Professional Identity in Tax Preparation Work." *Academy of Management Discoveries* 3 (2): 208–29.

Gauchat, Gordon. 2012. "Politicization of Science in the Public Sphere: A Study of Public Trust in the United States, 1974 to 2010." *American Sociological Review* 77 (2): 167–87.

Giannelli, Paul C. 1997. "The Abuse of Scientific Evidence in Criminal Cases: The Need for Independent Crime Laboratories." *Virginia Journal of Social Policy & the Law*, 4:439–78.

———. 2010. "Independent Crime Laboratories: The Problem of Motivational and Cognitive Bias Symposium—Lessons from the Lab: Implications of the 2009 National Academy of Sciences Report on the Future of Forensic Science." *Utah Law Review*, 2:247–66.

Giddens, Anthony. 1990. *The Consequences of Modernity.* Palo Alto, CA: Stanford University Press.

Gieryn, Thomas F. 1983. "Boundary-Work and the Demarcation of Science from Non-Science: Strains and Interests in Professional Ideologies of Scientists." *American Sociological Review* 48 (6): 781–95.

———. 1999. *Cultural Boundaries of Science: Credibility on the Line.* Chicago: University of Chicago Press.

Goddard, C. H. 1980. "A History of Firearms Identification to 1930." *American Journal of Forensic Medicine and Pathology* 1 (2): 155–68.

Goodwin, Charles. 1994. "Professional Vision." *American Anthropologist* 96 (3): 606–33.

Gorman, Elizabeth H., and Rebecca L. Sandefur. 2011. "'Golden Age,' Quiescence, and Revival: How the Sociology of Professions Became the Study of Knowledge-Based Work." *Work and Occupations* 38 (3): 275–302.

Hackman, J. Richard, and Greg R. Oldham. 1976. "Motivation through the Design of Work: Test of a Theory." *Organizational Behavior and Human Performance* 16 (2): 250–79.

Hallett, Tim. 2010. "The Myth Incarnate: Recoupling Processes, Turmoil, and Inhabited Institutions in an Urban Elementary School." *American Sociological Review* 75 (1): 52–74.

———, and Marc J. Ventresca. 2006. "Inhabited Institutions: Social Interactions and Organizational Forms in Gouldner's Patterns of Industrial Bureaucracy." *Theory and Society* 35 (2): 213–36.

Harcourt, Bernard E. 2007. *Against Prediction: Profiling, Policing, and Punishing in an Actuarial Age.* Chicago: University of Chicago Press.

Hartl, Daniel. 1994. "Forensic DNA Typing Dispute." *Nature* 372:398–99.

Heath, C. and Luff, P. 1998. "Mobility in Collaboration." In *Proceedings of the ACM Conference on Computer-Supported Cooperative Work*, 305–14. New York: Association for Computing Machinery.

Henderson, Kathryn, 1991. "Flexible Sketches and Inflexible Data Bases: Visual Communication, Conscription Devices, and Boundary Objects in Design Engineering." *Science, Technology & Human Values*, 16 (4): 448–473.

Herzberg, Frederick. 1964. "The Motivation-Hygiene Concept and Problems of Manpower." *Personnel Administration* 27:3–7.

Hess, Edward D., and Katherine Ludwig. 2017. *Humility Is the New Smart: Rethinking Human Excellence in the Smart Machine Age.* Oakland, CA: Berrett-Koehler.

Hsu, Spencer S. 2017. "Sessions Orders Justice Department to End Forensic Science Commission, Suspend Review Policy." *Washington Post*, April 10, 2017. https://www.washingtonpost .com/local/public-safety/sessions-orders-justice-dept-to-end-forensic-science -commission-suspend-review-policy/2017/04/10/2dada0ca-1c96–11e7-9887-1a5314b56a08 _story.html.

Hughes, Everett C. 1994. *On Work, Race, and the Sociological Imagination.* Chicago: University of Chicago Press.

Huising, Ruthanne. 2015. "To Hive or to Hold? Producing Professional Authority through Scut Work." *Administrative Science Quarterly* 60 (2): 263–99.

Hyman, Louis. 2018. "It's Not Technology That's Disrupting Our Jobs: The Insecure Nature of Work Is a Result of Decisions by Corporations and Policymakers." *New York Times*, August 18, 2018. https://www.nytimes.com/2018/08/18/opinion/technology/technology-gig -economy.html.

Jacobs, Sally. 2013. "Annie Dookhan Pursued Renown along a Path of Lies." *Boston Globe*, February 3, 2013. https://www.bostonglobe.com/metro/2013/02/03/chasing-renown-path-paved -with-lies/Axw3AxwmD33lRwXatSvMCL/story.html.

Jasanoff, Sheila. 1998. "The Eye of Everyman: Witnessing DNA in the Simpson Trial." *Social Studies of Science* 28 (5/6): 713–40.

———. 2003. "Breaking the Waves in Science Studies: Comment on H. M. Collins and Robert Evans, 'The Third Wave of Science Studies.'" *Social Studies of Science,* 33 (3): 389–400.

———. 2005. "Law's Knowledge: Science for Justice in Legal Settings." *American Journal of Public Health* 95 1, supplement: S49–58.

Jordan, Kathleen, and Michael E. Lynch. 1998. "The Dissemination, Standardization, and Routinization of a Molecular Biological Technique." *Social Studies of Science* 28 (5/6): 773–800.

Keller, Evelyn Fox. 1984. *A Feeling for the Organism, 10th Anniversary Edition: The Life and Work of Barbara McClintock.* New York: Henry Holt.

Kington, Tom. 2011. "Amanda Knox DNA Appeal Sparks Legal Battle by Forensic Experts." *Guardian*, July 24, 2011. https://www.theguardian.com/world/2011/jul/24/amanda-knox-dna-appeal-threat.

Kohler-Hausmann, Issa. 2018. *Misdemeanorland: Criminal Courts and Social Control in an Age of Broken Windows Policing*. Princeton, NJ: Princeton University Press.

Koppl, Roger. 2005. "How to Improve Forensic Science." *European Journal of Law and Economics* 20 (3): 255–86.

Kruse, Corinna. 2015. *The Social Life of Forensic Evidence*. Berkeley, University of California Press.

Kuhn, Thomas S. 1962. *The Structure of Scientific Revolutions*. Chicago: University of Chicago Press.

Lander, Eric S., and Bruce Budowle. 1994. "DNA Fingerprinting Dispute Laid to Rest." *Nature* 371 (6500): 735–38.

Latour, Bruno. 1987. *Science in Action: How to Follow Scientists and Engineers through Society*. Cambridge, MA: Harvard University Press.

———, and Steve Woolgar. 1979. *Laboratory Life: The Construction of Scientific Facts*. Princeton, NJ: Princeton University Press.

Lave, Jean. 1988. *Cognition in Practice*. Cambridge: Cambridge University Press.

———, and Etienne Wenger. 1991. *Situated Learning: Legitimate Peripheral Participation*. Cambridge: Cambridge University Press.

Lebovitz, Sarah, Hila Lifshitz-Assaf, and Natalia Levina. 2020. "To Incorporate or Not to Incorporate AI for Critical Judgments: The Importance of Ambiguity in Professionals' Judgment Process." Working paper, https://ssrn.com/abstract=3480593 (accessed June 2, 2020).

Legal Information Institute. 2009. "Daubert Standard." November 9, 2009. https://www.law.cornell.edu/wex/daubert_standard.

Leibel, Esther, Tim Hallett, and Beth A. Bechky. 2017. "Meaning at the Source: The Dynamics of Field Formation in Institutional Research." *Academy of Management Annals* 12 (1): 154–77.

Leicht, K. T., and M. L. Fennell. 1997. "The Changing Organizational Context of Professional Work." *Annual Review of Sociology*, 23:215–31.

Lewontin, Richard. 1994. "Forensic DNA Typing Dispute." *Nature* 372:398.

Lichtblau, Eric. 2006. "US Will Pay $2 Million to Lawyer Wrongly Jailed." *New York Times*, November 30, 2006. https://www.nytimes.com/2006/11/30/us/30settle.html.

Lynch, Michael E. 1985. *Art and Artifact in Laboratory Science: A Study of Shop Work and Shop Talk in a Research Laboratory*. Boston: Routledge & Kegan Paul.

———. 1988. "The Externalized Retina: Selection and Mathematization in the Visual Documentation of Objects in the Life Sciences." *Human Studies* 11 (2/3): 201–34.

———, and Steve Woolgar. 1990. *Representation in Scientific Practice*. Cambridge, MA: MIT Press.

———, Simon A. Cole, Ruth McNally, and Kathleen Jordan. 2008. *Truth Machine: The Contentious History of DNA Fingerprinting*. Chicago: University of Chicago Press.

Mahony, Martin. 2014. "The Predictive State: Science, Territory, and the Future of the Indian Climate." *Social Studies of Science*, 44:109–33.

McAfee, Andrew, and Erik Brynjolfsson. 2017. *Machine, Platform, Crowd: Harnessing Our Digital Future*. New York: W. W. Norton.

Melendez-Diaz v. Massachusetts. 557 U.S. 305. 2009. US Supreme Court.

Mergel, Ines, David Lazer, and Maria Binz-Scharf. 2008. "Lending a Helping Hand: Voluntary Engagement in Knowledge Sharing." *International Journal of Learning and Change* 3:5–22.

Merton, Robert K. 1973 [1942]. "The Normative Structure of Science." In *The Sociology of Science: Theoretical and Empirical Investigations*, edited by Robert K. Merton, 267–78. Chicago: University of Chicago Press.

Miller, J., and M. McLean. 1998. "Criteria for Identification of Tool Marks." *Journal of the Association of Firearms and Tool Mark Examiners* 30 (1): 15.

Mills, S., and M. Possley. 2001. "Report Alleges Crime Lab Fraud: Scientist Is Accused of Providing False Testimony." *Chicago Tribune*, January 14, 2001. https://www.chicagotribune.com/investigations/chi-010114roscetti-story.html.

Mnookin, Jennifer L., Simon A. Cole, Itiel E. Dror, and Barry A. J. Fisher. 2010. "The Need for a Research Culture in the Forensic Sciences." *UCLA Law Review* 58 (3): 725–80.

Moore, Solomon. 2009. "Science Found Wanting in Nation's Crime Labs." *New York Times*, February 4, 2009. https://www.nytimes.com/2009/02/05/us/05forensics.html.

Murphy, Erin E. 2015. *Inside the Cell: The Dark Side of Forensic DNA*. New York: Nation Books.

Myers, Natasha. 2008. "Molecular Embodiments and the Body-Work of Modeling in Protein Crystallography." *Social Studies of Science* 38 (2): 163–99.

National Research Council. 1992. "DNA Technology in Forensic Science." https://www.nap.edu/catalog/1866/dna-technology-in-forensic-science (accessed June 2, 2020).

———. 1996. "The Evaluation of Forensic DNA Evidence." https://www.nap.edu/catalog/5141/the-evaluation-of-forensic-dna-evidence (accessed June 2, 2020).

———. 2008. "Ballistic Imaging." https://www.nap.edu/catalog/12162/ballistic-imaging (accessed June 2, 2020).

———. 2009. "Strengthening Forensic Science in the United States: A Path Forward." https://www.nap.edu/catalog/12589/strengthening-forensic-science-in-the-united-states-a-path-forward (accessed June 2, 2020).

Nelsen, Bonalyn J., and Stephen R. Barley. 1997. "For Love or Money? Commodification and the Construction of an Occupational Mandate." *Administrative Science Quarterly* 42 (4): 619–53.

O'Neil, Cathy. 2016. *Weapons of Math Destruction: How Big Data Increases Inequality and Threatens Democracy*. New York: Crown Books.

Orlikowski, Wanda. 1992. "The Duality of Technology: Rethinking the Concept of Technology in Organizations." *Organization Science* 3 (3): 398–427.

Orr, Julian E. 1996. *Talking about Machines: An Ethnography of a Modern Job*. Ithaca, NY: Cornell University Press.

Pegues, Jeff. 2018. "Fingerprint, DNA, and Cellphone Tracking Led Investigators to Mail Bomb Suspect Cesar Sayoc." CBS News, October 26, 2018. https://www.cbsnews.com/news/fingerprint-dna-and-cellphone-tracking-led-investigators-to-mail-bomb-suspect-cesar-sayoc/.

Peters, Jeremy W. 2009. "Report Condemns Oversight of New York State Police Crime Lab." *New York Times*, December 17, 2009. https://www.nytimes.com/2009/12/18/nyregion/18statepolice.html.

Podlas, Kimberlianne. 2006. "The *CSI* Effect and Other Forensic Fictions." *Loyola of Los Angeles Entertainment Law Review* 27 (2): 87.

Porter, Theodore M. 1996. *Trust in Numbers*. Reprint. Princeton, NJ: Princeton University Press.

Rakoff, Jed. 2019. "Jailed by Bad Science." *New York Review of Books*, December 19, 2019. https://www.nybooks.com/articles/2019/12/19/jailed-bad-forensic-science/.

Rip, Arie. 2003. "Constructing Expertise: In a Third Wave of Science Studies?" *Social Studies of Science* 33 (3): 419–34.

Saks, Michael, and Jonathan J. Koehler. 2005. "The Coming Paradigm Shift in Forensic Identification Science." *Science* 309 (5736): 892–95.

Samydurai, Kuzhalan. 2016. "Technology: A Key to Patient Satisfaction?" Managed Healthcare Executive, April 10, 2016. http://www.managedhealthcareexecutive.com/connectivity/technology-key-patient-satisfaction.

Scarselletta, Mario. 1997. "The Infamous 'Lab Error': Education, Skill and Quality in Medical Technicians." In *Between Craft and Science: Technical Work in US Settings*, edited by Stephen R. Barley and Julian Edgerton Orr, 187–209. Ithaca, NY: Cornell University Press.

Schön, Donald A. 1983. *The Reflective Practitioner: How Professionals Think in Action*. New York, NY: Basic Books.

Schuster, Henry, and Terry Frieden. 2006. "Lawyer Wrongly Arrested in Bombings: 'We Lived in 1984.'" CNN, November 30, 2006. http://www.cnn.com/2006/LAW/11/29/mayfield.suit/index.html.

Schuppe, Jon. 2017. "Epic Drug Lab Scandal Results in More than 20,000 Convictions Dropped." NBC News, April 18, 2017. https://www.nbcnews.com/news/us-news/epic-drug-lab-scandal-results-more-20-000-convictions-dropped-n747891.

Schwartz, Barry. 1974. "Waiting, Exchange, and Power: The Distribution of Time in Social Systems." *American Journal of Sociology* 79 (4): 841–70.

Scott, W. Richard. 1995. *Institutions and Organizations: Ideas, Interests, and Identities*. Thousand Oaks, CA: SAGE.

———, Martin Ruef, Peter J. Mendel, and Carol A. Caronna. 2000. *Institutional Change and Healthcare Organizations: From Professional Dominance to Managed Care*. Chicago: University of Chicago Press.

Shapin, Steven. 1989. "The Invisible Technician." *American Scientist* 77 (6): 554–63.

Shelton, Donald E., Young S. Kim, and Gregg Barak. 2006. "A Study of Juror Expectations and Demands Concerning Scientific Evidence: Does the '*CSI* Effect' Exist?" *Vanderbilt Journal of Entertainment and Technology Law*, 9:331–68.

Silverberg, Bret. 2014. "Inspector General Says Annie Dookhan 'Sole Bad Actor' at State Drug Lab." Patch, March 4, 2014. https://patch.com/massachusetts/jamaicaplain/inspector-general-says-annie-dookhan-sole-bad-actor-at-state-drug-lab.

Smith, Jordan Michael. 2014. "Forget *CSI*: A Disaster Is Happening in America's Crime Labs." *Business Insider*, April 30, 2014. https://www.businessinsider.com/forensic-csi-crime-labs-disaster-2014-4?op=1.

Smith, Merritt Roe. 1994. "Technological Determinism in American Culture." In *Does Technology Drive History? The Dilemma of Technological Determinism*, edited by Leo Marx and Merritt Roe Smith, 1–36. Cambridge, MA: MIT Press.

Smith, Tovia. 2012. "Crime Lab Scandal Rocks Massachusetts." NPR Morning Edition, September 12, 2012. https://www.npr.org/transcripts/161502085.

———. 2013. "Crime Lab Scandal Leaves Mass. Legal System in Turmoil." NPR Morning Edition, March 14, 2013. https://www.npr.org/2013/03/14/174269211/mass-crime-lab-scandal-reverberates-across-state.

Starr, Douglas. 2016. "When DNA Is Lying." *Science* 351, no. 6278:1133–36.

Stern, Mark Joseph 2014. "Forensic Science Is Biased and Inaccurate, but Juries Believe It and Convict the Innocent." Slate, June 11, 2014. https://slate.com/technology/2014/06/forensic-science-is-biased-and-inaccurate-but-juries-believe-it-and-convict-the-innocent.html.

Strathern, Marilyn. 2003. *Audit Cultures: Anthropological Studies in Accountability, Ethics and the Academy.* New York, NY: Routledge.

Strauss, Anselm. 1978. "A Social Worlds Perspective." *Studies in Symbolic Interaction* 1:119–28.

Strickland, Eliza. 2019. "How IBM Watson Overpromised and Underdelivered on AI Health Care." IEEE Spectrum, April 2, 2019. https://spectrum.ieee.org/biomedical/diagnostics/how-ibm-watson-overpromised-and-underdelivered-on-ai-health-care.

Susskind, Richard E., and Daniel Susskind. 2015. *The Future of the Professions: How Technology Will Transform the Work of Human Experts.* Oxford: Oxford University Press.

———, and Daniel Susskind. 2016. "Technology Will Replace Many Doctors, Lawyers, and Other Professionals." *Harvard Business Review,* October 11, 2016.

Thompson, Sandra. 2015. *Cops in Lab Coats: Curbing Wrongful Convictions through Independent Forensic Laboratories.* Durham, NC: Carolina Academic Press.

Thompson, William. 2015. "A Setback for Forensic Science." *Washington Post,* May 8, 2015. https://www.washingtonpost.com/opinions/a-setback-for-forensic-science/2015/05/08/540273f2-f350-11e4-84a6-6d7c67c50db0_story.html.

Timmermans, Stefan. 2007. *Postmortem: How Medical Examiners Explain Suspicious Deaths.* Chicago: University of Chicago Press.

———, and Marc Berg. 2003. *The Gold Standard: The Challenge of Evidence-based Medicine and Standardization in Health Care.* Philadelphia, PA: Temple University Press.

Toobin, Jeffrey. 2007. "The *CSI* Effect." *New Yorker,* May 7, 2007. https://www.newyorker.com/magazine/2007/05/07/the-csi-effect.

Trager, Rebecca. 2017. "Thousands of US Drug Convictions Overturned by Rogue Chemist's Actions. "*Chemistry World,* December 6, 2017. https://www.chemistryworld.com/news/thousands-of-us-drug-convictions-overturned-by-rogue-chemists-actions-/3008385.article.

Traweek, Sharon. 1992. *Beamtimes and Lifetimes: The World of High Energy Physicists.* Rev. ed. Cambridge, MA: Harvard University Press.

Van Cleve, Nicole Gonzalez. 2017. *Crook County: Racism and Injustice in America's Largest Criminal Court.* Palo Alto, CA: Stanford University Press.

Van Derbeken, Jaxon. 2010. "Overworked SF Drug Lab Was Sloppy, Audit Says." *San Franscico Chronicle,* March 31, 2010. https://www.sfgate.com/bayarea/article/Overworked-S-F-drug-lab-was-sloppy-audit-says-3268828.php.

Van Maanen, John. 1988. *Tales of the Field.* Chicago: University of Chicago Press.

———, and Stephen R. Barley. 1984. "Occupational Communities: Cultural Control in Organizations." *Research in Organizational Behavior,* 6:287–365.

Watkins, Ali. 2019. "Old Rape Kits Finally Got Tested. 64 Attackers Were Convicted." *New York Times*, March 12, 2019. https://www.nytimes.com/2019/03/12/nyregion/rape-kit-tests .html.

Weissmann, Jordan. 2018. "Amazon Created a Hiring Tool Using AI. It Immediately Started Discriminating against Women." Slate, October 10, 2018. https://slate.com/business/2018 /10/amazon-artificial-intelligence-hiring-discrimination-women.html.

Worland, Justin. 2019. "Trump Said 'We Need' Global Warming to Deal With Record Cold Temperatures. Here's Why That Doesn't Make Sense." *Time*, January 29, 2019, https://time .com/5515340/trump-climate-change-weather/.

Wynne, Bryan. 1996. "May the Sheep Safely Graze? A Reflexive View of the Expert-Lay Knowledge Divide." In *Risk, Environment, and Modernity: Towards a New Ecology*, edited by Scott Lash, Bronislaw Szerszynski and Brian Wynne, 44–83. London: SAGE.

———. 2003. "Seasick on the Third Wave? Subverting the Hegemony of Propositionalism: Response to Collins & Evans (2002)," *Social Studies of Science*, 33 (3): 401–17.

Zetka, James R., Jr. 2003. *Surgeons and the Scope*. Ithaca, NY: ILR Press.

INDEX

alleles, 26, 27–28

American Academy of Forensic Science (AAFS), 62, 149

American Board of Forensic Toxicology, 62

American Society of Crime Lab Directors (ASCLD), 62, 149, 161–62

anticipation, 75; by educating outside audiences, 85–93; how experts work with, 75–77; implications across social worlds, 178–80; by incorporating outside expectations, 78–85; manifestation of, 77–78; neutrality of criminalists and culture of, 16, 99–110; as routine, 104–10; testimony and, 145–47; waiting and, 101–4; while negotiating and resisting requests of criminal justice representatives, 93–97

applied science, forensic science as, 57, 62–66

Association of Firearm and Tool Mark Examiners (AFTE), 62, 155

autonomy of criminalists, 176–77

biology, forensic. *See* DNA profiling

Barley, William, 76

boundary work of experts, 186–88

capillary electrophoresis, 24

chemistry units. *See* narcotics labs

Christin, Angèle, 185

comparative evidence, 19

consequences of testifying, 114–18

contamination, 26

crime labs: case notes on ethnography of, 189–98; chemistry unit, 40–48; contamination in, 26; culture of anticipation in (*see* anticipation); different units of, 18–19; firearms, 30–40; forensic biology, 19–30; taming, questioning, and framing across, 54–56; toxicology, 48–54; understanding the culture of, 3–5

criminalists: author's observation of, 3–5; autonomy of, 176–77; as captive communities, 101–104, 114, 147, 174–75; characteristics of expert work by, 174–76; credibility of, 135–45; cultural tropes about, 70–72; documentation by, 81–82; education and training of, 17–18, 62–63; expertise of, 8–10, 173–74; gunshot residue (GSR) and, 57–61; legal considerations for, 61, 64–69; neutrality of, 16, 99–110; as part of community, 63; professional organizations for, 62; role of, 15–17; sought after jobs of, 180–81; taming, questioning, and framing across labs, 54–56; testimony by (*see* testimony); value in studying, 7–11; as voice of the evidence, 133–45; working in science, criminal justice, and the public arena, 57

criminal justice system, 1–3, 15–16; anticipating while negotiating and resisting requests from representatives of, 93–97; criminalists as neutral experts within, 99–110; forensic science in, 66–69

crystal testing, 44

CSI, 1, 85, 195

CSI effect, 72, 87–88

DNA profiling, 55; anomalies in, 26; and change in forensic science, 168–72; compared to firearms analysis, 153–60; compared to narcotics analysis, 164–68; compared to toxicology, 160–64; as complex, uncertain, and fallible, 151; DNA envy and, 151–53; documentation in, 26–27; educating outside audiences on, 88–91; as gold standard of forensic evidence, 150–53; graphs of, 25–26; as legitimated scientific inquiry using statistical inference, 19–21; locus in, 24; negotiating and resisting requests of

DNA profiling (*continued*)
  criminal justice representatives on, 93–97;
  public and scientific acceptance of, 148–50;
  reports in, 27–33; sample analysis in, 23–27;
  sample collection for, 22–23; statistics in,
  27–28; technical reviewer in, 29; testimony
  on (*see* testimony); waiting and making
  anticipation routine and, 102–10
documentation, 81–82

education of outside audiences, anticipating
  by, 85–93
enzyme immunoassay screening (EIA), 51
expertise of criminalists, 8–10, 173–74;
  autonomy and, 176–77; boundary work
  and, 186–88; characteristics of, 174–76;
  objectivity and, 184–86; technology
  impact on, 181–83

firearms labs, 55, 168; compared to DNA
  profiling, 153–60; gun knowledge of
  criminalists in, 38–39; role in the criminal
  justice system, 39–40; safety in, 34–35;
  tasks in, 33; test-firing in, 35–36; testimony
  by criminalists in, 37–38; textbooks for,
  35–36; training of criminalists in, 33–34;
  work practices in, 30–33
Forensic Alcohol Supervisors (FAS), 53
forensic biology. *See* DNA profiling
forensic science, 1–3, 15–16; as applied science,
  57, 62–66; as captive occupation, 76; in
  criminal justice world, 66–69; DNA
  profiling and change in, 168–72; in the
  public sphere, 69–72
forensic scientists. *See* criminalists

gas chromatography/mass spectrometry
  (GC/MS), 44–45, 51, 164–68, 169
Goddard, Calvin, 39
gunshot residue (GSR), 57–61

International Association for Identification,
  62

loci, DNA, 24, 27

media portrayals of criminalists, 70–72
Melendez-Diaz vs. the State of Massachusetts,
  83, 100

narcotics labs, 18, 55; compared to DNA
  profiling, 164–68; handling of evidence
  by, 43, 46, 82–85; reports in, 45–46; role
  in the criminal justice system, 46–48;
  types of tests in, 43–44; typical substances
  analyzed by, 43; work practices in, 40–42
National Academy of Sciences (NAS), 5, 71,
  148–49, 177; on firearms analysis, 153–60;
  on toxicology, 161–64
National Institute of Justice, 62
neutrality of criminalists, 16, 98, 101–4

objectivity, 184–86
outside expectations, anticipating by
  incorporating, 78–85

public sphere, forensic science in the,
  69–72

reports, DNA profiling, 27–33; review
  process for, 29–30
review process, DNA profiling report,
  29–30

safety, firearms, 34–35
short tandem repeats (STRs), 23, 24
"Strengthening Forensic Science in the
  United States: A Path Forward," 71

technology: impact of, on criminalists,
  181–83; objectivity of, 184–86
testimony, 2–3, 11, 37, 53–54, 98–99, 113–14;
  adversarial relationship between lawyers
  and criminalists and, 122–25; anticipation
  and, 145–47; consequences of, 114–18;
  credibility of, 135–45; criminalists as
  voice of evidence through, 133–45;

criminalists' partial membership in the
criminal justice community and, 129–33;
lawyers' lack of knowledge and criminalists',
125–29; specter of, 118–33
toxicology labs, 18, 55, 80; collaboration
in, 51–53; compared to DNA profiling,
160–64; evidence handling by, 50;
machines used in, 51–52; reports in,
49, 53; types of tests in, 51; work practices
in, 48–49

voice of the evidence, criminalists' testimony
as, 133–45

waiting, time spent, 101–4
wet chemistry techniques, 44